LIVES OF THE
GREAT SONGS

LIVES OF THE
GREAT SONGS

EDITED BY TIM DE LISLE

PAVILION

Lives of the great songs
/

First published in Great Britain in 1994 by
Pavilion Books Limited
26 Upper Ground
London SE1 9PD

Text selection and introduction copyright © 1994 by Tim de Lisle
For individual text copyright, see individual articles
For photographic acknowledgements, see page 143
Front cover artwork copyright © 1994 by Paul Burgess

Designed by Grahame Dudley Associates

A CIP catalogue record for this book is available from
the British Library

ISBN 1-85793-0517

Typeset by Dorchester Typesetting Group Ltd in Garamond

Printed and bound in Great Britain by Hartnolls, Bodmin

2 4 6 8 10 9 7 5 3 1

This book may be ordered by post direct from the publisher.
Please contact the Marketing Department.
But try your bookshop first.

CONTENTS

INTRODUCTION

BY TIM DE LISLE

THEY'RE the sound that fills the dancefloor, even if it hasn't much of a beat. They're the jangle and whine of the busker, ricocheting down the tunnel. They're the whistle of the milkman, drifting down the street. They're the muffled thump of the jukebox, breaking the ice of the pub. They're the wheeze and ripple of muzak, leaking into the lift. They're the plunk of the piano in the restaurant, stuck in the key of romance.

They're a finger on your pulse, and a shot in the arm. They're a sudden shift of mood (how strange the change from major to minor). They're the language of love, and a kick in its direction: a voice for the tongue-tied, a shove for the shy. They're a thrill, a pill, a sweet, a treat. They're an aide-memoire ("These Foolish Things" reminds me of you), and a memory in themselves. They're a bond, a knot, a lasting link: you may leave your lover, but the two of you will still have your tune (play it, Sam!). And so they're the ghost of love, a congenial form of torture (if she can stand it, I can). They're a melody from a symphony by Strauss. They're the top. They're the great songs.

THE MOST recorded song in the world is, by general consent, "Yesterday", written by Paul McCartney. But you won't find an entry for it in *The Oxford Companion to Popular Music,* or *The Faber Companion to 20th-Century Popular Music,* or *The Guinness Encyclopedia of Popular Music,* or even the 1,378 pages of *The Penguin Encyclopedia of Popular Music.* They mention it, of course. One calls it a "sentimental standard"; another runs to "lovely", and notes that the song has been recorded about 2,000 times; another cites it as an example of how McCartney was best at sad songs. The fourth offers no description at all.

This is not to suggest that they are bad books. Other kinds of rock literature are also strangely silent on songs: there are biographies of all creatures great and small, from the Beatles to Take That, but only one book, as far as I know, that is devoted to a song – *Louie Louie: History and Myth* by Dave Marsh. Despite spending many happy hours in the music sections of bookshops, I have never actually seen a copy.

Somewhere along the line, we have got something wrong. We have lingered on the singer at the expense of the song. This book is an attempt to put that right. It's no encyclopaedia, but it is a start: a set of critical biographies of three dozen songs, including "Yesterday", each one short enough to be read at a sitting, but long enough to capture the magic of the song, as well as follow its progress from one singer to another, from one meaning to the next, across oceans, generations and genres.

The odd thing about this idea is that no one has had it before. At least they probably have, but if so, they don't seem to have turned it into a book.

I wouldn't have thought of it myself if I hadn't been approached one day in the summer of 1992 by my then boss, Richard Williams, editor of the *Independent on Sunday* Review. He said he had a rather odd idea for a piece. There was this Ry Cooder song, "Across the Borderline", which he kept coming across. He'd heard Bob Dylan do it on television the other night, at a guitar festival in Seville. Then he'd found it on a Springsteen bootleg, a live recording of a concert in Los Angeles. It was a great song and he'd like to do a piece about it, talking to Cooder, and looking at what it was that made it special.

I didn't know the song, but I liked the idea. I liked it better when Williams' piece appeared, and gave evident pleasure. It seemed a natural idea for a weekly series.

I called the series "Lives of the Great Songs" and commissioned eight articles. It was June 1993 before we had enough of them in the can to launch (give any self-respecting journalist a timeless idea, and he will take his time with it). The series seemed to go down well. Radio and TV producers wrote saying they'd like to turn it into a series of programmes (this, I was to discover, is a very different thing from saying they were going to make the programmes). Fellow journalists rang offering contributions. Publishers wrote asking if they could turn the series into a book. *Private Eye* put a line from one of the pieces in

Pseuds' Corner (quite unjustly, of course). A second series began in November 1993, and ran for 10 weeks, making a total of 19 pieces that had appeared in the paper. For the book, I commissioned a further 17, so what you hold in your hand is like a good cover version, half old and half new.

THE BRIEF the writers were given was brief. It was up to them what sort of piece they wrote, as long as it was persuasive, informative and entertaining: it could be an essay, built on thought and hard listening, or a feature, drawing on interviews; or, most likely, something between the two.

There were three rules governing the choice of song. First, it needed to have had an interesting life: there had to be at least three significantly different recordings of it. This hurdle proved too much for dozens of great records, from "Only the Lonely" to "Every Breath You Take". Second, it had to fit into the line-up of the series: we make no claims to completeness - among the songwriters whose work you will not find in these pages are Leiber and Stoller, Irving Berlin, John Lennon, Burt Bacharach, David Bowie, Bob Marley and Prince - but we havé tried to give a fair spread, to do something like justice to pop's rich tapestry. Since the subjects range from a setting of Goethe by Schubert to a song by Kurt Cobain, it may not be too immodest to claim that we have managed this. Third, the writers had to be convinced that their song was great (it was at this fence that "Macarthur Park" fell). Which brings us to the question, what makes a great song?

Simple, really: it must be simple, and real. It must put its finger on some everyday predicament, some democratic emotion. I want to hold your hand. My baby left me, never said a word. And it must be tuneful. There is no element of a song that is not liable to change as it goes forth and multiplies: tempo, key, arrangement, instrumentation, even lyrics are all up for grabs. But the melody is unlikely to change more than a shade. (John Coltrane's versions of "My Favourite Things" – pages 61-64 – are the exception that proves this rule.) Together, the theme and the tune must move you: they must make your heart sing.

As somebody said of jazz, these qualities are hard to define but not hard to recognise. "Yesterday" has all of them: with about as little doubt as there can be, it is a great song. "Paperback Writer" is not: it's fun, but it's not moving. "Bridge over Troubled Water" is, "Bright Eyes" isn't: it's not unemotional, but the emotion is a bit cheap, a bit slushy.

To some extent, you can measure a song by the people who have sung it. Take the song I've written about myself, "Take Me to the River": you may or may not like it, but you have to be impressed by the fact that it's a black, southern-soul song that has been covered by two outstanding white art-school acts, Talking Heads and Bryan Ferry, as well as Levon Helm, of The Band, Tina Turner and several others. However, this yardstick becomes less useful as you go back to the days of pre-rock pop, when every song worth its salt appears to have been recorded by every singer worth his or hers.

Most of all, the test these songs have passed is that of time. There is a paradox here. As art forms go, pop music is here today, gone tomorrow. This book, being partly a collection of journalism, is therefore in danger of being the ephemeral in pursuit of the disposable. But an art form is an art form, and if something is good, you don't throw it away. All the songs here are still giving pleasure, long after their release. The youngest is four years old ("Smells Like Teen Spirit"), the oldest 67 ("How Long Has This Been Going On?"). The average is somewhere over 29 – 1965 was a golden year – and under 40.

The test of time is a long-distance race, and it's best not to hit the front early on. One or two of our songs were instantly recognised as classics: "Everything about this record is an overwhelming gas," said *Melody Maker* when it heard the first single by a band called Procol Harum. But again, this is the exception. "Yesterday" was scoffed at by the three Beatles who didn't play on it. "Blowin' in the Wind" was hailed by Bob Dylan's friend and mentor Dave van Ronk as "an incredibly dumb song!". Mick Jagger and Keith Richards didn't think "Satisfaction" was good enough to be a single. Louis B Mayer, finding that *The Wizard of Oz* was too long, thought the solution was to drop "Over the Rainbow".

X

IF YOU'VE already looked at the contents page, it may have struck you as a mixture. There are the great songs of rock 'n' roll, and the great songs of pre-rock pop, the Broadway tradition. The split is roughly even, with one classical number, Schubert's "Erlkönig", to hold the balance of power. You can only be rough about it, because the two categories overlap. 'You Are the Sunshine of My Life" was written and sung by a rock star, but soon hijacked by men wearing tuxedos and Brylcreem. "Fever" has travelled in the opposite direction, from Peggy Lee to Madonna.

The distinction, none the less, is a sharp one. A lot of people who call themselves music-lovers have never bought a Sinatra album. A lot of Sinatra fans have never deigned to investigate Simply Red. This goes back to the Beatles. By making it big on the strength of their own songs, they put the cover version out of fashion as surely as short hair. This was a bit rich considering they'd started as a covers band (most bands do), but it happened, and the great interpreters suffered as a result.

In 1973, there was a partial reconciliation between rock and the music of Sinatra, Crosby and Fitzgerald. They met on *These Foolish Things*, the excellent solo debut by Bryan Ferry, the leader of Europe's most stylish group of the moment, Roxy Music. Then, about 15 years later, in a quiet period for new music, there arose a strange coalition of London advertising people, who saw the potential of great songs to lend their product the aura of a classic, and dance-music boffins, who needed solid structures to do their thing to. There was a boom in revivals and remakes. Since then, the past has never been entirely out of fashion. But still most record collections are biased one way or the other.

Greatness doesn't work like that. A great song can come from any genre: it's the genres it moves into that are more revealing. Our 36 songs have one thing in common, over and above the qualities I have mentioned. They bring something out of people. They are the canvas as well as the picture.

A WORD about the lyrics. If you are putting a song under the micro-
scope, you need to quote some of the words. But they were not written
to be read. If you read them to yourself like the rest of the words in the
book, they will seem thin, maybe bathetic. After sustained delibera-
tion, I have come up with the answer to this problem: you should sing
them as you read. This solution rather falls down if you don't know the
tune. But if you don't know the tune, you won't get full pleasure out of
the piece, so you may as well put the book to one side now, and go and
find it.

To help you do this, we have tried to give details of every recording
that is mentioned more than in passing. These occur in the text, and
consist of an album title, a label and a year. There is only one for each
recording, though some pop up on dozens of albums. The idea is to
give the information you need to run a record to ground, without
turning the book into a list.

xii

BRIDGE OVER TROUBLED WATER

BY GILES SMITH

ART GARFUNKEL sang this song, but Paul Simon wrote it and he thought it could have turned out differently. "The demo of 'Bridge over Troubled Water' will show you that it was a much less grandiose thing than the record. It was a humble little gospel hymn song with two verses and a simple guitar behind it . . ."

So much for that. By the time Simon and Garfunkel came out of the studio with the finished version, the song had grown a third verse and had sprouted strings and cymbals and a drum which goes off like a cannon. It had become not a hymn but a giant pop ballad, and simplicity (and, perhaps, humility) was somewhere in its past.

Still, people liked it that way – liked how the song welled up gradually from its quiet opening until it rang in their ears, liked how Garfunkel's voice started out soft and then pulled itself gradually higher to the sustained note at the end. This wasn't one of those pop numbers that drove a catchy idea round the block a few times: it unfolded across its four minutes and 50 seconds, developing like a drama. As a result, you couldn't really drop in and pick up the plot at any point; to make it work, you had to start at the top and follow it all the way through.

But millions gladly gave up the time. In February 1970, "Bridge over Troubled Water" went to No 1 in America and sat there for six weeks. It was No 1 in Britain for just three, but the Simon and Garfunkel album of the same name stayed in or around the charts for 18 months. Ask most people what they think of when they think of Simon and Garfunkel and they will say "Bridge over Troubled Water".

In 1971, at the Grammy Awards, to nobody's big surprise, the song cleaned up: Record of the Year, Song of the Year, Best Contemporary Song, Best Arrangement Accompanying Vocalists, Best Engineered Record. Covers happened quickly. Aretha Franklin recorded her version in August 1971 and Stevie Wonder had it on a live album within the year (*At the Talk of the Town*). In October 1973, when Capital, the first British commercial radio station, launched, the first song it broadcast was "Bridge over Troubled Water". It was already that kind of record.

Ever since, though, Simon seems to have clung to some reservations about the song, or at least about what it became. "It has lived a long life," he said, "and I've gone through many different feelings about it, from negative to superlative." But more often than not, the feelings he has voiced publicly have been the negative ones. The song slipped loose of his intentions, but that's only part of the problem.

1

It took a colossal 800 hours of studio time to make the *Bridge over Troubled Water* album, Garfunkel quibbling with some anti-Nixon material that Simon wanted to include, and further annoying his partner by slipping off to Hollywood every now and again to chase his new career in the movies. This was their last album together – they had agreed to split before it even reached the shops. And strangely, some of the personal difficulties between them find a unique focus in (of all places) this hymn to the virtue of seeing another through.

In 1993, Paul Simon put together a boxed selection of his work (*Paul Simon, 1964/1993*) and threw in the demo of "Bridge over Troubled Water" so we could hear for ourselves how the song started out. There he is, 28, picking quietly at an acoustic guitar and singing in a small, struggling falsetto, based, he would later recount, on Reverend Claude Jeter of the Swan Silvertones, Simon's favourite gospel group. (Jeter would later sing on Simon's "Take Me to the Mardi Gras".)

The first line of the melody is askew and the descent of the chords under the chorus isn't quite worked out. There's a patch of mumbling where words have yet to come and a couple of duff lines which would become strong ones eventually ("when evening turns you blind" became "when evening falls so hard I will comfort you"). And after two verses it stops. A palpable hit? Well, yes, because of one thing – the chorus line: "Like a bridge over troubled water, I would lay me down". Garfunkel's version mends the grammar and changes it to "I will lay me down", but either way we're looking at a winner.

★ ★ ★ ★ ★ ★ ★ ★ ★ ★

It's a guaranteed show-stealer. And Garfunkel has never been shy about stealing shows with it.

★ ★ ★ ★ ★ ★ ★ ★ ★ ★

Where had Simon got this image from? From the Bible, perhaps: "I will lay me down in peace and take my rest" (Psalm 9). Or from "The Lord's My Shepherd" (Psalm 23): "He makes me down to lie/ In pastures green." In fact, the main influence was a line in the Swan Silvertones' version of "O Mary Don't You Weep". Simon recalled hearing this on his radio in 1957 and picking out a line of scat thrown in midway through by Claude Jeter: "I'll be your bridge over deep water if you trust in My name".

This is still some way from the grandeur of Simon's finished line. Yet, apparently no exact source exists for his words: you just feel there should be one. Here is a songwriter's dream – a phrase which not only seeps into the language, but seems to have lived there for years beforehand. (Simon would do it again later with "still crazy after all these years", a new coinage which immediately felt like old tender.)

Not that it caught on immediately with everyone. Jimmy Haskell, who arranged the strings for the final recording, misheard the demo's chorus altogether and wrote on the title page of his sheet music, "Like a Pitcher of Water". Simon framed it.

What Garfunkel made from the bones of the demo is something Simon is in awe of and, at the same time, something he has never quite forgiven him for.

Garfunkel's soprano delivery is faultlessly sweet, floating on a studio-contrived reverb effect which picks up the merest hint of sibilance (in the words "small", "tears", "eyes"), magnifies it and flings it away as if into the far corner of some giant cavern. People tend not to remark on the piano playing by Larry Knechtel, but it is formidable and essential – not just the rolling and gradually quietening storm of the introduction, but the whole performance. It is an object lesson in accompaniment, intricate but never intrusive, supporting and meeting the tune at intervals, then ducking away to allow the voice to be heard.

Slowly, Garfunkel gathers strength, pushing the words ever harder to the conclusion which Simon originally planned at the close of the second verse. "I'll take your part when darkness comes and pain is all around, like a bridge over troubled water, I will lay me down". And then the third verse starts, with distant crashes, as of waves on pebbles. Low strings are heard. A bass guitar pops in and slides up.

Simon said this part of the song put him in mind of the Righteous Brothers – the voice is doubled, a bass drum presses the song forward, the strings well up rapidly. The lyric, meanwhile, after the simple clarity of the first and second verses, now veers away into pop vernacular. "Sail on silver girl, sail on by, your time has come to shine, all your dreams are on their way." (It has been argued – normally in tones of outrage – that these lines champion a drug experience, the "silver girl" referring to the needle on a syringe. Simon maintains they relate quite innocently to his wife who had just discovered her first grey hairs.) And gradually, drawing longer breaths, Garfunkel carries himself to the huge, open-throated cry at the end of "I will ease your mind" as the cellos come sawing through the air underneath him.

It's a real party piece, a guaranteed show-stealer. And Garfunkel has never been shy about stealing shows with it. In the reunion concerts at the Paramount Theatre, New York, in 1993, all he had to do was come on and hit that high note and everyone was out of their seats. What can it have been like for Simon, when the signal moment in a concert of his own music didn't involve him? During a recent *Omnibus* documentary on BBC1, he was candid, confessing that hearing the extraordinary ovations which would greet Garfunkel's performances of the song, he would frequently find himself sitting there, ignored, thinking: "Author! Author!".

Not that he has ever suggested that Garfunkel's vocal delivery wasn't a superb thing in its own way – "astounding," he told me, "a real virtuoso performance". Yet his own, solo live performances of the song (there's one on the *Live Rhymin'* album, CBS 1974) have tended to be modest, Simon accompanied at the piano by the late Richard Tee, who would make the chords tremble in a churchy kind of way, as if attempting to lead the song back. And further elaborating the distinction between his demo and the record, Simon put it this way: "Artie's version is much more white gospel." Then a pause. "More *Methodist* than Baptist."

What of those who have carried the torch from there? Chiefly (perhaps bearing out Simon's greatest fears) the cover artists are the big stars of Radio

3

2, the light-entertainment crew, attracted as ever to a warm sentiment gently expressed, but also to what the song offers in the way of a work-out or challenge – the assault on Mount Garfunkel. Why do they do it? Because it's there. Tom Jones, Andy Williams, Shirley Bassey, Nana Mouskouri – each of them has headed for the summit, coming on all dreamy and comforting in the foothills and ascending with various degrees of smoothness to wax noisy and masterful in the third verse. It is the choirboy Aled Jones who gets closest to Garfunkel's unstrained purity (*Best of Aled Jones*, BBC 1985), but as his voice hadn't broken when he made his attempt, he may have to be disqualified for cheating.

But vocal heavyweights, too, have gone for the song. Paul Simon said, directly after its composition, that he could hear Aretha Franklin singing it and Franklin's 1971 recording (*Aretha's Greatest Hits*, Atlantic) makes a different kind of music altogether, hearing those gospel traces in the tune and lyrics and pursuing them hard. Itself a Top 10 American hit and a Grammy winner, her version glows like a devotional candle.

Elvis Presley, meanwhile, was in a position to go either way with the song: much to Simon's disappointment, what the King delivered on *Magic Moments* was more Andy Williams than Aretha Franklin.

"It was in his Las Vegas period and done with conventional thinking: it kind of imitated the Simon and Garfunkel record. He sang it well, but it would have been nice to hear him do it gospel because he did so many gospel albums and was a good white gospel singer. It would have been nice to hear him do it that way, take it back – as opposed to the big ending; he seemed to end everything with a karate chop and an explosion. So he didn't really add anything to the song. It's not nearly as significant as the Aretha Franklin recording. It's just a pleasure for me that Elvis Presley recorded one of my songs before he died."

But to what extent is "Bridge over Troubled Water", as Simon put it, "a tiny little, humble country church song", even in essence? Hymns and gospel tunes are more often second-person than first and any phenomenal curative powers are normally ascribed to God. Here, the capacity to cope and assuage which the song triumphantly celebrates belongs to the singer – who further illustrates this strength within him or herself by turning in a particularly belting third verse. If you go through the song substituting "He" for "I" ("When tears are in your eyes, He will dry them all", "He's on your side when times get rough" etc), you end up with something closer to gospel. The song has an element of self-promotion that church music does not readily admit – unlike pop songs, which revel in that kind of business. You could argue that Garfunkel's instinct with "Bridge over Troubled Water" – to make it dazzling, to command your awe, to give it the showbiz treatment – was an accurate response to the material to hand, rather than, as Simon has sometimes seemed to imply, a wilful requisitioning of it.

As Simon says, it could have been different. But it couldn't have been better.

ACROSS THE BORDERLINE

BY RICHARD WILLIAMS

RY COODER was into the chorus of "Across the Borderline" when I glanced along row D of the Hammersmith Odeon stalls and saw a girl crying quietly to herself. She didn't look in distress, exactly, but these weren't tears of joy either. It seemed like a complicated set of emotions going on, and I thought: this must be some kind of song.

> When you reach the broken promised land
> And every dream slips through your hand
> Then you'll know it's too late to change your mind
> Because you've paid the price to come this far
> Just to wind up where you are
> And you're still just across the borderline

Listening to Cooder's warm, artless voice, his sweetly gliding bottleneck guitar and the band's swaying Tex-Mex rhythm, it certainly wasn't hard to share some of the same emotions. And since that night in March 1992, when Cooder and Little Village performed it at the first of their London concerts, the song has kept turning up. First there was Bob Dylan singing it on television, at the "Guitar Legends" festival in Seville. Then, picked up from a market stall, there was a £5 bootleg cassette of Bruce Springsteen using it to finish his set at a 1990 charity concert in Los Angeles. More polished versions appeared later on records by Flaco Jiminez (*Partners*, 1992), the accordionist who has often worked with Cooder, and Willie Nelson, as the title song of an exceptional album.

But Dylan and Springsteen: here are two fellows you'd trust to know a good tune when they hear it. Between them, they've composed many of the most significant songs of the last 30 years. So what drew them to a song that neither of them wrote, that wasn't written with any very profound purpose in mind, and that has never been a hit in any shape or form? And what is it that can make people cry when they hear it?

"*HE JUST* said, 'I want a song that tells the story of the film.' " Ry Cooder is thinking back to 1981, to when the British director Tony Richardson was briefing him on the soundtrack assignment for a movie called *The Border*, starring Jack Nicholson as a frontier guard fending off the wetbacks down El Paso way.

Cooder is a veteran soundtrack composer; it's how he's made his living since he realised that touring the world with a band was neither financially

5

viable nor a civilised way for a grown man to spend his time. *Southern Comfort*, *The Long Riders* and *Paris, Texas* are among his credits. He has a reputation for capturing and enhancing the moods of the southern states, thanks to his knowledge of blues, gospel, country and Tex-Mex music. So Richardson's request wasn't a surprise; but it was, in its way, a challenge.

"It's a very good film," Cooder remembers, "but a bleak and nasty one. There was Jack Nicholson with a bad haircut and a worse attitude, portraying the corruption of the immigration service. People didn't want that then, but Tony was a very uncompromising guy."

Richardson, says Cooder, wanted a song to start the film off. "You have the opening sequence of a girl and her brother trying to get across. It's about three-and-a-half minutes long, and I had to fit the tune into that space. I thought, what can I do? Woody Guthrie already wrote the anthem of those people when he came up with 'Deportees'. It's easy to fit a piece of instrumental music into a space like that, but it's hard to fit a song with lyrics.

"Well, I got lucky. I was watching the piece of film over and over again, and a little chord progression came into my mind. Then I found a little rhythm, and a tempo, and I found I had the chord structure of a melodic ballad. From what I'd already done, I knew I had a good thing. So the next job was to get a chorus. A chorus can pull people in, and I liked the little melodic thing I came up with. Then one day I was out jogging and I thought of the words for the first verse – that yellow-brick-road thing, 'There's a land, so I've been told/Every street is paved with gold . . .' Well, you've heard that a million times in gospel and pop songs, but it's still a great idea – this need that people have to feel that where they're going is better than where they've been. Little do they know! But they're driven by hope, otherwise they wouldn't go through it. Once I had that scoped out, I knew I had something I could take to John Hiatt."

> *"Which bit did I write?" says John Hiatt. "The good bit, of course!" He's right. His line is the key to the song.*

Now a fellow member of Little Village, Hiatt is a singer and songwriter who had first gone on the road with Cooder in the mid-seventies. "I drove up to his place in Topanga Canyon with a guitar and an amplifier," Cooder says. "He was asleep. But Tony was coming back from France and he needed the song. So I set up in Hiatt's yard, plugged in and played. I said, 'John, I'm in a hurry.' He said, 'Play the chorus again.' By this time he was brushing his teeth. And he stuck his head out the window and sang: 'When you reach the broken promised land . . .' The whole chorus. And I said, 'That's it, I'm outta here.' "

"Which bit did I write?" says John Hiatt. "The good bit, of course!" He's right, in that his line about "the broken promised land" is the key to the song, the idea that unlocks the emotions. It has its own specific and metaphoric meanings within the lyric, but it also resonates with rock'n'roll history.

CHUCK BERRY was sitting in jail in Springfield, Missouri in 1962, serving part of a three-year sentence for transporting an under-age girl across a state line, when he wrote a song called "The Promised Land". Aged 32, Berry had already written "Johnny B Goode", "Roll Over, Beethoven", "Sweet Little Sixteen" and a dozen other classics of early rock'n'roll. To help him write this one, though, he needed a road atlas of the United States – something that the penal authorities were reluctant to provide to a potential escapee. But he got it, and with it he wrote a song that embodies more vividly than any other the geographical and emotional reality of moving west across the USA.

On 25 February 1964, fresh out of jail, Berry recorded the song at the Chess Studios in Chicago. It gets its momentum not just from his guitar, which whines like a jet engine, but from the fact that the words don't repeat: like the journey it describes, it takes the listener from A to B, no detours.

On 15 December 1973, in one of the last genuinely creative acts of his life, Elvis Presley entered the Stax Studio on East McLemore Avenue, Memphis and cut his version of "The Promised Land". The notion of Presley, the King of Rock'n'Roll, singing his poor-boy's song of liberation is poignant enough; the spontaneous intensity with which he delivers it, snarling back at the dirty guitars of James Burton and Johnny Christopher on the sloping floor of the old cinema where Otis Redding had made his masterpieces, turns it into something else: the ultimate statement of the Tennessee truck driver who took the world, a tragic tale of desires fulfilled.

7

> I left my home in Norfolk, Virginia
> California on my mind
> I straddled that Greyhound
> And rode him into Raleigh
> And on across Carolin'

No doubt Bruce Springsteen, who could play guitar like Chuck Berry and was fixated by the destiny of Elvis Presley, knew both versions when, in 1977, he wrote his own song called "The Promised Land". Like many of the songs he composed for *Darkness on the Edge of Town*, it dealt with the frustrations caused by lawsuits between him and his former manager, which had stalled his career just when it seemed ready to take off.

These songs were about life and work, about broken promises and the ties that bind. On stage he mixed "Badlands" and "Racing in the Street" with Woody Guthrie's "This Land is Your Land", creating lengthy sequences that burned with a bitter, sullen rage.

> There's a dark cloud rising from the desert floor
> I've packed my bags and I'm heading straight into the storm
> Gonna be a twister to blow everything down
> That ain't got the faith to stand its ground

Whatever may have happened to him since then, the shadowy, fearful Promised Land that Springsteen created out of his own tribulations remains an unforgettably disturbing vision.

"*SO NOW*," Cooder resumes, "I needed a second verse, which had to take the story a little further. So I called Jim Dickinson in Memphis and played the song to him over the phone. He gave me the poetic heart of the song, the subtext. I was very appreciative."

> Up and down the Rio Grande
> A thousand footprints in the sand
> Reveal a secret no one can define
> The river flows on like a breath
> In between our life and death
> Tell me who is next to cross the borderline

"I wrote it in a hotel room in New Orleans," says Dickinson, once the pianist with the Dixie Flyers, who has worked on many of Cooder's projects. "When I heard that Dylan had done it, that was the thrill of a lifetime for me. He changes the tune and the chords a little bit. And he's the only one who really gets the meaning of that last line. Now I sing his version. I figured, who's right, me or Bob Dylan?"

In fact the first person to record the song was the singer Freddy Fender, bought in by Cooder for the soundtrack session. Fender sang it with beautiful delicacy, despite being, in Hiatt's recollection, "a little less than sober that day". Cooder himself recorded it on *Get Rhythm*, a largely unnoticed 1987 album; a third verse, half in Spanish, had been added for the actor Harry Dean Stanton to sing.

"Jackson Browne's been doing it, too," Cooder told me, "at some of his benefit concerts." But while Browne, performing it at a Sandinista fund-raiser, would be thinking of the original meaning of the song, Dylan and Springsteen surely find within it a different kind of truth. Cooder does, too. "To me," he says, "that borderline may be inside yourself."

Dickinson agrees. "It doesn't have to be about illegal aliens," he says. "It's about people who're trapped."

"I guess the larger metaphor is that there are borders we all have to cross in our lives," Hiatt adds. "It's a pretty gosh-darn powerful song."

THE WAY YOU LOOK TONIGHT

BY ROBERT CUSHMAN

POPULAR songs freeze the moment. That is what they're best at. Some of the finest – the Gershwins' "How Long Has This Been Going On" for example, or Rodgers and Hart's "I Didn't Know What Time It Was" – celebrate the moment of falling in love, and are bemused rather than euphoric. The joy is tempered with a wistful incredulity. How could this have taken so long to happen? How can it possibly last? My favourite song, "The Way You Look Tonight", music by Jerome Kern, lyric by Dorothy Fields, does all this and more.

It evokes the moment of discovery, drama-tises it, and – the last and most brilliant refine-ment – discusses it. It is, in the least pretentious way, about itself.

Nobody but Astaire could be so urbane and so diffident at the same time.

Like many songs of its era, it leads a double life. If you hear it as an independent pop song it seems to be about a first, rapturous meeting or – perhaps more likely – about the start of a date. Man greets woman, who is looking especially radiant, and compliments her. You can, within limits, construct your own scenario; and it helps if you have someone in your mind to attach it to. But it was written for a specific situation in a still-current film; Fred Astaire sings it to Ginger Rogers in their 1936 film *Swing Time*.

The extra-musical portions of *Swing Time* are, for me, the hardest to sit through of any in the Astaire-Rogers canon. This is largely because Astaire's usual comic foil, the heavyweight bumbler Edward Everett Horton, has been replaced by Victor Moore, whose clowning is so gentle as to be practically invisible. Also, the film's planned opening number was cut, so there is an interminable wait before any singing or dancing gets done. When it does, and for as long as it does, the film is a masterpiece. Song by song, it may have the best score of the series; certainly the numbers are the best-integrated with one another and with the plot. In fact the songs *are* the plot.

"The Way You Look Tonight" has a modest setup. There isn't even any dancing. Fred sits at a piano while Ginger is showering in the next room. As he plays and sings, she appears with her hair all suds and enchantedly drinks in the praise. It's absurd that *this* should be the way he is vowing to remember her: absurd and totally endearing. His singing is straightforward, with a hint of melancholy; the tone, in the fashion of the time, is surprisingly formal, though the phrasing isn't. The song, interestingly, jumps straight into sadness: "Someday when I'm awfully low/And the world is cold . . ." Having admitted the odds the song makes its first and most important statement with a slight but definite lift in the melody: "I will feel a glow/Just thinking of you/And the way you look tonight."

Then comes the masterstroke. "Oh, but you're lovely . . . ". That "oh, but", deftly fitted by Fields to Kern's pick-up notes, forestalls any chance of the second eight bars being mere repetition. Disarmingly conversational, it also suggests uncertainty, inability to find words, a sense of how-could-you-be-so-lovely, and of "lovely", though conventional (and more or less patented by Kern's contemporary Irving Berlin), being the only possible word. The song then proceeds to specific compliment: "your cheek so soft . . . your smile so warm . . . with each word your tenderness grows tearing my fears apart". The qualities praised are gentleness, wit and compassion; and the song exemplifies them even as it cites them. Kern's middle eight, trim but expansive, is remarkable even for him (by this point, it seems, an orchestra has crept into the room); and Fields's climactic bouquet – "that laugh that wrinkles your nose touches my foolish heart" – clinches both the romance and the reality. A person is being sung to, whether it's Ginger or another. And that "foolish heart" phrase has been plundered by other lyricists ever since.

The last section begins by repeating and savouring the word "lovely": this time without the hesitation. The song and the singer have moved on to a new plane of confidence. "Never never change/Keep that breathless charm/Won't you please arrange it . . ." Obviously she can't – nobody can – and in making the request the song acknowledges its impossibility. Nobody but Astaire could be so urbane and so diffident at the same time. But of course he and his writers have worked the trick anyway. As long as the song lives, so will the beauty it commemorates. Shakespeare and Keats had observed this phenomenon for their respective centuries. Kern and Fields have done it for ours.

As well as the soundtrack (reissued as *Swing Time and The Gay Divorcee*, EMI 1970), Astaire made a commercial recording of the song, done in suave dance-band fashion (Brunswick 1936, reissued on *Starring Fred Astaire*, CBS 1987). It's more insistently rhythmic than the film version, more obviously *sung*, but also more acted. "Your cheek so *soft*" is gently emphasised; "never, never change" is quietly pushed home; "breathless charm" has a tremble to it. Astaire's great singing years, though, were the fifties when the voice was lighter, more intimate, and, if I may, de-theatricalised. His film vocals of this time were a marvel, and a three-LP set (*The Astaire Story*, Mercury 1952, reissue DRG) on which he reprised his classics with a jazz quartet led by Oscar Peterson must be the most charming (among other things) vocal record ever made. He murmurs a lot here, moving at a conversational rubato through the opening section, caressing the first "tonight", then picking up a moderate tempo, kicking the beat with an amiable desperation on "there is *no-thing* for me but to love you". That "for me", by the way, is a hidden rhyme with the "warm" in the previous line; it keeps other lyricists goggling.

Though nearly everybody you would expect has recorded the song since, nobody but Astaire has come close to owning it. Billie Holiday, who spent most of the thirties singing inferior songs, never seemed to realise her luck

10

when, as here, she got a great one (*The Quintessential Billie Holiday*, Vol 2, Brunswick 1936). Her version is jaunty, no more. (Her records of the fifties tell a different story, but this song is not part of it.) Like nearly everybody, including Astaire, she neglected the song's coda; a series of precisely notated hums that balance the stammers of the beginning. (Once we couldn't find the words; now we don't need them.) Most singers leave these sighs to their accompanists; a happy exception is Peggy Lee, who recorded the song with Benny Goodman in 1942 (Columbia, reissued on *A Portrait of Peggy Lee*, CBS/Sony). Cool and tingling, it's one of the few mementoes of her band-singing days that forecast greatness.

My two favourite instrumental versions date from the early fifties, and both emphasise joy, not regret. A buoyantly rhapsodic interpretation by Coleman Hawkins (with Miles Davis in support; *Blowin' up a Breeze —Coleman Hawkins Plays the Windy City*, Spotlite 1963) does especial justice to the coda. Sonny Rollins's work-out with Thelonious Monk ("The Way You Blow Tonight", *Sonny Rollins*, Prestige 1954) is an amiable hurricane. Its vocal counterpart is Mel Tormé, paying tribute to Astaire in 1956 (*Mel Tormé loves Fred Astaire*, Bethlehem) and sailing exhilaratingly through and around a fast West Coast arrangement. He *starts* with a coda: "lovely . . . never never change". There seens no chance that she will. There is no uncertainty in Tormé's version, no psychological progression; the drama comes from his exploration of Kern's harmonic possibilities and from the insouciant accuracy of everything he does. Dick Haymes, magnificent balladeer, took the opposite tack (*Moondreams*, Capitol 1957). He starts sombre: "AWFULLY low . . . the world is COLD." He is wonderstruck, and he is halfway through the song before he can believe his good fortune. His final "I LOVE you" is triumphant (it helps that he can hit the note so ringingly) but the possibility of loss still hovers.

11

Neither Ella Fitzgerald nor Frank Sinatra got to the song till the early sixties: a little late, I think. Both used arrangements by Nelson Riddle. Ella's (*The Jerome Kern Songbook*, Verve 1963) is a lullaby version: sweet of course but too slow to flow. And since she isn't a dramatic singer, the pauses don't mean anything. Sinatra (*Academy Award Winners*, Reprise 1964) merely crosses the song off his list: a swinging lovers' treatment, without the commitment. Neither he nor Ella explores the song as they could. They should have exchanged tempos. More recently and eccentrically Peter Skellern (*Astaire*, Mercury 1979) offers one of his passionately sedate, oddly touching Astaire homages; Kiri Te Kanawa (*Kiri Sings Kern*, EMI 1983), though less overbearing than often in this territory, glides through the song without leaving a mark.

The song itself glides. That is the mark of an Astaire, even one that excludes dance. But I can imagine it being sung out of tempo all the way through: thoughtfully, musingly, ecstatically. With each word its tenderness grows; and the encounter might as easily be sexual as social. The voice I hear in my head is that of Rosemary Clooney, who today sings classic pop more warmly and expressively than anyone: she has never recorded this song, and might do it definitively.

Recently, "The Way You Look Tonight" has gone back to the movies. It is a grace note in the British film *Peter's Friends* (1992): a quiet moment in the otherwise stormy reunion of half a dozen college friends. Hugh Laurie sits down at the piano and dreamily plunks it out; Imelda Staunton, the singer of the bunch, begins it sweetly; the others – Kenneth Branagh, Alphonsia Emmanuel, Emma Thompson, Stephen Fry – gradually drift over and join in. Whether the writers chose the song purposefully or whether anything equally "squishy" (their word) would have done as well, remains uncertain. But the song brings the friends together as almost nothing else does (the hangers-on they have brought to the party remain pointedly outside the circle): a hedge against the world for them, the poignantly miserable, just as it was for Fred and Ginger, the poignantly happy. The song, concerned with preserving the present, began by projecting itself into a chilly future which it proceeds to redeem. It seems to have got it right.

ALWAYS ON MY MIND

BY BEN THOMPSON

IT'S not every day you find yourself sharing a misconception with Roger Whittaker. I'm holding in my hand a CD copy of Roger's 1986 album *His Finest Collection* (Tembo). There's a version of "Always on My Mind" on it. It's not a great version – the mood is funereal and the trademark Whittaker whistle is too far down in the mix – and the song is credited to Willie Nelson, legendary cowboy-pothead, the first man to smoke marijuana in the White House and talk about it. I thought it was by him too. So did a passing librarian at the National Sound Archive.

There is a gentle irony in the fact that Willie Nelson is best known for a song he didn't actually write, given how many instant standards – "Crazy" and "Funny How Time Slips Away" not least among them – he has penned for other people. "Always on My Mind" is actually the work of the less than celebrated American songwriting team of Johnny Christopher, Wayne Thompson (no relation) and Mark James. It was first recorded in March 1972, in

★ ★ ★ ★ ★ ★ ★ ★ ★ ★

"I thought I sounded very sincere and my voice was dripping with emotion," Neil Tennant says, *"until people started congratulating me on being so deadpan."*

★ ★ ★ ★ ★ ★ ★ ★ ★ ★

the MGM studios in Los Angeles, by Elvis Presley (who was singing the odd Willie Nelson song at the time, but this wasn't one of them). The band featured, among others, James Burton on guitar, Ronnie Tutt on drums, and J. D. Sumner and the Stamps on backing vocals. The song was released on *Separate Ways* (RCA), the album that also gave the world "Old Shep".

The cover of this record features the white-spangled, Vegas-era Elvis, more badly drawn than at any other point in his career. His legs are planted on divergent roads – a clever visual image, I'm sure you'll agree – and it looks like he's about to be run over (which, I suppose, is pretty much what eventually did happen, though no-one knew that Elvis himself would be driving the car). "Always on My Mind" did go its separate ways. In America it languished in album-track obscurity. In Britain – which has always appreciated a fine whine – it was released as a single, getting no higher than No 9 in the charts, but hanging around for 18 weeks, and in the process establishing itself as a pub-jukebox classic.

It's one of those songs, like the Bee Gees' "More than a Woman", whose words get more disturbing the more you think about them. "Maybe I didn't treat you quite as good as I should have," Elvis admits, ungrammatically. "Maybe I didn't love you quite as often as I could have . . . but you were always on my mind." Oh well, that's all right then. If you were *thinking* about me, that makes it OK that you were running around with all those drum-majorettes.

"Little things I should have said and done," Elvis continues – showing off now – "I just never took the time . . . but you were always on my mind. You were always on my mind." You'd think this would be the time for the confessing to stop and the repenting to start, but he just has to keep rubbing salt into the wounds. "Maybe I didn't hold you all those lonely lonely times, and I guess I never told you I'm so happy that you're mine. If I made you feel second best, girl I'm so sorry I was blind: you were always on my mind. You were always on my mind." How comforting can that last repetition be? Not comforting enough.

At last, it's pay-off time. But instead of falling on his paper knife in an act of ritual seppukku, the dirty stopout still has the nerve to make requests, and does so with all the cringing self-righteousness of the true miscreant. "Tell me, tell me that your sweet love hasn't died. Give me, give me one more chance to keep you satisfied." Only a really great singer could make this work, and Elvis does, his gentle repetition of "satisfied" carrying the day. The strings glisten, the tune is hymnal, and the singer had lost his own wife by this time, so he knew a thing or two about remorse. When he goes over his crimes again to the fade, it does sound as if he's truly sorry. "Little things I should have said and done, I just never took the time, but you were always on my mind, you were always on my mind."

An alternate take of this version appeared on the soundtrack of the 1981 film *This is Elvis* (Warner Bros), but it was not until a year later, ten years after it was first recorded, that "Always on My Mind" got the respect it deserved in the land of its birth. Johnny Christopher offered it to Willie Nelson, tactfully neglecting to mention that Elvis had already recorded it. Nelson liked it, and wanted to record the song with his partner in outlawdom, Merle Haggard. Haggard didn't fancy it, so Nelson sang the song on his own, with the first two lines swapped, to put oftenness of loving before goodness of treating. His version was a massive crossover hit – No 5 in the US pop charts – and was voted best country song of 1982.

The difference in the two singers could hardly be greater. Elvis' voice is deep and voluptuous, Nelson's is crisp and nasal; but Nelson has a way of half-speaking a line that lodges it in your brain. If there was any liquid in it, his voice would ooze conviction (Nelson, old devil that he is, was already on his third marriage by then). The backing is sparser too – it starts with a simple, courtly piano; and there's no big orchestral flourish, just a plaintive little solo from Nelson's faithful, one-step-behind-the-beat guitar, known as Trigger.

The little Latin theme which Nelson's solo brought out was expanded upon by Laurindo Almeida – Stan Kenton's old guitarist and first evangelist of bossa nova – in a version of the song on his 1984 album *Artistry in Rhythm* (Concord Jazz). "This album will provide three-star restaurants with a perfect backdrop for dining," the sleeve notes claim, somewhat ominously, but there's rather more to it than that. Almeida's is a delicate, mischievous cover, with a lovely bass part from former Buddy Rich sideman Bob Magnusson.

"Always on My Mind" is now part of the scaly skin of every self-respecting lounge lizard, but few dare to take real liberties with it. The underrated Joe Longthorne adds a nice pedal-steel and a bit of high-quality chicken-in-the-basket quavering on *The Joe Longthorne Songbook* (Telstar 1988), but then allows the whole thing to be cocked up with a horrific guitar solo. Vince Hill (*Lovesongs*, Pickwick 1987) ushers in the eccentric harmonica part the song was always crying out for, but then as the inner sleeve points out, "since the mid-sixties the name of Vince Hill has been synonymous with quality".

The meaning of the song changes in an interesting way when a woman sings it. It would be nice to hear Madonna or Sinead O'Connor have a go at "Always on My Mind", and be really unrepentant. Brenda Cochrane gives it her best shot though. Cochrane's version, on her 1991 album *In Dreams* (Polydor), can call upon the full might of Gavin Wright and his orchestra, but it still veers a little too strongly towards atonement for my liking.

There is one great female recording. Cissy Houston – Whitney's mum – gives "Always on My Mind" its most dramatic reading; frogmarching the song into the back room and scolding some moral sense into it. It's not just her frighteningly disciplined vocal pyrotechnics, or the sublimely funky piano-and-organ tussle in mid-song, that make Houston's powerhouse gospel version (*I'll Take Care of You*, Shanachie 1992, with Chuck Jackson) stand out. The way she opens the song up to new interpretations is also remarkable – as a religious confession maybe, or even, in the closing whoops that sound almost like "mama", as a declaration of love for a parent. Coming from a great singer who is now best-known as a lesser singer's mother, this has several layers of subtext.

Bert Weedon, on the other hand, turns the song into "Cherry Pink and Apple Blossom White" (*Once More with Feeling: 16 Great Love Songs*, Pickwick 1988). "Music should in sound convey what dying lovers dare not say," it says on the cover, "We think that Bert's playing does just that."

If you had been asked, in 1987, to pick the band least likely to record "Always on My Mind", the Pet Shop Boys would have been on the shortlist. But then an American TV company rang them up, asking if they would be one of several groups doing Elvis covers for a show marking the 10th anniversary of his death. "We got a huge pile of Elvis cassettes to pick a song off," Neil Tennant remembers. " 'Always on My Mind' was on the first one, *Magic Moments of Elvis*. Chris [Lowe] and I both liked the song, and we decided to do it so we wouldn't have to listen to all the others. All the Americans kept asking us why we were doing a Willie Nelson song – we had to explain to them about the Elvis version."

Legend has it that the Pet Shop Boys' intentions towards the song were not entirely honourable. "Oh no." Tennant is shocked. "We'd never actually do a song that we didn't really like. The only challenge was that we knew everyone else was going to do their songs very much in the style of Elvis Presley, so we wanted to make sure ours was very different. It was around the time that Acid House was starting, and everyone had their own idea of what it might sound like, so we wanted this to be ours."

Does he think there's anything strange about the singer's point of view in the song? "Not really. It's very much a country sentiment, that the man should be a bastard." The nine-minute album version (on *Introspective*, EMI 1988) even fills out the singer's point of view, with Tennant's voice intoning at varying speeds "I worked so hard, I thought you knew/ My love I did it all for you". The seven-inch version is the best – a delirious and economical hi-energy stomp which successfully translates the simple country chord changes of the original into the language of the dancefloor, in which they are just as, if not even more, effective.

Neil Tennant's voice was, as so often, misunderstood. "I thought I sounded very sincere and my voice was dripping with emotion," Tennant says, "until people started congratulating me on being so deadpan. That was when I realised that there was a big difference between how I thought my voice sounded, and how everyone else did." Well meant as it was, the Pet Shop Boys' restructuring of the song would have dire consequences. It went to No 1 in Britain and brought the darkest forces of MOR into the open. The Shadows recorded a truly horrific version of the Pet Shop Boys' version, complete with proto-rave drum bump, on their 1989 album *Reflection* (Polydor). Hank Marvin wrestled that "Mind" note into heartbreaking contortions, but the coup de grace was left, appropriately enough, to the great James Last.

16

The year is 1990. The album is *Dance Dance Dance* (Polydor). Last, vicious post-modernist that he is, puts the song in a medley. Try and guess the two songs he puts it in with. Yes, that's right, the Timelords' "Doctor in the Tardis" and Sinitta's "So Macho". Doctor Who-oo, in the tardis. He's gotta be . . . so macho! You were always on my mind. It makes a warped kind of sense. Especially with party noises in the background and the final chorus sung by a posse of drunken English-as-a-Foreign-Language students. You can hear the song talk in Last's version though, right at the start, where a warped voiceover chants in tribute to the Pet Shop Boys, "What have I, what have I, what have I done to deserve this".

As if "Always on My Mind" hadn't suffered enough, it was then condemned to eternal damnation in video karaoke hell. On *The Original Karaoke Volume Seven* (Picture Music International, 1992), the music is Willie Nelson's arrangement played by robots. The words come up on the screen with a colour band moving across to show you when to sing, and the song's story is acted out by catalogue models. A neglected young wife hands her husband a beer. He snubs her and carries on playing his guitar. A hotshot producer whisks him off to Hollywood where he records the song, and is too busy to ring her up. She decides to leave him, packs her bags and walks out to the jeep, but he returns, having walked out on a recording session to be with her. She looks doubtful for a moment but then they kiss, and the reconciliation is complete. Go on then, sing along, see if you can make it convincing.

OVER THE RAINBOW

BY MARY HARRON

IN *1983*, Jerry Lee Lewis played the Wembley Country Music Festival. He flew into London shrouded in scandal. Drugs and alcohol had left him with a quarter of his stomach, the US government was pursuing him for tax evasion, he had shot his bass player in a fit of pique, and there had been the mysterious death of his fourth wife (not to be confused with the mysterious death of his third wife). He seemed to be riding out his own damnation. Jerry Lee probably wouldn't show, and if he did he'd do only country music, as it pleased him to frustrate his fans by refusing them his greatest hits.

He did turn up, and it was the greatest live performance I ever saw. It was not so much a revival as a resurrection of the spirit that made audiences in the fifties tear theatres apart. For an hour or so he pulverised the audience with incandescent rock'n'roll. Then he sat back at the piano and muttered a few words at us in his incomprehensible Louisiana swamp drawl.

His hand fluttered moodily, absent-mindedly, over the keys, and he began to sing:

> **Somewhere over the rainbow, bluebirds fly**
> **They're flying high over that old rainbow . . .**
> **I wonder why, oh Lord, why can't I?**

It was understated, delicate even, and electrifyingly sinister. It was as menacing as the black clouds that hover over Dorothy's farmhouse in *The Wizard of Oz*: the lyrics, with their candy-coloured visions, were shown to be full of latent evil. (Only in concert, by the way. The studio version, on *Killer Country*, Elektra 1980, doesn't come close.) There was deep irony, but also regret, as if Jerry Lee were the serpent in the Garden of Eden, longing for a paradise that his presence had destroyed.

Naturally, he customised the lyric:

> **Somewhere over the rainbow, way up high**
> **You know there's a land old Jerry dreamed of,**
> **Once in a lullaby.**

He knew how well the song played into his mythic past, the astonishing early stardom, the vertiginous fall, and a life spent lurching from one violent tragedy to another. "Over the Rainbow" became a testament to his own bewilderment at all the things that had slipped from his grasp. (And being Jerry Lee, there was a ripple of evil amusement running through it.) The song had a history he could work with. It already belonged to Judy Garland, Judy the abused child star, with her drink and drugs, her showbusiness martyrdom. Jerry Lee simply let his myth resonate against hers.

The memory of that night is superimposed with another, 15 years earlier, when my parents took me to one of Judy Garland's last shows. Teetering like a bird on frail little legs, body bloated with alcohol, she was in her mid-forties but seemed 60. When the time came to sing "Over the Rainbow", she sat down by the footlights and, unable to make the high notes, wryly made the audience sing along. It was said that those last performances were ambulance chases, that people came to see Judy Garland fail, but to me it was charming and heroic.

"Over the Rainbow" is not my favourite song, although Harold Arlen's music is lovely; but no other has such a strange psychic pull. I first heard it, of course, in *The Wizard of Oz*, but I forget when: the movie runs through childhood like the letters in a stick of rock, one Christmas viewing blurring into another.

In the beginning, it was only a song for children. The story of *The Wizard of Oz* was an American classic that MGM hoped could rival the screen success of *Snow White*, filmed two years earlier in 1937. They wanted Jerome Kern to write the tunes, but he wasn't available, so they asked Harold Arlen, who had written "Stormy Weather" and would go on to write the music for *A Star is Born*. The lyricist was E. Y. (Yip) Harburg, who'd done "Brother, Can You Spare a Dime" and "April in Paris". In David Shipman's excellent biography of Judy Garland (*The Secret Life of an American Legend*, Hyperion 1992), Harburg says: "Judy was an unusual child with an ability to project a song and a voice that penetrated your insides . . . She was the most unusual voice in the first half of this century . . . Judy Garland was to singing what Gershwin was to music. They brought a quality and vitality that was typically and uniquely American."

> ★ ★ ★ ★ ★ ★ ★ ★ ★ ★
>
> *If a producer called Arthur Freed hadn't talked Louis B. Mayer out of it, the most famous song in motion pictures would have ended up on the cutting-room floor.*
>
> ★ ★ ★ ★ ★ ★ ★ ★ ★ ★

The early story is filled with near-misses. MGM nearly cast Shirley Temple as Dorothy, hideous thought. Once the film was made, the first previews suggested it was too long. Louis B. Mayer thought the answer was to drop "Over the Rainbow": if a producer called Arthur Freed hadn't talked him out of it, the most famous song in motion pictures would have ended up on the cutting-room floor.

In 1939, the song won an Academy Award. Within a few months, the war was giving those yearning lyrics a whole new meaning. The song's transformation had begun.

Even in 1939, it had undercurrents. Dorothy sings it at the start of the film, when her happy home is disrupted because her neighbour wants to destroy her pet dog, and her beloved aunt and uncle agree. She wants to go over the rainbow because her own world is no longer a sanctuary: childhood is over, paradise is lost.

But Judy Garland was not a child when she sang the song. She was 16, with her bust rigidly corseted to make her look younger. Sung by an adolescent, the song reveals a hidden psychodrama of sexual fear and unease: "Toto, I have a feeling we're not in Kansas any more." The society that produced this sweet confection was sleazy and corrupt.

Perhaps that's why the movie's vision of paradise was so kitsch, with its candy colours and artificial flowers: an innocence that parodies itself.

Where troubles melt like lemon drops
Away above the chimney tops . . .

Like a photograph in a darkroom tray, the campness in "Over the Rainbow" revealed itself slowly. It was a natural favourite among the friends of Dorothy. Drag queens emoted to it, Liberace took it to Las Vegas. The song's appeal lay in Garland's tragic glamour: the irony that the little gingham-clad farm girl had actually spent her childhood on a movie set, fed a steady diet of amphetamines so she could work longer hours. Camp is a winking acknowledgement of the deceptions that lie beneath the surface, and *The Wizard of Oz* is camp to us because we know now what the real Hollywood – so corrupt, so sexualised – was like.

The best recent commentary on "Over the Rainbow" is in a movie where the song is never played. Almost 50 years after *The Wizard of Oz*, David Lynch made *Blue Velvet* with a heroine named Dorothy. Instead of ruby slippers, she wore red high heels. (The part of Jerry Lee Lewis was played by Dennis Hopper.)

Lynch, who is from the Mid-West, is obsessed with *The Wizard of Oz*. Early drafts of the script of *Blue Velvet* are sprinkled with references to it, and there were more in his next film, *Wild at Heart*, which ends with the Good Witch Glinda descending in a bright pink bubble.

Lynch was giving us *The Wizard of Oz* for adults only. He showed how Hollywood kitsch had permeated our dreams. We absorbed its brilliant blue skies and picket fences, and they became our emblems of security, but at the same time we took in Hollywood's unease. We sensed that there was something darker, some web of guilty secrets, beneath the too-bright surface. *The Wizard of Oz* teaches us disillusion: there is a wicked witch at the end of the yellow brick road, and the wizard is a fake.

The level of irony in "Over the Rainbow" depends on how the singer feels about paradise. In the original, Garland's tone is deep and mature but she has the clarity and freshness of a child. In 1960 when she recorded the song again (*Judy Garland: The London Sessions*, Capitol) the childlike lyrics were delivered with hopeless melancholy. It had become a lament for her own life.

As her biographer writes, "the song no longer belonged to Dorothy; it belonged, forever, to Judy Garland".

Because it deals with innocence and experience, dream and disillusion, "Over the Rainbow" seems capable of infinite adaptations. A few years ago a male falsetto version stormed the gay clubs of New York; it could be taken

19

first as a triumphant anthem of sexual liberation and later as a requiem for Aids.

The song can be high camp or showbusiness melodrama or delicate jazz. It has been recorded by Basie and Brubeck, Sinatra and Fitzgerald, Max Bygraves, Richard Clayderman, Patti Labelle, Melissa Manchester, John Martyn and Willie Nelson. But only one version I know rivals Garland's. It's by Aretha Franklin, and was part of her first major-label recording session, in 1961 (*The Great Aretha Franklin, The First Twelve Sides*, Columbia 1972). She was 18: like Garland, a teenager who combined youthful exuberance with the power and technique of a mature woman. Her delivery was elegant and truthful, with a simple jazz backdrop and no stylistic excesses, just a voice brimming with feeling. Only in the last verse did she let fly with gospel emotion. The best versions of "Over the Rainbow" come from extremes. You have to be very young or very disappointed to do this song justice.

LEFT: Patsy Cline was reluctant to record "I Fall to Pieces", which had been turned down by other artists. However, she was persuaded to make a recording of it in 1960 and it transformed her career.

★ ★ ★ ★ ★ ★ ★ ★

RIGHT: "The Way You Look Tonight" was written for a specific situation: Fred Astaire sings it to Ginger Rogers in the 1936 film Swing Time. *Billie Holiday recorded a jaunty version of it, also in 1936, but only Astaire has come close to owning it.*

BELOW: Composed by a teenage Franz Schubert in 1816, "Erlkönig" has been a favourite with Lieder singers ever since. The baritone Dietrich Fischer-Dieskau's version succeeds in conveying the thrill and excitement of the story. It is a treasurable piece of scene-setting.

★ ★ ★ ★ ★ ★ ★

ABOVE: The Rolling Stones recorded "(I Can't Get No) Satisfaction" in Chicago in 1965. It went to No 1 in both the States and the UK, and was the band's first US chart-topper. At last the Stones had found a sound to match their fury.

RIGHT: Neil Young was reluctant to analyse the meaning of "Only Love Can Break Your Heart" which appeared on his 1970 album After the Goldrush. *He commented, "It was written for somebody – I think it was Graham Nash".*

★ ★ ★ ★ ★ ★ ★ ★ ★ ★ ★

BELOW: Frank Sinatra recorded "My Funny Valentine" in 1953. His intimate and informal version moved it out of the theatre and into the nightclub.

RIGHT: "Over the Rainbow" seems capable of infinite adaptations. But, as Judy Garland's biographer writes, "the song no longer belonged to Dorothy; it belonged, forever, to Judy Garland".

ABOVE LEFT: *Ry Cooder composed "Across the Borderline" as part of a soundtrack assignment for the 1981 film* The Border *which starred Jack Nicholson. "It's a very good film," Cooder remembers, "but a bleak and nasty one."*

LEFT: *One of Bob Dylan's biographers claims that "Blowin' in the Wind", written in 1962, may be the only song from the 1960s that will be remembered 100 years from now. Dylan also wrote the plainest of country songs "I'll Be Your Baby Tonight".*

★ ★ ★ ★ ★ ★ ★ ★ ★ ★ ★ ★ ★ ★ ★

CENTRE: *The debut single from Procol Harum, "A Whiter Shade of Pale", was the surprise hit of summer 1967. The title has the authority of a line of Shakespeare and is as catchy as the most persistent jingle.*

BELOW: *Rodgers and Hammerstein wrote "You'll Never Walk Alone" for the musical* Carousel *in 1945. Gerry and the Pacemakers took it to the top of the British charts in 1963. Six weeks later someone sang it on the terraces of Anfield, where it has remained for over thirty years.*

★ ★ ★ ★ ★ ★ ★ ★ ★

CENTRE: First recorded by Elvis Presley in 1972, "Always on My Mind" reached No 9 in the UK charts. It remained there for eighteen weeks and in the process established itself as a pub jukebox classic.

FAR RIGHT: "Girl from Ipanema" made an overnight star of the unknown Brazilian Astrud Gilberto, whose charming, tremble-free recording became a hit in the States in 1964 and won a Grammy Award for Best Song.

RIGHT: The best jazz/pop record of "You're the Top" is Ella Fitzgerald's version, recorded as part of her Cole Porter Songbook *in 1956. It is warm and precise over an uninventive but invigorating arrangement.*

BELOW RIGHT: Perhaps the best known recent recording of "These Foolish Things" is by Bryan Ferry. It appeared on his solo debut album in 1973 and led the jazz critic Francis Davis to describe him as "the British postmodern crooner".

★ ★ ★ ★ ★ ★ ★ ★ ★ ★

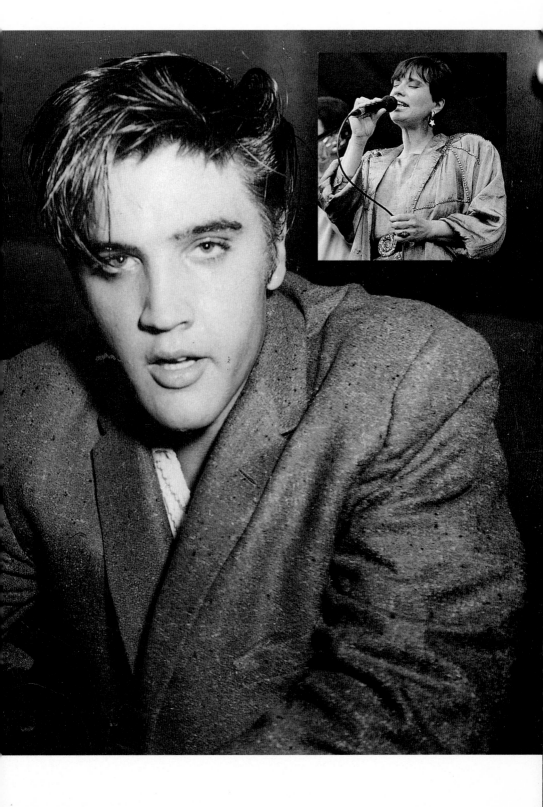

ABOVE: "Body and Soul" has provoked some of the most important jazz performances of the century. Legend has it that Billie Holiday performed it as an audition for her first job in New York in 1930.

LEFT: "How Long Has This Been Going On?" is a comfortable choice for non-singers. Audrey Hepburn's rendition in Funny Face, in which she starred with Fred Astaire in 1957, suited the shy character she played.

★ ★ ★ ★ ★ ★ ★ ★ ★ ★ ★ ★ ★

TAKE ME TO THE RIVER

BY TIM DE LISLE

BEFORE rock'n'roll meant music, it meant sex. It was a piece of slang, used by black Americans, especially in the south. Black music, at the time, meant either jazz, or blues, or (especially in the south) gospel. When blues lightened into rhythm and blues, and then gospel and country-and-western (the white man's music) were added to the stew, the result was steamy enough to be called rock'n'roll. So sex and religion, sin and sanctity, are there in rock's genes, deep in its DNA.

The same combination can be found in dozens of the stars' CVs – stepping out of the choirstalls and into the studio – but none illustrates it more vividly than Al Green. Before he was ten, Al was singing in a gospel quartet with his brothers, Walter, William and Robert. At 13, he left the group: the story goes that he was fired by his father, after being caught listening to the profane music of Jackie Wilson. At 18, in 1964, he became a profes-

★ ★ ★ ★ ★ ★ ★ ★ ★ ★

Al Green's original doesn't sound like a nine-piece band playing: it sounds like nine instruments humming.

★ ★ ★ ★ ★ ★ ★ ★ ★ ★

sional club singer, and formed a band of his own, the Creations. Seven years later he was a star, crossing over from the *Billboard* R'n'B chart to the pop chart with the silkiest, slinkiest string of hits that soul music has known. On record sleeves he wore a white suit. In concert he was more often topless. The term "sex god" was much used.

In 1976 he was ordained a pastor of the Full Gospel Tabernacle. He bought a church on the outskirts of Memphis and became its minister. He's still there today. He did not stop making records, though for a long time they were gospel, not soul, and when they are soul, they are not very physical – the words are all about love, and general enough to apply equally well to God and woman.

It wasn't always so. Al Green's spiritual rebirth is variously dated 1973 and 1974. He has tended to say '73; others have argued for '74, the year that he had a brush with death. An ex-girlfriend, Mary Woodson, burst into his house in Memphis while he was having a shower. She poured boiling grits over him, then shot herself dead with his gun. He went to hospital with sec-ond-degree burns.

That was in October. In December he released the album *Al Green Explores Your Mind*, and on it was a song called "Take Me to the River". Musically, it was much like any other track sung by Green and produced by Willie Mitchell, the southern soul maestro who ran Hi Records, the Memphis Horns and the Memphis Strings: R'n'B with lashings of subtlety, a light, easy, late-night sound, in which the horns, the strings, the organ, the guitars and that honey-vinegar voice blend into a single swinging, winning thing. It doesn't sound like a nine-piece band playing: it sounds like nine instruments humming.

Lyrically, the song was something else. If Green's career crystallises something about rock in general, this lyric does the same for Green in general. This is where the two Als meet. In the verses, it's the sex god speaking:

> I don't know why
> I love you like I do
> With all the changes
> That you put me through.
>
> You take my money,
> My cigarettes.
> And I haven't seen
> How to have you yet.
>
> I wanna know,
> Won't you tell me,
> Am I
> In love to stay?

In the chorus, the servant of God takes over:

22

> Take me to the river
> Wash me down
> Won't you cleanse my soul
> Put my feet on the ground

But not for long:

> Hold me, squeeze me
> Love me, tease me
> Till I can't – till I can't
> I can't take no more.

So: he's in love, and he doesn't know whether she's in love with him. Why this need for baptism, for ritual purification? The answer has to wait until the fifth verse:

> Love is a notion
> that I can't forget
> My sweet sixteen
> I would never regret.

The split personality doesn't extend to the music. When the words tear themselves away from romance, the music goes on boiling up, so there's a delicious contrast: it's the oldest game in town, body vs. soul, and judging by "hold me, squeeze me", soul is not the winner.

"It's almost a gospel song," Willie Mitchell says. "The music is R&B all the way, but the words – it's really a message song." I asked if he had rated it as a great song at the time. "Of course," he said, with a twinkle in his voice.

In fact he didn't put it out as a single, and the only evidence that he had a high opinion of it is that he was at the console again a year later, when the first cover version was done. The singer was the Chicago blues-and-soul-man Syl Johnson. As well as Green's producer, he had most of the same musicians – the Hi house band, featuring the Hodges brothers, Leroy (bass), Charlie (organ, piano) and Mabon (guitar). "Take Me to the River" was one of several songs written by Green with Mabon Hodges, the youngest, known as Teeny. "Al would do the words," Mitchell says, "and Teeny'd do the music – well, he and Al together."

Syl Johnson kept the same chugging rhythm and the gentle swelling horns, but added his own instrument, the harmonica. His voice was grittier, more assertive than Green's, and behind it Mitchell put the crisper, more northern soul sound that he had deliberately weaned Green away from. This time the song was a single: it reached No 7 in the American R'n'B chart. The album, now reissued on CD, was called *Total Explosion*.

Another year on, and "Take Me to the River" was recorded by white people for the first time: Foghat, a blues-rock quartet whose sleeve photograph (for *Night Shift*, on Rhino) reveals not just the shoulder-length perms that were *de rigueur* at the time, but shoulder-length permed moustaches too. Why they recorded "Take Me to the River" is not entirely clear. If they had to do yet another fast loud heavy jam, you would have thought they could do it without desecrating a soul tune.

At this stage few people would have called the song great. That changed in 1978, when it was sung by two singers who had already achieved a measure of greatness and a third who was heading that way. Levon Helm, drummer and singer with The Band, included it on his second solo album, *Levon Helm* (MCA, USA). One of The Band's hallmarks had been a powerful sense of southern history. Helm cut his record at Muscle Shoals, Alabama, one of the south's historic studios, and used some of the crack players he had grown up listening to, including Steve Cropper, who had co-written both "Knock on Wood" and "Dock of the Bay". The result was impeccable, but not very interesting: a photocopy of Syl Johnson, with a little more shading on the horns.

Meanwhile, in Montreux, Switzerland, Bryan Ferry was recording "Take Me to the River" for his fifth solo album, *The Bride Stripped Bare* (Polydor). "I did it in quite a traditional way," Ferry says. "I love the Al Green. I'm one of his greatest fans. I love the feel of it – all that music that comes out of Memphis has always been quite magical for me." In fact his version is unassumingly different. There are four people playing, not nine or ten: just two guitars, bass and drums. For the first time, the bass is not just a base: you can

23

hear it meandering along, with unexpected elegance, while the guitars have a nice conversation – one bluesy and crunchy, the other shiny and countrified, with a twang that Teeny Hodges would approve of. The singing is very Ferry, stylised but not unfeeling.

Meanwhile, in London and New York, a New Wave had broken, and men like Helm and Ferry were being made to feel old by a generation of angry young punks. Among the new bands was an East Coast art-school quartet called Talking Heads. They weren't punks at all, but they played fast and tight enough to attract the same sort of press. When they toured Britain with the Ramones, Dee Dee Ramone was shocked. "They were so strange. We were into the Sex Pistols and stuff like that, and they were into this whole funky thing. They were listening to Al Green."

On that tour Talking Heads met Brian Eno, who had been in Roxy Music with Ferry until they discovered that the band wasn't big enough for the both of them. For their second album (*More Songs About Buildings and Food*, Sire), Talking Heads went to Nassau, with Eno as producer, and recorded "Take Me to the River". It was the only cover version they ever did. "Unfortunately," Ferry says, "their one was very good. They turned it inside out. And it was their breakthrough record."

What Talking Heads had done was pull an art-school trick: apply an idea, a little lateral thought, to something familiar. "We played it live in the studio," Tina Weymouth, the bass player, said later. "It sounded so great when we listened to the playback that we immediately imposed a rule on ourselves – that this song would have no additional playing on it, except single notes. Just one *ping* or *bop* or *pang*."

Thanks to Eno's sense of space, the backdrop is wide open, with a huge drum in one speaker, a cymbal in the other, and a big, juicy bassline oozing between the two. On top, you get these wonderful splashes and sploshes, dabs of organ and guitar, in patterns of endless variation, and over that, Byrne's voice, suddenly growing into something like soulfulness. Every sound is distinct: Willie Mitchell's soup has been replaced by a stir-fry. This, not the original, is the standard by which other versions will be judged.

America saw this, and gave the group, and the song, their first run in the pop chart. (It reached No 29. It has yet to be a hit in Britain, a fact that will one day be rectified by an advertising agency.) It set Talking Heads on a new path: two years later they went on tour as a nine-piece funk band, aiming for the ecstatic release that Byrne had found in African music. "Take Me to the River" would always come near the end of the show, a natural climax.

You can hear how it sounded on *The Name of This Band is Talking Heads* (Sire 1982, recorded in '81) and the album or video of Jonathan Demme's great concert film, *Stop Making Sense* (Sire 1984). In '81 the expanded band did something unheard of: it had two bass players, Tina Weymouth for the upper octaves and Busta Jones for the lower. The effect is almost too good. The song, like the band, kept on growing. In '81 they added gospel backing vocals; in '84 they got really carried away, and included a guitar solo.

24

Next came another twist: the song was sung by a woman. It was 1985, the age of the toy boy: the woman was Diane Schuur, a mature mainstream jazz singer, who did it with more power and gloss than feeling (*Schuur Thing*, GRP). In 1987 Tina Turner followed suit, on the 12-inch single "What You Get Is What You See" (Capitol). Her comeback had begun with an Al Green song, "Let's Stay Together". Here she had the same producer, Martyn Ware of Heaven 17, without the same dividends. Tina got overexcited, yelling "Wash meh!" before the music started. Ware felt the need to use all 48 tracks, and both forgot that what had made "Let's Stay Together" so good was its restraint.

In 1988 the song appeared on another 12-inch B-side, "There's No Deceiving You" by the Blue Ox Babes (Go! Discs). They sped it up, and added a promising boogie-woogie piano and a country fiddle. But the singer was a bored punk who didn't wake up until the final chorus. Finally, in 1991, the song was recorded, as all great soul tunes had to be, by the Commitments, for Alan Parker's film of the same name (MCA). Their version is big without being moving (the race is not to the swift, nor the battle to the Andrew Strong). But it's fun. It sounds like a dozen Irish people having a good time, which is what it is.

THE SONG still holds some mysteries. Who was the 16-year-old? Why did Al Green feel so bad about her, especially if he hadn't had her yet? Was Little Junior Parker, the "cousin o' mine" to whom he dedicates the song, the same Little Junior Parker who had recorded the original version of the seminal "Mystery Train"?

To find out, I rang the Rev Green in Memphis. Did he remember writing the song? "Sure I remember. Yes sir." Could he tell me about it? "I just made a new record, and it's called *Don't Look Back*. And that's what I'm doin'."

I tried rephrasing the question. He wasn't fooled.

It didn't matter. The great songs are greater than the sum of their facts. They are canvases, spaces which allow musicians to express themselves, and listeners to draw their own conclusions. For me, it's all in the third line. "I don't know why/ I love you like I do/ With all the changes/ That you put me through." It's odd that he says "changes". You'd expect "trouble" – and when the verse is reprised, you get it. Why "changes"?

Because this is a song about transformation. It marked Al Green's change from heart-throb to pastor. It marked Talking Heads' change from a nervy, nerdy, white sound to a big fat black sound, from four-piece to nine-piece, from post-punk to post-funk. The message is clear: if this song doesn't change you, you won't get much change out of it.

25

MY FUNNY VALENTINE

BY GILES SMITH

ELLA SANG it slow and Frank made it swing. Tony Bennett kind of spoiled it and Miles Davis made it last for 15 minutes. Elvis Costello did it on his own, cocktail pianists can't leave it alone, and Rickie Lee Jones . . . well, we will get to Rickie Lee Jones. Most people can hum it, many people know the lyrics but nobody has the last word on "My Funny Valentine".

It takes a flexible kind of number to attract pop singers and jazz players and rock stars alike. But "My Funny Valentine" is nothing if not broad in its appeal. So many love songs are breathless with hyperbole, big on euphemism. But this one comes right out and says what's on its mind. "Your looks are laughable/ Unphotographable/ Yet you're my fav'rite work of art." This is the love song for people excluded by love songs – a fairly large catchment area. Is your figure less than Greek? Is your mouth a little weak? Then this is your song.

> ★ ★ ★ ★ ★ ★ ★ ★ ★ ★
>
> **This is the love song for people excluded by love songs – a fairly large catchment area.**
>
> ★ ★ ★ ★ ★ ★ ★ ★ ★ ★

"My Funny Valentine" was written in 1937 by the Broadway team Rodgers and Hart. Lorenz Hart, who was busy partying a lot of the time, tended to leave his lyrics to the last possible moment, so the music came first – just 32 bars, in the economical Tin Pan Alley style. This format was a battered old cliché even in 1937 – but Richard Rodgers performs a small miracle of invention, squeezing the genre just enough to make something conventional and yet utterly distinct. The most striking tribute to his construction is that people rarely meddle with the tempo. Van Morrison slips a verse, just for fun, into the middle of the live version of "Moondance" on *A Night in San Francisco* (Polydor 1994), which belts along at a crisp lick. But it would probably be unwise to tackle the whole song at this pace. Contrast "Where or When", another Rodgers and Hart number, which Sinatra alone has recorded at four different speeds. No one would be daft enough to risk a rhumba version of "My Funny Valentine".

But that doesn't mean the song is set in its ways. The tone is always open to interpretation. Sometimes the tune appears to ring like a nursery rhyme, which is hardly surprising. The melody for the lines "My funny Valentine/ Sweet comic Valentine" repeats, three notes higher, on the lines "Your looks are laughable/ Unphotographable"; in other words, "My Funny Valentine" shares a crucial compositional device with "Three Blind Mice". And yet the song is built around an evenly descending bass-line, and the slight rise of the melody against the slow fall of the bass can come over you like melancholy. Hart, it might be useful to remember, spent much of his life in despair and died an alcoholic. Cutesy ditty or rueful lament? This is the gap the singers step into.

Kim Novak sings the song in the film of the musical *Pal Joey* (1957) and most people assume that this show is where it belongs. In fact, it was written for the Broadway musical *Babes in Arms,* in which Betty, smart and self-possessed, sings it to a character actually called Valentine, a dope who has failed to notice her affection for him. But at the same time, the song was built to stand alone. When *Babes in Arms* was converted into a movie in 1939, "My Funny Valentine" got jettisoned along with all the other Rodgers and Hart songs bar one. (Film companies frequently threw out the original tunes to save on publishing fees.) Later, though, the song was press-ganged into the movie *Gentlemen Marry Brunettes* (1955). From early on, nobody was going to pin "My Funny Valentine" down, although, like most songs, when it moved in with Frank Sinatra, it threatened to stay for good.

Sinatra recorded it in November 1953 for his album *Songs for Young Lovers* (Capitol). This was his first ten-inch long-playing record. "My Funny Valentine" was track one. A small band sets up a straight beat, brushes skipping the drums, the bass gently pushing the arrangement along. And in comes Sinatra, relaxing the rhythm by taking each line slightly late, working easily through the song, and finally drawing one extraordinary, casual breath which carries him right through the closing lines: "Stay little Valentine, stay/ Each day is Valentine's Day." The effect is intimate and informal, which is a small step for Frank, but one giant leap for "My Funny Valentine". The song moves out of the theatre and into the nightclub.

The pace allows Sinatra to work in the half-rhyme of "is your" with "figure" in the line "Is your figure less than Greek?". That is the only ornate poeticism in Hart's lyric – and this from a writer who was regularly lavish. An old joke about Hart runs like this: "Larry Hart can rhyme anything – and does." Here, though, he sat back, turning on the style just once – that triumphant "Unphotographable", where one word unfolds to fill an entire line. There's a crafty rhyme in the lines "Don't change a hair for me/ Not if you care for me", but more prominent are the non-rhymes, in which the same words chime quietly together: "My funny Valentine/ Sweet comic Valentine" and "Stay little Valentine, stay". They partly explain the song's muteness, the sense that all is not quite bright in its world. (The movie *The Fabulous Baker Boys* [1989] takes this angle. Michelle Pfeiffer plays a half-decent lounge singer with a two-bit piano duo, and you hear her sing "My Funny Valentine" over the closing credits. Her delivery is respectable and no more – but that's the point. The song is a smart choice to cap a film about settling for second best.)

Ella Fitzgerald proceeds untroubled through a lusher arrangement than Sinatra's – all thick string slides and woodwind counterpoint. Her version came three years later than Sinatra's but, recorded for her *Songbook* series (Verve

27

1956), which attempted to catalogue and fix the work of the great American songwriters, it can be fairly said to look backwards, rather than forwards.

Fitzgerald restores the original introductory verse, which preceded the song in the stage show. (This is a piece of consciously antiquated whimsy, but it has the effect of masking the familiar tune into which it finally slides: "Behold the way our fine feathered friend his virtue doth parade/ Thou knowest not, my dimwitted friend, the picture thou hast made . . . You're/ My funny Valentine . . .") But, perhaps more than Sinatra, she attends to the needs of the words, drawing them out, singing through each line in one long breath, so that the song picks up a lucid, hypnotic sway.

Tony Bennett recorded a version in the early 1970s (collected on *The Good Life*, CBS 1990), and it is clear that he'd been listening to Fitzgerald for phrasing and Sinatra for attitude. The song is arranged for a slow-burning, late-night jazz trio – tipsy bass, half-cut piano, drunk drums – against which Bennett stretches the words as far as his breath will take them. At the end of "Yet you're my fav'rite work of art", the studio staff must have been tempted to phone out for an oxygen cylinder.

But Bennett, more than anyone up to that point, exposed the weight of melancholy at the song's heart. Unfortunately, in a tragic lapse of taste, he broke the word "laughable" over a hiccupped giggle – as if this lyric, of all lyrics, needed subtitles. This is the trouble with a portable song: there's nothing to stop someone scooping it up and taking it off to Las Vegas.

It's possible that Bennett borrowed his mournfulness from the jazz version of "My Funny Valentine" recorded in September 1952 by the trumpeter Chet Baker with the Gerry Mulligan Quartet (*Gerry Mulligan Quartet with Chet Baker*, Giants of Jazz). Baker also sang a version of the song, but the performance with this piano-less quartet, in which the trumpet and the saxophone lean into one another for support, brings home more vividly the ache in the tune. Miles Davis fastened on to that too, getting inside the melody's phrases and pushing them outwards in great despairing curves for 14 minutes and 54 seconds on *My Funny Valentine*, the live album (Columbia, February 1964). Kenneth Tynan said of Davis's playing generally that it displayed "the minimum of fuss, the maximum of restraint". In "My Funny Valentine", Davis found a tune to answer directly to those powers.

Davis prised the tune apart with virtuosity; Elvis Costello could barely play it. "I couldn't say I really arranged it in any way. I just played it on an electric guitar, fed through some kind of electric device. I didn't even fill the chords out, just picked at the guitar with the pads of my fingers, rather than the nails, so that there's no point on the front of the note. What struck people was that it seemed so at odds with the tone of the times. But I've known that song longer than I've known any of my own songs."

Costello's version was based on Sinatra's, which his father played around the house. It went on the B-side of his biggest hit, "Oliver's Army" (Radar 1979). The performance and the lyrics had a mutual awkwardness, a raw poignance. The song had never sounded so bare, nor so strong.

When Rickie Lee Jones reaches the song (on the ten-inch album *Girl at her Volcano*, Warner Bros 1983), she is at a piano on her own in front of an audience. She takes all manner of liberties with the tune and lets the tempo fluctuate at will. She even inserts the word "please" ahead of the line "don't change a hair for me", which would be a kind of sacrilege, except that her delivery of the word is one of the most eerie things you will ever hear – a long down-bending cry, sung from the stomach and starting way out on a mad tangent from the song's key. It is a voice imitating the arc of Miles Davis's trumpet, just as Jones's understated piano accompaniment seems to have heard Tony Bennett's version and her phrasing to have caught something from Fitzgerald. Hers is a portfolio of every "My Funny Valentine" you have heard, though it must resign itself to sounding incomplete eventually. There will be others.

I PUT A SPELL ON YOU

BY BEN THOMPSON

JALACY, "Screamin' Jay", Hawkins was born in Cleveland, Ohio, in 1929. Like James Brown, he had a boxing career before a musical one (he won a Golden Gloves amateur middleweight title in 1947). But by 1952 the gloves were off, and Jay was playing piano and singing with Tiny Grimes and his Rockin' Highlanders. They gave him his first shot at solo recording – "Screaming Blues", for Atlantic Records in 1953 – but this was not a success. The young producer told him to lighten up and sing more like Fats Domino. Jay had a vocation flashback and tried to punch him. Since the name of the producer was – according to which version of the story you believe – either Ahmet Ertegun or Jerry Wexler, this was not what you'd call a career move.

★ ★ ★ ★ ★ ★ ★ ★ ★ ★

How then did Screamin' Jay Hawkins come to make one of the most extraordinary records in all rock 'n' roll?

★ ★ ★ ★ ★ ★ ★ ★ ★ ★

The record was never released. Hawkins left Grimes' group, was thrown out of a black Muslim ensemble called the Lynn Hope Band for eating chitlings, and soon tired of playing back-up piano for (cruel fate) Fats Domino, so he had little option but to go out on his own. How then did he come to make one of the most extraordinary records in all rock'n'roll? He was driven to it by a woman.

Some time in the summer of 1954, Screamin' Jay was in the middle of his set at Herman's Bar in Atlantic City when his girlfriend of the time approached the stage, threw down the keys to their apartment, and walked off. Returning home to find that she'd left him with no keepsake but "Goodbye my love" written in lipstick on the bathroom mirror, Jay let out a single, unearthly scream; "out of my big mouth, directly through my heart and guts," he would explain later. Then he sat down on the bed and wrote a song to get her back.

An early version of the song was released on Philadephia's Grand Records (with a co-writer's credit guaranteeing immortality to one Herb Slotkin of that company), but the definitive cut was made by Okeh Records, a division of Epic, in 1956. At producer Arnold Maxin's suggestion, the recording session became a drunken revel. The "I Put a Spell on You" that emerged was a masterpiece of tortuous simplicity. A slow, tight waltz, built around a compressed, meandering bass and a guitar that sounds like a banjo, the song has a vocal so demented that it will still make the hair on your palms stand on end.

"I put a spell on you," Jay affirms, "because you're mine." Well, that seems fair enough. "You'd better stop the things you're doing *ha ha ha what's up* I ain't lying. Yeah. I can't stand *oh no* you're running around, I can't stand no, you're putting me down. I put a spell on you . . . because you're mine."

At this point the singer's tenuous self-control dissolves in a mess of delirious "oh yeah"s. He regains it, albeit briefly, in the respite of a ripe and mellifluous sax break. "You'd better stop the things you do," he warns, "Oh I ain't lying. I love you baby" – he's howling now – "I don't care if you don't want me, I'm yours right now. I put a spell on you . . . because you're mine *woooh aaoo ha ooh had had had grunt grunt ooh.*" Some radio stations deemed two bars' worth of these groans to be "cannibalistic", and they had to be cut out.

The song breaks down at the end into gibbering insanity, but the path of Screamin' Jay Hawkins' professional career was firmly set. Screamin' Jay Hawkins made plenty of other records. Some, like "Alligator Wine", were good; others, like "Constipation Blues", were not, but "I Put a Spell on You" would always be his signature tune – whether on stage, rocking up a storm at the Town & Country Club a couple of years back, or on film, in his justly acclaimed performance as the hotel maître d' in Jim Jarmusch's *Mystery Train.* The flamboyant, voodoo-tinged stage act Hawkins built around the song on the rock'n'roll package tours of the fifties – Alan Freed paid him $2,000 to get out of a coffin onstage for the first time – supports him to this day.

He also got his woman back. She liked the B-side. Allegedly.

Gerri Hershey's living-history book *Nowhere to Run: The Story of Soul Music* (Pan Macmillan 1984) begins with Screamin' Jay and "I Put a Spell on You". It's the early eighties and he's the support act on the New York leg of a massive Rolling Stones tour. The pioneering showman cuts an uncluttered figure amid the bloated paraphernalia of stadium spectacle, with only Henry, his human skull on a stick, for company. "This guy's ripping off the Sabbath," observes one Stones fan, a decade before *Wayne's World*. "Nah, this guy's ripping off Kiss," says another. Hawkins does his pièce de résistance and the fans are impressed. "Hey," says one, knowledgeably, "that's a Creedence song." Hershey tells Hawkins this when she goes to see him afterwards. Furious, he brandishes a fan letter from Creedence Clearwater Revival (who had a hit with "I Put a Spell on You" in 1968) and proclaims: "The statue of justice in Washington DC is not only blind – she is retarded."

The first, and best-known, cover version of "I Put a Spell on You" gave no sign of the privations the song was later to suffer. Nina Simone recorded it for Colpix Records in the US, a version which – insultingly – scraped into the British Top 50 when released as a single on Philips in 1965. Simone rendered the song opulent and seductive, her sublime voice all tangled up with a tinkling piano on a bed of ululating strings. The performance is sprinkled with mellow scat interludes, but still reaches a compelling climax with Simone's four repetitions of "I love you". It was the kind of song, she said, that "no one could ignore".

These words proved prophetic, as "I Put a Spell on You" became one of the building blocks for the British beat boom. Manfred Mann were first off the mark, also in 1965, with a version that oozed English reserve, Paul Jones

31

bringing the song to a comically polite conclusion – "Oh that is why I'm gonna put a spell on you, because you oughta be mine" (*The R&B Years*, See For Miles 1986). Eric Burdon and the Animals' attempt, recorded just after they split from Mickie Most and released on their album *Animalisms* (Decca) in 1966, was rougher and more ready, but the only English performer to have a hit with the song was their newly departed keyboard player Alan Price. His Alan Price Set got to No 12 with it in the same year; theirs was a jaunty but lightweight rendition, distinguished only by some characteristically dextrous organ manipulation and the faintest trace of a Geordie accent.

Them, Van Morrison's tough Dublin bar-band, gave the song some of its rawness back (*Them Again*, Parrot 1966), with a rasping vocal and some eloquent saxophone squelches. The Crazy World of Arthur Brown put it in touch with its inner child. Brown, the crazed psychedelicist, had, like many others, been much influenced by Screamin' Jay's British appearances of the early Sixties. The version of "I Put a Spell on You" which appears on The Crazy World of Arthur Brown's eponymous 1968 Polydor album next to songs like "Fire" and "Spontaneous Apple Creation" is not as wild as some they performed, but it's wild enough, especially when Brown shouts "Stop it stop it stop it". Creedence Clearwater's saner, more earthbound approach to the song earned them a big hit in America in the same year (*Creedence Clearwater Revival*, Fantasy).

A successful cover version usually condemns a song to a few years of obscurity, and so it was with this one. A little-remembered London progressive-rock quartet called Audience recorded it on the 1971 Charisma (by label, but not by contents) album, *The House on the Hill*: it was studiously rearranged for "electric classical" guitar and – I'm sorry but it's true – flute solo. The next recorded version came ten years later and was, if anything, even more bizarre. When Tim Curry, star of the profoundly Screamin'-Jay-influenced *Rocky Horror Picture Show*, decided to make an unlikely bid for svelte crooning stardom with an album called *Simplicity* (A&M), what could be more twisted than that he should employ top session players like Earl Slick and David Sanborn to drain the blood from "I Put a Spell on You"?

Far truer to the spirit of the original was the haunting, hollering adaptation which Nick Cave and the Bad Seeds used to play live in 1984–85 (it appeared on the *NME* compilation tape *Department of Enjoyment* as the work of Nick Cave and the Cavemen), complete with evil guitar rumbles from Blixa Bargeld and a wonderfully asthmatic harmonica.

"I first heard the song in a bar somewhere when I was very young," Cave remembers, "and I'd never heard anything like it. The performance seemed so brutal and outrageous." In Australia in the mid-seventies, Cave and his "school" band the Boys Next Door made it a central plank of their set. Their interpretation was not as respectful as it might have been. "I'm certainly not going to tell you how we changed the lyrics," he says. "It was very adolescent."

Once the Bad Seeds emerged from the savage catharsis of Cave's next group, The Birthday Party, vandalism was no longer on the agenda. "We were inclined to be more faithful when we did a cover version, there wasn't any need to destroy them any more." But personal experience has shed a harsh light on Cave's view of his youthful inspiration.

"I have some difficulties with Screamin' Jay as a person, which have rather prejudiced me against his music," Cave admits. "He is a man with a somewhat bloated ego. We did a tour with him in Australia and he couldn't come to terms with the idea of himself, as a legend of rock'n'roll, supporting a band of musically incompetent upstarts. I suppose he had a point in some ways, but after a while I found him quite intolerable." What about the song though? "As Screamin' Jay loved to explain to anyone who had the misfortune to be sitting next to him on long transcontinental flights, it is a masterpiece. I prefer Creedence's version now myself; it's simpler and more direct."

The simplest and most direct "I Put a Spell on You" of all was recorded by Rocking Richard and Whistling Vic Templar, a mysterious north Kent skiffle phenomenon of the late 1980s. Their version, on a 1988 Hangman Records album called *Tea & Baccy*, seems to have been sung in a toilet with a cardboard box over the singer's head. The accompaniment is just a snare drum and a tinny guitar. The effect is a happy one – of early Sun rockabilly played by idiots – and there's a great ad-lib from Whistling Vic. "What's up with you woman? Let's get this straight once and for all: I ain't no bit of rubbish."

The song has been subjected to three desecrations, all of them comparatively recent. American "blues" guitarist Leslie West, a fat white man with an earring and a headless guitar that sounds like Gary Moore's but uglier, put a truly horrific version on his album *Alligator* (IRS 1989), in which he ad-libs, slobbering, "Put your knees behind my neck baby; lift them high, feel my spell." Screamin' Jay himself was party to a nightmarish "I Put a Spell on You Dance Mix" on his album *Black Music for White People* (Demon 1991). And in 1993 Bryan Ferry – usually such an astute judge of material – got it badly wrong on his covers album *Taxi* (Virgin). Languid detachment was not something this song was ever meant to convey, and the session-lizard guitars are an insult. The Future Sound of London remix on the single is better, but only because they've taken all the singing off.

Pain and fury and the desire for revenge are what "I Put a Spell on You" is all about. The interpreter who has done it most justice is a past mistress at expressing – and provoking – these feelings. Diamanda Galas, the New York composer and vocal improviser who uses her voice as an instrument of terror, put an extraordinary version of the song on *The Singer* (Mute 1992). She grew up playing it, it turns out, in war veterans' bars and masonic lodges with her dad's band Jim and the Flames. Now she opens and closes the song with a characteristically unnerving piece of chattering improvisation – "devil, devil, devil". In between there's a huge rolling piano and the words are amplified by a selection of moans and shrieks that would chill Bessie Smith's blood.

Galas' opinion of Screamin' Jay is not mixed. "That man is a fuckin' genius," she says firmly. "It's a really *bloody* song: it's not bathetic, there's no

33

whingeing, and it just never stops moving." Why did she add a bit in the middle then, about snakes and sharks and vultures lying in wait? "The woman who is tracking somebody down, that's always been one of my big themes, and to me this is like an animal-tracking song: whatever your opinion as the loved one happens to be is pretty irrelevant, and I like that."

YOU'RE THE TOP

BY ROBERT CUSHMAN

ON A broad view, most songs are list songs. I'm thinking especially of songs in the standard or Broadway tradition, but I suspect that it applies across the board. Popular songs fasten on a single idea, a single conceit, and spin out examples of it or variations on it until the music stops. "My Funny Valentine" is a list song. It catalogues the beloved's physical limitations, and the irrelevance of those limitations, one at a time. Most lyrics are collections of one-liners, for fairly obvious reasons. The demands of rhyme and scansion – we're talking here about conscientious lyricists – are easier to negotiate if you confine yourself to one thought per line or, more important in practical terms, one line per thought. The musical line, generally pretty simple, encourages that discipline anyway, and if you get it right, a certain elegance will result. It is a rare lyricist who can construct in paragraphs: who can spin out a thought over half-a-dozen lines without clumsiness or padding. PG Wodehouse, long ago, could do it. Oscar Hammerstein did it, though so unspectacularly you hardly notice, and Frank Loesser, who could do almost anything. This is beginning to sound like a list song itself – appropriately, since the great master of the long form, the one who told the suavest stories (cf. "Begin the Beguine") was Cole Porter who, most unfairly, was also the virtuoso of the list song in its purest state. As far as lists are concerned, Porter consummately did it, all the way back to "Let's Do It".

★ ★ ★ ★ ★ ★ ★ ★ ★ ★

It takes some cheek to claim authorial inadequacy while laying a perfect quadruple rhyme over a jauntily undulating rhythm.

★ ★ ★ ★ ★ ★ ★ ★ ★ ★

Actually he did it even before that, but to admit it would have ruined my punch line.

Let me distinguish the pure list from the sort-of-list. Using "Funny Valentine" again as an example of the latter: it gathers its items up, over just one chorus, into an argument that is summed up in a clinching line we haven't heard before: "each day is Valentine's Day". "Let's Do It" delivers its title-line, which is also its message, a quarter of the way through and repeats it twice more at salient moments as a kind of marker. It doesn't build, it accumulates; and the accumulation is the point of the song. To prove it, and to stun us into delight at his ingenuity, Porter writes five complete choruses. The pattern is the same in "Anything Goes", from the 1934 musical of the same name; and so it is in another Porter list song, introduced in the same show by William Gaxton, who is now virtually forgotten, and Ethel Merman, who isn't: the incomparable catalogue of comparisons known as "You're the Top".

The obvious danger in a song of this kind is monotony. Porter avoids it with a musical device that Alec Wilder in his book *American Popular Song* reckoned to be unique. The title which starts the song off and recurs four more times in every chorus, is delayed at every appearance except the last, by a two-beat instrumental phrase, "*Da-da*! You're the Top!" It's like bending back a piece of elastic and then releasing it. The music kicks the words, the words kick the song, and the song kicks the show. The sharp, jerky rhythm has a 1930s hedonism – a shrugging, mature pursuit of happiness rather than the self-consciously manic kind that preceded the Depression – pulsating inside it.

There is a kind of generic introductory verse to a song that I think of as the "I've-written-you-a-love-song-and-this-is-how-it-goes" approach. Porter used it a lot, sometimes with brazen simplicity, but more often he put a literary, self-mocking spin on it. Here he starts with a confession:

> At words poetic, I'm so pathetic
> That I always have found it best
> Instead of getting 'em off my chest,
> To let 'em rest unexpressed.

It takes some cheek to claim authorial inadequacy while laying a perfect quadruple rhyme over a jauntily undulating rhythm. He confounds the impertinence by switching to his musical deficiencies ("I hate parading/My serenading,/As I'll probably miss a bar"), excuses himself with a basic compliment ("At least it'll tell you/How great you are"), and proceeds to business.

> You're the top!
> You're the Colosseum.
> You're the top!
> You're the Louvre Museum.

This, obviously, is compliment on a monumental scale, but rendered engaging by its speed and snap: one cultural tourist attraction, and then on to the next. We then get a more leisurely accolade – "You're a melody from a symphony by Strauss" – followed by a return to shopping-list economy, three items carried on a single arching musical wave: "You're a Bendel bonnet, A Shakespeare sonnet, You're Mickey Mouse." The last brings us down to earth a bit in the conventional cultural scale, just as the melody descends a step before re-charging for its second half. But then Shakespeare and Henri Bendel, New York ladies' outfitter, are hardly neighbours in the official pantheon. Porter anticipates a modern arts editor or hip academic in the range of his enthusiasms, but he is not out to deconstruct the canon. He merely took what he needed for his own prosodic purposes from wherever he needed it, though he was certainly well aware of the comic possibilities of unlikely juxtaposition. He wanted to extend standards of excellence, not to debunk them. We end up with an increased respect for Shakespeare and Disney alike, not to

36

mention Mahatma Gandhi, Napoleon brandy, and the nimble tread of the feet of Fred Astaire. Porter actually values, however flippantly, the things he extols. That's what gives the song its energy.

As it progresses – there are seven choruses preserved in the *Collected Lyrics* – he leaps, with apparent effortlessness, through breezily disrespectful diminutives ("You're an O'Neill drama/You're Whistler's mama") into bizarrely inevitable reversals:

> You're a rose.
> You're *Inferno's* Dante.
> You're the nose
> On the great Durante.

Few singers have been able to resist an impromptu impersonation on that one.

The fecundity of those seven refrains is part of the message, part of the joy. At one level it's Porter showing off, but at another the sheer volume of hyperbole is its own love-offering.

Each stanza concludes with an ironic avowal of the singer's own inadequacy. These disclaimers balance the song lyrically and also musically; after the staccato fusillades of compliment, words and tune briefly stretch their limbs in a full sentence, each one incorporating a snappily satisfying internal rhyme while travelling towards the crucial moment at which Porter must rhyme his title. We get the ground-laying "I'm a worthless check, a total wreck, a flop"; the insolently delightful "I'm just in the way, as the French would say *de trop*"; the deceptively conclusive "I'm a lazy lout that's just about to stop"; and the deliciously inspired "I'm a frightened frog that can find no log/To hop" – each leading into the final admission:

> But if, baby, I'm the bottom,
> You're the top.

But as the song is a duet, neither baby, even by their own reckoning, has to be the bottom. Each has been pummelled with praise, though it hardly matters who gets what; the song is impeccably non-gender-specific. They are *both* the top: and the singular coinage may have been Porter's own. Think how incomparably less effective it would have been had he settled for the commoner "You're the Tops". (There are those who refer to the song that way but they belong with those who spell Richard Rodgers' surname without the 'd', in the lowest circle of *Inferno's* Dante.)

The nature of the song means that interpretations don't vary much; it demands, and invariably gets, crispness and enthusiasm. There is an original cast recording, or half of one, with Merman (Gaxton, as far as I know, never cut a disc in his life) accompanied by a choice society dance-band; still young, she is ebullient but not over-bearing, precise but not pedantic (recorded

1934, reissued on *Merman Sings Merman*, Decca). She doesn't sing much of the song, though. Porter himself recorded a far fuller text, backed by his own rum-ti-tum piano; he has a brusque mandarin delivery which is fine for the occasional outing, and his phrasing is suitably exemplary (Victor 1934, reissued on *The Song Is Cole Porter*, ASV). The song in its utter entirety can only be heard on the 1989 EMI recording of the *Anything Goes* score in the delighfully spruce 1934 orchestrations. Kim Criswell, who does a very good Merman, duets here with Cris Groenendaal, under the purist baton of John McGlinn. They offer a note-and-letter-perfect rendition, that might have benefited from some loosening up. With seven choruses you can afford some variation; neither Merman nor Porter was averse to playing with the rhythm on occasion. The recent excellent New York revival (RCA 1987) yielded a performance by Howard McGillin who has the raffish-romantic thirties style down to perfection, and Patti LuPone who honks anachronistically. The arrangement is a spirited best of both worlds.

A song so crammed with local and topical references has of course been altered over the years. (Needlessly, I feel. The chances are that many of the original audience didn't get all the references, either. They were happy to pretend that they did. Now it all adds to the flavour.) The rewriting process started as early as 1935, when Charles B. Cochran presented the show in London, and engaged P. G. Wodehouse to make the lyrics comprehensible: to change, for example, a Bendel to an Ascot bonnet (this version can be heard sung by Jack Whiting and Jeanne Aubert on a 1935 Columbia 78, reissued on *Cole Porter in London*, World Records). Among the other obscurities he purged was, surprisingly, Ovaltine, which on Broadway had made a triumphal appearance on the heels of Botticelli, Keats and Shelley. (It rhymed with "too, too deveen".) Wodehouse was a fine lyricist himself and at least one of his additions is treasurable: "I'm a son of a gun, an underdone chump chop." He also managed to retain, more or less, Porter's dazzlingly tortuous resort to Brooklynese:

> **You're my thoist,**
> **You're a Drumstick lipstick,**
> **You're da foist**
> **In da Irish svipstick.**

The best jazz/pop record of the song is Ella Fitzgerald's, warm and precise over an uninventive but invigorating arrangement, a few notches down from the theatrical temperature and tempo. It's one of the best tracks on her *Cole Porter Songbook* (Vol 2, Verve 1956). More extreme examples of fifties and early-sixties style can be sampled in performances by Anita O'Day and Buddy Greco. Both sing a fairly faithful verse and first chorus, and then get hip. O'Day, by changing the title-line to "you're the bop", more or less makes her own rules and keeps them with such mad authority that purist objections wither in the breeze (*Anita*, Verve 1956). Greco, updating more recklessly

38

while singing the fastest version ever, is another matter (*Buddy's Back in Town*, Epic 1961). His inventions include "you're like church-bells ringing . . . you're Sinatra singing". The second might pass but the first, apart from the fearful banality of the image, disqualifies itself by being a simile. Porter deals entirely in metaphors: hence his authority. He never says you're like something. He says you are that something. That's why you're the top. That's why the song is.

THESE FOOLISH THINGS

BY ROBERT CUSHMAN

SOME list songs are sad songs. "Thanks for the Memory" is one, an artful catalogue of reminiscence guaranteed to strike a chord in anyone who has enjoyed nursing a broken heart while pretending to ignore it; it's the classiest of all tear-jerkers. "It Never Entered My Mind", a masterpiece by Rodgers and Hart, takes a subtler tack; rather than list the happy moments of a past affair it recalls the warning signs that the singer disregarded as the relationship approached its end. The time-scheme here is quite complicated, as the warnings were explicit ones, issued by the absconding partner: forecasts of the singer's likely fate when left alone. One example, marvellous in its detail and surprise:

> Once you told me I was mistaken
> That I'd awaken with the sun
> And order orange juice for one
> It never entered my mind.

40

This is a song written largely in the future conditional. It reverts, though, to the simple present in the middle sections of the melody, where it's confirmed that all these prophecies have in fact come true.

> You have what I lack myself
> And now I even have to scratch my back myself.

The main strain compiles the list; the middle – variously known in the trade as the bridge, channel or release – extrapolates, generalises, draws conclusions. The same pattern occurs in "Thanks for the Memory" (where the bridge summarises "many's the time that we feasted, and many's the time that we fasted") and it seems endemic to songs of regret. The paradigm is "These Foolish Things", music by Jack Strachey and Harry Link, lyric by Holt Marvell.

Those are not household names, and one of them isn't a name at all. Holt Marvell was a *nom de plume* for Eric Maschwitz, who in the 1930s was a scriptwriter for the BBC. In urgent need of a song for a radio revue, he ground the words out one Sunday morning and read them over the phone to Strachey. (As for the mysterious third name on the credits, the missing Link: Harry Link was an American whose name also crops up as co-composer of Fats Waller's "I've Got a Feeling I'm Falling". Presumably he had something to do with sprucing up "These Foolish Things" for the US market, though it's hard to tell what. Maybe he was just good at royalties.)

Perhaps it's hindsight, or whatever the aural equivalent may be, but the tune sounds as if it were dictated by the words in more than the literal sense. It's a compelling melody but repetitious: compelling because repetitious. The principal task is to provide a long wistful line to accompany each of the foolish things and – what Strachey does best – to build to a climax, philosophic or despairing as the singer chooses, on the final "oh, how the ghost of you clings". Strachey never wrote another tune as resonant but Maschwitz, who went on to great success as a BBC executive, has some claim to be considered the leading British lyricist of his era, Noel Coward notwithstanding. Two of his songs – this one and the contrastingly happy "A Nightingale Sang in Berkeley Square" – have become nostalgic shorthand for old Mayfair. Angels dining at the Ritz, and candle-lights on little corner tables: the debutante-and-guardsman set succumbing decorously to passion or, when it's over, keeping a stiff but remarkably loquacious upper lip.

"These Foolish Things" attracted little attention on its radio debut, and not much more when it was sung in a 1936 West End revue called *Spread It Abroad*. Still unpublished, it was discovered – as a manuscript on a piano, according to Maschwitz – by London's reigning cabaret entertainer, the singer-pianist Leslie A. Hutchinson, alias Hutch.

Hutch, born in Grenada, professionally blooded in New York and Paris, was English society's pet exotic, exposed to a wider audience by records, radio and the last gasps of the music hall. Right into the 1950s he remained the living definition of a certain idea of sophistication. There is a controlled ardour about his performances that is rather intimidating. Mabel Mercer used to say that her function was to sing her audience's emotions back to them, and she did it by making musical conversation. Hutch was more stylised; he served his public by reflecting, as in a shiny chafing dish, their own grandest conceptions of wit and high romance. Mostly he used American material – he was London's most reliable conduit for the songs of Cole Porter and his peers – but in "These Foolish Things" (HMV 1936, reissued on *Hutch at the Piano*, World Records 1975) he found a native work that suited him and them to perfection. The words with which Maschwitz unfolds his roster of regrets may not be greatly witty but they are certainly evocative. The first image is enough in itself to create a feeling and a world: "A cigarette that bears a lipstick's traces."

So it's a shock to find that that line – which I had always assumed made the song's fortune – does not figure on Hutch's classic recording. Maybe it was written in later, after the song took off; maybe Hutch simply preferred other bits of the lyric. He had plenty to choose from; the song, copious as a list song should be, boasts three choruses, of which he sings two.

★ ★ ★ ★ ★ ★ ★ ★ ★ ★

When Sinatra is not on his best behaviour vocally, when the vowels get broad and the consonants sibilant, he can sound surprisingly like the late Sid James.

★ ★ ★ ★ ★ ★ ★ ★ ★ ★

He also sings a verse: one that begins, after a brief snatch of muted trumpet has set a properly anguished mood, with the blunt inquiry "Oh, will you never let me be?". It goes on to set up the song with a reference to "those little things . . . that brings me happiness and pain." Most singers have tipped that balance in one direction or the other. Hutch keeps it exquisitely poised; he suggests that he has the heart for grief but would never dream of wallowing in it. He could plainly give any of his patrons a lesson in *noblesse oblige*. His voice, famously, throbs; but it throbs with dignity. He is suffering greatly, but he knows how to live with it. The cut-glass precision of his diction, with its outlandishly elegant vowels, actually contributes to his haunted sound: the upper crust of soul. He must have sensed that in this still obscure song he had found a perfect spectral showcase. He sings it as if it were already a standard.

In place of the opening cigarette, he offers us a more rarefied commodity, though one conceivably available at an adjacent counter of the same smart store: "gardenia perfume lingering on a pillow". Maybe the explicit sexuality of that image alarmed the publishers; Hutch's version certainly got air-play but subsequent singers, if they have used the line at all, have pushed it way down the song. It goes with "wild strawb'ries only seven francs a kilo", a rhyme that Hutch's accent makes more plausible than most have managed. This, we are being signalled, is a lusciously cosmopolitan affair, the kind we would all like to be regretting; we are expensive travellers but we can still appreciate a mouth-watering bargain. Another of the key memories is "the Ile de France with all the gulls around it", again somewhat dubiously rhymed with "the park at midnight when the bell has sounded". Maschwitz was not always too scrupulous in the way he combined his images, but he was a whiz at picking them.

The sights and scents are well enough but what have always struck home are the sounds. For happiness, "the tinkling piano in the next apartment"; for pain, the universal ache of "a telephone that rings, but who's to answer?" a brilliant blow below the belt, real *chanson noire*. Hutch serves them all up polished and gleaming, at a pace noticeably faster than later generations would think proper for a ballad.

In New York in 1936 pianist Teddy Wilson, in a model of understated swing, set an even jauntier tempo to usher in a single chorus from the 21-year-old Billie Holiday. She brings a new note to the song: disappointment verging on anger. Hutch sang of loss; Holiday sings of betrayal (Brunswick 1936, reissued on *The Quintessential Billie Holiday*, Vol 2, CBS). When she refers to "those stumbling words that told you what my heart meant" she isn't congratulating herself on her own bashfulness, she's asking how she could have been such a fool. Indeed on her lips the title sounds less affectionate and more bitter than on any others. She injects acid into the regrets, and erotic pain as well, gilding "a fairground's painted swings" – one of the more hackneyed items on the agenda – by italicising "swings" with a vocal shiver.

Most striking is what she does with the bridge. "You came, you saw, you conquered me . . ." Hutch sang that melodramatic observation from the heart, which in his case seems to have been the site of conquest; Holiday is unmistakably physical. Again, the song's middle interrupts the catalogue to offer a comment. Musically, too, it makes a break; Strachey abruptly offers a new if foreshortened musical idea. It's less satisfying than the release of "You're the Top" (or of another great Porter list song, "At Long Last Love"), which develops seamlessly out of the main strain and is in fact an extension of it. Strachey's bridge, though an effective point of rest, is pop-song routine.

In 1961 the song turned up on the Frank Sinatra LP *Point of No Return*, the last of the six great ballad albums he recorded for Capitol. Each of them had its own distinctive mood; this one, following on the sustained angst of *Only the Lonely* and the bleak hopelessness of *No One Cares*, settles on a plateau of acceptance, lost love recollected in something approaching tranquillity. "An airline ticket to romantic places" is the line most savoured; the ghost of you still clings, but it imparts a glow rather than a chill. Forsaking the deep cello timbre of his previous laments, Sinatra sings here with a light, burned-out quality and with an unexpected casualness of tone. When he is not on his best behaviour vocally, when the vowels get broad and the consonants sibilant, he can sound surprisingly like the late Sid James.

I suppose the best-known of recent versions is Bryan Ferry's (on his solo debut, *These Foolish Things*, Island 1973). It's also textually the fullest. He starts by resurrecting the verse on which Hutch sounded stricken but powerful. Ferry, who seems to have his mike turned way down low at his entrance and only becomes fully audible at the end of the first line, is a broken man. He sings out of tempo, in traditional verse manner, but he's backed by a piercing trumpet and exaggeratedly docile piano: a Brecht and Weill combination. The jazz critic Francis Davis describes the record, approvingly, as "fiendishly syncopated"; to my ears, certainly on first hearings, the reggae beat to which Ferry submits the bulk of the song is remarkably foursquare, flattening out melodic shape and verbal nuance. Coming back to it, I can hear more. There is a point in each of the song's long lines where the tune turns a corner; Ferry pounces on and isolates each of these moments, almost regardless of what the lyric might be doing at the time. We get "the winds of March that make my – heart a dancer" and even "first daffodils and long ex–cited cables". The equivalent pause in "but – who's to answer" makes obvious dramatic sense, though, and nobody could accuse Ferry of swallowing the words. They all come out clear if somewhat odd; the park at evening becomes "the park a tevening", reminding me of Ken Tynan's comment on an especially eccentric performance by Ralph Richardson: "a mode of speech that democratically regards all syllables as equal". My very favourite item – "the sigh of midnight trains in empty stations" – seems to appeal to Ferry too: he is momentarily gleeful, while "the smile of Garbo" makes him come over all knowing.

All the elements of the song are laid out – the elegance, the nonchalance, the driven misery – but dislocated and jumbled, so that Ferry seems simultaneously to be commenting on traditional pop style and re-enacting it. In this he was a harbinger. Davis calls him "the British postmodern crooner", and he seems to enjoy tipping his hat to Bing. (That's on the line "the song that Crosby sings", which, if you'll follow me into the hall of mirrors for a moment, "These Foolish Things" had actually become. He recorded it in 1955, though without the self-reference. The Groaner reserved his postmodernism for jokey duets.) The most disconcerting thing about Ferry's performance – I have no idea whether or not it's intentional – is its persistent refusal to honour the final resolution of Strachey's melody; the foolish things sound as if they are going to be around for a while yet, all three choruses of them. Since I'm a sucker for completeness, Ferry's sweet-sour version might be the one I would play on my Platonic ideal of a radio programme.

If, though, I were simply going for the best post-war recording of the song, I would have to choose between a pair of chartered cabaret singers, one old, one young. Mabel Mercer, the doyenne, sang "These Foolish Things" in concert at New York's Town Hall in 1969 (*Mabel Mercer and Bobby Short Second Town Hall Concert*, Atlantic 1969). She was 70 and had a cold; her delivery was husky and very conversational. But she still had power in reserve, and it is fascinating to hear when she decides to unloose it. Or perhaps when it's decided for her; there is a definite sense as she proceeds of the song taking her over.

She sings two choruses, both rubato, easing in on the cigarette line before the inevitable applause of recognition. At the mention of "romantic places", her voice begins a steady climb up to the first climax of "still my heart has WINGS". Mercer, renowned for her treasuring of a song's lyrics, had one especially tasteful and cunning method of illuminating them. She rarely stressed an adjective; she knew that if they were any good, they would do their own work. So she sings "THESE foolish things" and "those stumbling WORDS"; treating the descriptive words as functional, she makes them all the more striking. It isn't an inflexible rule; she lingers irresistibly on "LONG excited cables", though it's still the noun that brings out the wonder in her. That wonder increasingly predominates, lighting up whole phrases, even including the most awkward rhyme in the song, "the beauty that is spring's". And there's yearning in it, giving great strength to "you conquered me" and reaching a tantalising peak unscaled by other singers in the hushed rapture of "silk stockings THROWN ASIDE", which in her version is the song's penultimate image. At the close her voice breaks, and it hardly matters whether that's an emotional effect or a technical defect; it's moving anyway. Mercer enjoys some of the memories, cherishes all of them, but finally arrives at a grief as wrenching as Billie Holiday's and rather nobler. Hers is the most balanced account of the song since Hutch's, and a lot more approachable.

A more extreme treatment is Andrea Marcovicci's. Marcovicci is an actress turned singer, and when she sang this (it was released in 1990, on *What is Love?*, DRG, but I think recorded earlier) her voice was flawed; the last note is brayed rather than sung. But she overrides her imperfections in an insistently on-the-beat treatment that rarely isolates a phrase (though she does highlight "the waiters whistling as the last bar closes", a late and magical item that less patient singers never reach) and drives through on a controlled arc of intensity.

When she has finished, her accompanists take the tune out: piano, sax and violin in a shrill chamber-music frenzy. This may owe something to the solemnly intoning Peter Skellernish choir who round off the Ferry version, but it has a force of its own. It echoes a possibility already raised by Marcovicci's escalating stress on the thrice-repeated "oh, how the ghost of you clings". She may be coming to terms not with an unfaithful lover but with a dead one. No previous singer has made me take the words that literally. I doubt if the writers did. But after all these years of harmlessly foolish things it makes startlingly good sense.

TWIST AND SHOUT

BY PHIL JOHNSON

IT'S A rock'n'roll Boy's Own story: on Monday 11 February 1963, the Beatles are at Abbey Road studios, coming to the end of a 12-hour shift spent recording the whole of their first album. John Lennon strips to the waist before going for a take on a last number which has only just been agreed.

Taking a swig of milk, a last Zubes cough sweet from the glass jar on top of the piano to ease his throat, and a final counteractive puff on a Peter Stuyvesant, he sits out the intro to a song then best-known as a hit for the Isley Brothers. Then he begins: "Well shake it up baby, twist and shout." His voice is nearly gone, a wild, hoarse roar, thick with mucus, lisping at the consonants. By the time he gets over the penultimate bridge of harmonies – the soon-to-be-famous *aaah, aaaahh, aaaaahhh, aaaaaahhhh* – Lennon is screaming. Although George Martin coaxes him into a second take, his voice has gone and it's the first take that makes it on to wax. It's long past the studio's bedtime and when the Beatles ask to hear a playback of the song, Brian Epstein has to agree to take the second engineer home in his Ford Anglia, in case he has missed the last bus.

★ ★ ★ ★ ★ ★ ★ ★ ★ ★

To be able to see and hear a white man scream was, in 1963, quite new.

★ ★ ★ ★ ★ ★ ★ ★ ★ ★

46

Just as "Twist and Shout" closed *Please Please Me* (Parlophone 1963), it also closed the Beatles' concerts, and for years it was their most popular live number. In its many subsequent interpretations, the song has remained a closing number, held back for encores – notably by Bruce Springsteen, Peter Gabriel and Sting on their Amnesty International tour of 1988 – to summon up the essence of uncomplicated good-time pop and soul. At its worst, in cynical versions by Lindisfarne or Black Lace, it's the musical equivalent of a Party Four can of bitter, but for all that, it remains "Twist and Shout". Like "Louie Louie", it is strong enough to survive the abuse to which it has been subjected.

On the Beatles recording Lennon's laryngitis came across as the nearest a white English boy had yet got to soul. "Twist and Shout", like "Money (That's What I Want)" on the follow-up album *With the Beatles*, was Lennon *in extremis*, so out of control, so cheeky-rough (as opposed to Paul's cheeky-nice) and so sexy that at the time it seemed to mark a peculiarly English catharsis; to be able to see and hear a white man scream was, in 1963, quite new. When "Twist and Shout" was released on an EP in July, with its cover shot of the Fab Four caught in a mid-air jump, the song and the photo became the group's most powerful icons yet. In the playground at primary school we practised the jump, sang the aaaahhmonies and trilled Paul's trademark "oooh". "Twist and Shout" also became important in retrospect, as proof that the Beatles could indeed rock, and weren't just boring latter-day Schuberts, as the critic Tony Palmer would have them.

Like the rest of the songs on the album, "Twist and Shout" had been in the Beatles' stage act for at least a year. You can hear an early version recorded live at Hamburg's Star Club in 1962 and it's faster and even more raucous than the studio track (*Live at the Star Club, Hamburg*, Bellaphon). Lennon is only slightly less hoarse, so maybe the legend of the cold has been tricked up a bit for posterity. Or maybe he caught a lot of colds.

Credited to the pseudonyms Russell and Medley, the song was actually written by Bert Berns, the songwriter-producer who understudied Leiber and Stoller at Atlantic Records. The very first version of "Twist and Shout" was by the Top Notes, produced for Atlantic by Jerry Wexler and Phil Spector in 1961. While it's customary to prefer the original to a copy, the Top Notes' version is unbelievably bad – the Coasters crossed with Duane Eddy – and almost unrecognisable as the classic it was to become. "It was horrible," Jerry Wexler later remarked, while Berns, who had watched the session from the control booth, told Wexler and Spector: "Man, you fucked it up."

Berns took the song to the Isley Brothers and it is their version that becomes the *de facto* original, providing the model for the Beatles, "ooohs", "aaahs" and all (*20 Golden Pieces: Isley Brothers*, Wand Records 1963). Though it became a big hit, it's hard to rate the Isleys' version over the Beatles'. The vocals are soulful, but the arrangement is poppy and the middle-eight (which the Beatles did as a foot-tapping Shadows-ish guitar break) is a horn arrangement with a Mexican feel that sounds rather lame today.

47

The Mexican elements are important. Listen to any version of "La Bamba" and then start singing the words to "Twist and Shout". You'll find that they fit remarkably well. "La Bamba" was a hit for Richie Valens in 1958, but the melody is based on an ancient Mexican fisherman's song whose words reputedly changed according to how many fish were caught that day. Berns may well have borrowed the chord sequence from Valens, slowed it down and made it into just the kind of Latin-based call-and-response tune that was then all the rage in R&B.

After the Beatles came the deluge. Fellow beat group Brian Poole and the Tremeloes took the song to No 4 in Britain in July 1963 with an awful version, treacle-thick with echo (*Twist and Shout with Brian Poole and the Tremeloes*, Decca); the Searchers tried it, and so, unable to resist a song with "twist" in the title, did Chubby Checker.

The Shangri-Las did it as unconscious surrealism, all booming sound-effects (engines? rain?) with the girls' voices coming from an echoey distance in a Spectorish wall of sound (*Leader of the Pack*, Red Bird Records 1965). A live version by a still-obscure Jimi Hendrix, who had once played guitar with the Isleys, sounds terrible but is full of morbid interest (*20 Golden Pieces of Jimi Hendrix* Vol 1, Bulldog 1979). Picking up the chunka-chunka ska-like rhythm-guitar figure on the Isleys' version, it offers potential dissertation material: did Hendrix invent reggae?

For the next truly entertaining version we have to wait until 1969, when the song is sufficiently established even for Tom Jones's Las Vegas show (*Tom Jones Live in Las Vegas*, Parrot). Jones's opening enquiry, "Do you feel all right?", is delivered with all the leery menace of "Did you spill my pint?" The effect is much more British working-men's club than Vegas lounge and Jones is in glorious voice, tearing into quotes from "Land of a Thousand Dances" and Stevie Wonder's "Uptight" before the song succumbs to audience screams and the inevitable reprise of "It's Not Unusual".

When punk came along, there was a revival of interest in old beat stompers. In 1976, as part of the 100 Club's Punk Festival, a band of Siouxsie Sioux, Sid Vicious, Marco Pirroni and Steve Severin performed a medley of "Twist and Shout", the Lord's Prayer and "Knocking on Heaven's Door". An A&R rep from Island Records was reported as saying: "God, it was awful."

A live version by The Who, recorded on an American tour (*Who's Last*, MCA 1985), sounds like a closer not only for the show but for the song itself. It ends in a frenzy of guitar feedback, finally dissolving in a razor-slash of angry chords that continue to buzz resentfully until the fade. The song seemed doomed to be history repeated as farce, with Lindisfarne's ghastly version on *C'Mon Everybody: The Greatest Party Hits Album Ever* (Stylus 1987) and a less than crucial rap by Salt'n'Pepa (*A Blitz of Salt'n'Pepa Hits*, ffrr 1991).

48

As I write, "Twist and Shout" is back in the charts, as a reggae number by Chaka Demus and Pliers (*Tease Me*, Mango 1994). It has come full circle. "I heard the Isleys' version in an elevator in New York," Chaka Demus' producer, Sly Dunbar, told me, "and I reflected on 'Tease Me' and saw that it was the same tempo. If you divide rock'n'roll tempo by two, you get ska, and if you divide ska by two you get reggae."

It's a joyful sound, bubbling with life, and they even do the "aaaahhs" and the "ooohs". But, ultimately, this is "Twist and Shout" as post-modernism; the original innocence has gone, drained away through a sink of all the other versions. Still, it went to No 1.

A WHITER SHADE OF PALE

BY MIKE BUTLER

IT'S A summer song of pervasive dread, a wedding hymn riven with sexual anxiety, an epochal composition which routinely functions as background muzak for the keep-fit class (if you don't believe me, dig out Diana Moran's album *Get Fit with the Green Goddess*). Contradiction only bolsters the enigma of "A Whiter Shade of Pale".

The debut single from Procol Harum was the surprise hit of summer 1967. It captured listeners' imagination from the moment of its first toe-testing airing on Radio Caroline. "Everything about this record is an overwhelming gas," effused *Melody Maker* in May. In June, while *Sgt Pepper* topped the British album chart, "A Whiter Shade of Pale" (Deram) was the No 1 single.

It was among the first batch of songs produced by the songwriting team of composer-singer-pianist Gary Brooker and lyricist Keith Reid. *Melody Maker* of 3 June 1967 contains a contemporary account of the song's origin:

> *"I never understand when people say they don't understand it," said Reid. " 'We skipped the light fandango'. That's straightforward. 'Turned cartwheels across the floor.' It seems very clear to me."*

It was "sixth member" Keith Reid who had the idea for the song, at a "gathering". "Some guy looked at a chick and said to her, 'You've gone a whiter shade of pale'. That phrase stuck in my mind. It was a beautiful thing for someone to say. I wish I'd said it," laughed Keith, while Gary put down his cup of coffee and struggled with a nose inhaler.

Reid confirmed the account when I telephoned him in New York in 1994. "The title came first. It's always like that; like a puzzle. After the title you find the rest of the pieces to make a picture." The found phrase is felicitous. It has the authority of a line from Shakespeare, and is as catchy as the most persistent jingle – which, inevitably, was to be its fate. The ad, just as inevitably, was for Dulux.

Brooker's setting was a motley synthesis, derived from Bach (though Reid dissents: "It is not 'Air on a G-String' ") and Percy Sledge. "When a Man Loves a Woman", a hit of the previous year, had also had a hymnal quality, an integral part for organ, and a fervent, soulful delivery. Reid's cryptic lyrics inject some of the waywardness of the counter-culture. There's a tension between the placid majesty of the music and the paranoia and messiness of the subject-matter. The disjunction may account for the common perception of "A Whiter Shade of Pale" as impenetrable and obscure.

"I never understand when people say they don't understand it," said Reid.

'We skipped the light fandango'. That's straightforward. 'Turned cartwheels across the floor.' It seems very clear to me." Nervously, I hazarded my own reading, the summation of my voluntary immersion in the world of "A Whiter Shade of Pale", and much pondering on its significance. Is it about getting pissed and fancying the person opposite you? "It's a story, a journey, seen from the point of view of a man character."

The song explores what it means to be wrecked, in more than one sense of the word. A nervous seducer sustains his courage with alcohol. As he becomes more drunk, his impressions of his unfamiliar partner become confused by stray thoughts, fragments of childhood reading and his own faint-hearted aspirations. The song's recurring metaphor is of maritime disaster, and a parallel is drawn between romantic conquest and the allure and peril of the sea. The hero is a callow juvenile, far happier with a book than risking the emotional bruising of relationships. This ambivalence is underscored by frequent allusions to nausea.

As befits a night of excess, there are gaps in the telling. The evasive "And so it was that later . . ." is given weight by repetition and its positioning just before the hook ("Her face at first just ghostly / Turned a whiter shade of pale"). The listener is invited to fill the gaps with his or her own (prurient) imagination. An entire verse was dropped early in the song's gestation. Another is optional ("She said, 'I'm home on shore leave,'/ Though in truth we were at sea") and was excised from the recorded version at the insistence of producer Denny Cordell, to make the record conform to standard single-length.

50

For a pop song, "A Whiter Shade of Pale" carries an unprecedented amount of literary baggage. Although, Reid reveals, the reference to Chaucer is a red herring. "One thing people always get wrong is that line about the Miller's Tale. I've never read Chaucer in my life. They're right off the track there." Why did he put it in then? (In mild dismay at the peremptory demolition of this intellectual prop.) "I can't remember now."

The analogy with *Canterbury Tales*, whether welcomed by Reid or not, holds good. Both are quintessentially English works, the one established in the canon of literature, and the other a pop standard. Both have associations of piety and decorum. (The song has become a regular fixture of the wedding ritual, supplanting Handel's "Wedding March" as the tune to walk down the aisle to after the ceremony: it was played, indeed, at the wedding of Gary Brooker and Françoise, known as Frankie, with Procol Harum's Matthew Fisher in the organ loft.) Both, beneath their respectable surface, are puerile and sex-obsessed works.

Even discounting the Chaucer reference – the Miller's Tale is the usual mediaeval bawdiness, involving cuckoldry, bared buttocks, flatulence and a sadistic rear-end attack – the conviction remains that "A Whiter Shade of Pale" is all about sex, and juvenile sex at that. The following memorable couplet is the giveaway: ". . . [I] would not let her be/ One of sixteen Vestal Virgins . . ."

The Vestal Virgins were handmaidens of the Roman half-goddess Vesta (meaning hearth), whose job was to maintain a sacred and perpetual fire. The number of them is significant, invoking the biblical parable of the five wise and five foolish virgins, and, less edifyingly, the barrack-room ballad of ". . . four-and-twenty virgins . . . down from Inverness". Why Reid's lot should amount to 16 is one of the song's more imponderable details. Maybe it has something to do with 16 being the youngest a girl can be lusted after by a rock'n'roller with impunity ("You're Sixteen", "Sweet Little Sixteen", etc). The passing allusion to Lewis Carroll in the preceding couplet – "I wandered through my playing cards" – suggests that some of the obscurity of "A Whiter Shade", as in *Alice*, may be due to the broaching of taboo. The hesitant lover in the song is caught midway between the chivalry of "When a Man Loves a Woman" and the carnality of Jane Birkin in "Je t'aime" (a smash hit of the following year, blatantly modelled on the Procol Harum song).

The influence of "A Whiter Shade of Pale" is not confined to torrid French confections. Its success paved the way for pop music's assimilation of classical forms. Its progeny includes Queen's "Bohemian Rhapsody" and the complete works of Rick Wakeman. Its theme of romance on the edge, as viewed through the dregs of a bottle, struck a responsive chord elsewhere. It sometimes seems that Shane MacGowan's entire subject-matter is contained in "A Whiter Shade of Pale".

Certainly, the song received a generous endorsement when I canvassed the former Pogue's opinion. We met whilst rubbing shoulders at adjacent bins in a secondhand record shop in Camden Town, I fruitlessly searching for the Percy Sledge version. "'A Whiter Shade of Pale'," MacGowan said, "yeah man, that's one of my favourite records." MacGowan's speech is husky, but his judgement is unimpaired. "People say they nicked it from Bach. But it doesn't matter, because what they did with it was much better than what Bach did with it."

Percy Sledge is not the only soul singer to respond to "A Whiter Shade of Pale". For an example of the Motown studio system at its height, seek out Shorty Long's version on *The Prime of* (1969) and marvel at the bizarre and stilted trumpet solo (a rare lapse). Sledge's version would be fascinating – closing a circle of inspiration which links the tender balladeer from America's Deep South with London's barrier-smashing rockers – if only I could find it. King Curtis gives the definitive cover version, however, on *Live at Fillmore West* (Atco 1971). The tempo is slowed right down, and Curtis's bittersweet saxophone induces an insouciant euphoria.

This "Whiter Shade" plays over the opening credits of Bruce Robinson's cult British film, *Withnail & I* (1986), a nostalgic hark back to an age of innocent substance-abuse. Thus "A Whiter Shade of Pale", which orginally embodied sixties excess, becomes a threnody for a generation. King Curtis's own leave-taking was brutally final. He was stabbed to death in New York in 1971.

Willie Nelson on the *Always on My Mind* album (Columbia 1982) coaxes the words from his larynx shyly, bringing a new matter-of-factness to Brooker's

51

obtuse words. Waylon Jennings pitches in for a verse with his drier, slyer delivery. The two hell-raisers contrive to ditch every last trace of Eng Lit from the song. So "The Miller told his tale" becomes "the mirror told its tale". An alteration which, in fact, probably enhances its narrative clarity. "That's quite good," Keith Reid admitted, when I told him. "It's better. You can see why he's such a good songwriter, can't you?"

The Everly Brothers got their shot in early for the Nastiest "Shade of Pale" award with a misconceived attempt to appeal to the flower-children on *The Everly Brothers Sing* (Warner Bros 1967). The field subsequently became over-crowded. Bonnie Tyler switched the gender of the piece to no great effect on *Night Riding* (Night Riding 1990). Justin Hayward, abetted by Mike Batt and the LPO on *Classic Blue* (BMG 1989), is his usual fey and wispy self. A superfluous record, this, seemingly calculated to confuse all those who can't tell their White Shades from White Satin. Joe Cocker, in marked contrast, reveals the self-disgust at the song's heart (*Luxury You Can Afford*, Asylum 1978); his rawness is thrown into stark relief by Allen Toussaint's too slick production.

A disco version by Munich Machine touched the lower reaches of the charts for a few weeks in 1978 (Oasis). The most eccentric version comes from deconstructivist rockers Vibrating Egg, a band from Athens, Georgia. They restore the spookiness of the original by appending a tale told by a mad-man (*Come in Here if You Want to*, Dog Gone 1988).

Warlock and the London Symphony Orchestra vie for tastelessness with their respective treatments. Warlock (*Force Majeure*, Vertigo 1989) offer over-wrought corporate rock. The LSO (*Classic Rock*, K-Tel 1977) slum it by pretending to be a light orchestra. Both are lamentably conservative.

It is April 1994 and Gary Brooker is in a recording studio in north London, busy mixing *The Symphonic Music of Procol Harum*, an album of orchestrated versions of the band's songs. Daryl Way – best remembered as fiddler in Curved Air – picked the plum parts when he elected to arrange "A Whiter Shade of Pale" and the phantasmal "A Salty Dog". These new orchestral versions are so opulent they make the originals seem skeletal, bare bones to be adorned with bangles, frills and finery. Here they pirouette to a different dance.

Brooker takes time out from digitally tweaking a cor anglais to recreate, for my benefit, the inception of "A Whiter Shade of Pale". What does it owe to "Air on a G-String"? "Everything," Brooker says, and demonstrates his first, halting attempt to play the music from the Hamlet-cigar ad. He was messing it up. The bass line went on descending interminably, the trill in the right hand reduced to uncertain ornamentation. The stumbling coalesces into a pretty chord sequence. "Hello, if I get back to where I was, I can go round again." And so Brooker chases the tail of the sequence, and a familiar melody emerges.

How did you marry the tune to the words? "I just got them out." Brooker stoops. "I've got a pile of Keith's words here." He spreads imaginary papers on

52

the piano-stand, repeats the chord sequence, peers at imaginary words, and begins, "We skipped the light fandango . . ." "A Whiter Shade of Pale" was born fully formed.

More than fully, in fact. I ask about the missing verse. "I took it out because I was puffed." Brooker proceeds to sing it:

> If music be the food of love
> And laughter is its queen
> And likewise if behind's in front
> Then dirt in truth is clean
> My mouth by then like cardboard
> Seemed to slip straight through my head
> So we crashed dived straight way quickly
> And attacked the ocean bed.

No wonder it was dropped. The Shakespearean quote is a clunker, and pity Brooker stumbling over the back-to-back Ds on the awkward penultimate line. The crudity of the dénouement would surely have exposed the singer to ridicule. "A Whiter Shade of Pale", in this version, would have been sunk. And yet the verse is essential to an understanding of the song. We at last learn that the drunken seduction is consummated, and the sea metaphor reaches its apotheosis in the oblivion and forgetfulness of sex, with a neat pun thrown in as a punch-line. Meanwhile the edited version, which swam into the collective consciousness 27 years ago, still keeps its head above water.

53

NO FUN

By Ben Thompson

WAY BACK in dark, distant 1986, the cast of the British school soap opera *Grange Hill* had a hit with an anti-drugs anthem called "Just Say No". The authors of this infectious piece of improving pop music were playing with fire. The idea of negation is the first step along a delirious road to drug-crazed debauchery and poor personal hygiene.

The founding doctrine of punk rock was positive negativity – not no meaning no but no meaning yes. It was laid down by the Stooges in the song "No Fun", written by the singer, Iggy Pop (James Newell Osterberg to his mum), and guitarist Ron Asheton. "No Fun" is the fourth track on the Stooges' 1969 debut, *The Stooges* (Elektra). A half-formed drum fill kicks into a lazy loping beat – part handclap, part castanet – and a brutally simple guitar riff; a distant, degenerate cousin of Bo Diddley's primal rumble. The sound is a saturated tranquilliser haze, till Iggy's voice cuts through it like a hungry cat ruining a lie-in. "No fun," he yawls, "my babe. No fun."

★ ★ ★ ★ ★ ★ ★ ★ ★ ★

The asthma pills Iggy had to take as a child, a potent mix of uppers and downers, left him at ease with chemical interference.

★ ★ ★ ★ ★ ★ ★ ★ ★ ★

The guitar is choppy but opens out on the "babe", and Iggy expands on his theme. "No fun to hang around . . . feeling that same old way. No fun to hang around, freaked out . . . for another day". His voice is not pretty; nor are his prospects – "No fun to be alone, walking by myself. No fun to be alone, in love . . . with nobody else". Iggy runs through his options over a rudimentary middle eight – "maybe go out, maybe stay home, maybe call mum on the telephone" – but none has much appeal. It's still no fun to be alone, but Iggy picks himself up out of the void; yelping, eight times, "Well c'mon". Then, in a weird parody of gospel, he asks the guitarist to be his witness. "C'mon Ron," Iggy demands, "tell me how I feel." Ron obliges.

Iggy was not the first to grasp the no/yes impulse. There were glimpses of it in 1965, in the exhilarating whirl of doomy imagery on Bob Dylan's *Highway '61 Revisited*. And the Fugs (*aka* East Village beat poets Tuli Kupfenberg and Ed Sanders) stomped all over it a year later with "Nothing", a negativist mantra for tribal drum and wheezing harmonica. "Monday nothing, Tuesday nothing, Wednesday and Thursday nothing, Friday for a change a little more nothing . . ." The Velvet Underground took it somewhere new in 1967 with the deathly beauty of "Heroin", and then did so again a year later with the exhilarating tedium of "Sister Ray". By 1968, negativity was breaking out all over. The Beatles' "White Album" had a blank cover, "Helter Skelter" and "Happiness is a Warm Gun". The Rolling Stones' *Beggars Banquet* had "Sympathy for the Devil" and the deceptively gentle "No Expectations".

So what made the Stooges and "No Fun" special? Lester Bangs, writing a year or so after the song's release, described the band as an "escape": from "the folk/*Sgt Pepper* virus", to "something closer to the mechanical mindless heart of noise and the relentless piston rhythms which seemed to represent the essence of both American life and American rock and roll". This was not a popular view. Iggy's fondness for nudity, self-mutilation and hurling himself against stage walls and floor ("I felt I wanted to commune with the ground in some way", he said later, "I misjudged a little bit") had marked him out in the general perception as a psychotic loser. For Bangs, sickness and cure were inextricably linked. At a time when the new rock-based counter-culture was increasingly smug and self-satisfied, the advent of a new star with "not one shred of dignity or mythic corona left" could only be a good thing.

How did Iggy turn out this way? He was raised in a trailer home in the outskirts of Ann Arbor, Michigan; which would have been a one-horse town, if it had had a horse. As a child he enjoyed the electric whirr of the space-heater. "I wasn't brought up on the sizzle of mom's frying pan," he remembers in his autobiography *I Need More* (with Anne Wehrer, Karz-Cohl, 1982), "I was brought up on on the strange little red light on the aluminium plug of her electric frying pan." As a result, "just the sheer presence of electricity in large doses" has always made him feel "real comfortable and calm". The asthma pills Iggy had to take as a child, a potent mix of uppers and downers, left him similarly at ease with chemical interference.

By 1967, an early version of the Stooges was rehearsing in the Ann Arbor basement of brothers Scott and Ron Asheton. Practising wasn't easy. The Ashetons were classic suburban wasters, impossible to raise before noon, and the music had to stop by 3.30 when their mum came home from work. Iggy was the driving force. He'd been a drummer for a high-school band, the Iguanas, and a blues outfit, the Prime Movers. He'd played with older, black musicians in Chicago, whose music came "like honey off their fingers". He'd even held down two jobs ("that month of employment was the end of my rope"), selling burgers and in a record shop, earning enough money for a motley selection of amplifiers for his weird Hawaiian guitar. The four Stooges (now including doomed drummer Dave Alexander) made strange free-form whooshing sounds. Regulation Chuck Berry was beyond their compass.

Iggy had resolved that when he did get around to writing songs, they would be simple. And so it proved. The core of the first Stooges set was the immortal "1969" and "Now I Wanna Be Your Dog", the not so immortal "Dogfood", and best and simplest of all, "No Fun". "We had a sound and we always delivered," Iggy remembers with justifiable pride. "It was a sweeping sound, like Mongolian hordesmen charging in; thousands of them, little tartars with swords – frequencies only a geek can hear . . ."

By 1970, the original Stooges had folded, after Elektra had rejected their third album. It would be left to the lord of the geeks, David Bowie, to revive Iggy's career, seven years later. Before that, a new geek generation was discovered hanging around at Malcolm McLaren's clothes shop on the Kings Road.

The music they were listening to was a heady blend of old rock'n'roll, the New York Dolls, an early tape of the forthcoming Modern Lovers album (produced, like the Stooges' first, by Velvet Underground veteran John Cale) and the Stooges. Out of this fertile musical mulch crawled the Sex Pistols.

Their bassist, and chief tunesmith, was Glen Matlock. "We were constantly looking for other people's songs to do, like you do when you're a young band, cutting your teeth," Matlock says. "My whole thing was the Kinks, the Yardbirds, The Who. The point about them was that they were Mods – West Londoners, hip to what's going on, with a bit of money in their pockets – not wanting to be part of an underground, just being their own little clique and getting everyone to follow them. That's what we were about too really, but we wanted to show that we could turn our hands to something else as well."

Which was where, late in 1975, "No Fun" came in. "At Christmastime I think it was; it might even have been Boxing Day. John [Rotten] was gonna meet Steve [Jones] and Paul [Cook] in Chiswick – he went all the way over from Finsbury Park and they stood him up. At the next rehearsal, he was moaning and we were laughing at him – 'go on you miserable sod, let's do that one'. I think part of it was that we felt we had some kind of lyrical message to get across, and we weren't really sure what it was yet, but we knew that this song was part of the deal." They also wrote "No Feelings" and "Did You No Wrong"; and a song called "No Future", which was to become "God Save the Queen". "There were a lot of 'no's around at that time," Matlock observes.

"No Fun" eventually ended up on the B-side of the Sex Pistols' third single "Pretty Vacant" (Virgin 1977), having been recorded with producer Dave Goodman at the same time as "Anarchy", their first. "We were getting really fed up doing 'Anarchy' over and over again," Matlock says. "It was just getting faster and faster and no one had the bottle to say it was good enough, so we went on strike, and while they were trying to sort things out we started messing about doing lots of songs, and recorded 'No Fun' really quickly."

Quick in tempo as well as execution, the Sex Pistols' version moved much faster than the Stooges' – in part at least a reflection of changing trends in drug use. There were two other major changes. Jones's slashing guitar had no time for solos, and Rotten's gleeful, scorn-drenched vocal was in no mood to take prisoners. "Rrright, here we go now," he snarls, "a sociology lecture, with a bit of psychology, a bit of neurology, a bit of fuckology . . . No Fun." Mindful of his public image, he decides it's not "mum" he might call on the telephone but "somebody". He shakes the song till it rattles in a voice that is equal parts desperation and triumph – "It's no fun, all alone, I'm alive, All alone, It's no fun, All alone, It's not funny, All by myself – I'm alive".

The Sex Pistols were trying to play "No Fun" about ten o'clock on the evening of 13 June 1977, as their Thames cruiser Queen Elizabeth was pulled back to the landing stage by the long arm of the law, having just performed for the delectation of the Houses of Parliament. Rotten repeated the title as the power was turned off. It was also the last song of their final gig, at San Francisco's Winterland Ballroom on 14 January 1978. Rotten's expostulations

56

of disgust – "Ah it's awful . . . it's no good," and "Ever get the feeling you've been cheated" – seemed to be aimed, even more than usual, at himself as much as everyone else. Three days later the band went their separate ways – Jones and Cook to South America and the train-robber Ronnie Biggs; Rotten to New York and Public Image Ltd; and Matlock's replacement, Sid Vicious, to degradation and death.

"No Fun" was the first and the last breath of punk. The movement's nihilistic tendency, which Vicious came to personify, was eclipsed in the anti-fascist campaigning of Rock Against Racism. Many a bigot's graffito would be trumped (NF = No Fun, as well as National Front) with the help of the Stooges, whose drummer liked to wear an SS uniform on stage. Matlock (and later Jones) played with Iggy Pop for a couple of years. "I kept asking Iggy if we could play 'No Fun'," Matlock says, "but he wouldn't, because he said we'd done the definitive version, which was nice. He plays it now though."

He does too. In the summer of '93 at the London Forum, Iggy was still not sure whether to go out or stay home or call his mum on the telephone, 25 years on. He was still sharing his genitals with the crowd too. This man's lack of a mythic corona has become one of the biggest mythic coronas of all time.

That's not quite the end of the story. After the Sex Pistols, no new take on "No Fun" could ever really mean very much, but that hasn't stopped people having a go. Dr Mix and the Remix, *aka* Eric Debris of post-punk pioneers Metal Urbain, released a nice, clipped, vaguely electronic and stunningly inconsequential version on a Rough Trade single in 1979. And ambient-dub warriors The Orb dashed it off for a John Peel session 13 years later.

57

This was not quite the surprise development it might seem. Orb controller Alex Patterson began his musical life as a roadie for Killing Joke, the stern eighties proto-grungers. Their enigmatic mainman Jaz Coleman hated encores, and would encourage the star-struck Patterson to mess around singing "No Fun" after he'd left the stage. He sang it live in Chicago with Primal Scream once as well, and they've since taken to playing it on stage without him: a bar-room brawl of a version used to close the set throughout their 1994 "Rock'n'Roll Dreams Come True" tour, Denise Johnson's exceptionally feisty backing vocals giving the song a long-awaited female voice.

The Orb's version on the Peel session is basically a loving pastiche of the Sex Pistols', right down to the spoken intro and outro, with Patterson affecting a not entirely convincing Rotten-esque drawl, and just the odd plodding reggae bass-line and speeded-up-tape dub effect to remind you of the musical ground covered since.

Why did Patterson stay so faithful to the Sex Pistols? "Because of punk really . . . The Stooges' music has been more enduring. But the Sex Pistols were such a breath of fresh air at the time because they were so young. 'No Fun' is what life is all about really – it doesn't change.

"It's always no fun. You know where you are with that attitude – you don't get any illusions, like a lot of people do when they get a mortgage." Does he have a mortgage? "Yes, but I'm going to pay it off as quickly as possible . . ."

THE TRACKS OF
MY TEARS

By Richard Williams

THE FIRST thing you heard was Marvin Tarplin's guitar, finger-picked, lightly amplified, chiming like distant bells floating on the night air. Before anyone even had time to utter a word, here was a sound overloaded with memories, haunted by regret, hoping beyond hope, a sound of loss and lamentation. Within a few seconds, Smokey Robinson's swooning falsetto was along to give verbal expression to those emotions, and today it is Robinson whom we associate with one of the most affecting of all pop records. But "The Tracks of My Tears" started with Marvin Tarplin and his old black Gibson Les Paul Custom guitar, in more senses than one.

★ ★ ★ ★ ★ ★ ★ ★ ★ ★

For a few precious months in 1965, what pop music had to say was matched by its means of expression. And that summer, Tarplin's eight bars of finger-picked guitar rang clear and sweet across the airwaves.

★ ★ ★ ★ ★ ★ ★ ★ ★ ★

In the days when making a pop single was about structural ingenuity, about matters such as getting the hook-phrase in early and not bringing it back so often as to wear it out – in other words, in the days before James Brown and Andy Warhol conspired to establish the primacy of repetition and monotony – the intro was where, in a matter of seconds, a pop record could establish its claim to originality. Think of the electric 12-string guitar arpeggios that began the Byrds' "Mr Tambourine Man", the neck-snapping horn figures prefacing Otis Redding's "Mr Pitiful", the sleazy fuzz-guitar riff of the Stones' "Satisfaction", the haughty Hammond organ that paved the way for Dylan's "Positively 4th Street", the dramatic a cappella opening of the Righteous Brothers' "You've Lost That Lovin' Feelin'".

All those examples come from within a few months, practically a few weeks, of each other – from 1965, the year in which pop music achieved a perfect blend of innocence and experience, of intuition and craftsmanship. For a few precious months, what it had to say was matched by its means of expression. And that summer, Tarplin's eight bars of finger-picked guitar rang clear and sweet across the airwaves.

The song's origins were banal enough. Tarplin, born in Atlanta but raised in Detroit, had been the Miracles' guitarist since their first American No 1, "Shop Around', in 1960. In those days, a rhythm-and-blues vocal group would travel with a guitarist who acted as a musical director, teaching their arrangements to local rhythm sections and theatre orchestras. Tarplin played with the Supremes when they were still called the Primettes, which is how he came to the notice of Smokey Robinson, who, in his capacity as a Motown

Records talent scout, spotted the female trio's potential but managed to swipe the guitarist for his own group.

A quiet, humble man who preferred country-and-western to rhythm and blues, Tarplin had no pretensions beyond his accompanist's role, but was fooling about with his guitar one day early in 1965 when he came up with an idea inspired by an unlikely source. "Harry Belafonte had this song out," Tarplin told me a few years ago, in what seems to be the only interview he has ever given. " 'The Banana Boat Song' – that's where I got the idea. Belafonte had calypso-type tunes, and it's basically the same chord changes – three chords, turned around a little bit." He passed the result on to Robinson and another member of the Miracles, Warren "Pete" Moore.

"Marvin is a brilliant guitarist whose music has always inspired me to words," Robinson himself later told me. "I wrote all the words with the exception of about the first three lines of the chorus thing, the bit which says, 'Outside, I'm masquerading; inside, my hope is fading'. Pete Moore wrote that. But the first couple of verses and the ending – 'my smile is my make-up", all that stuff – I wrote that.'

Robinson, then aged 25, was in the middle of writing and producing a remarkable sequence of medium-tempo ballads, all characterised by a lush, swooning mood. Within the span of 1965, he wrote and produced "My Girl", "It's Growing", "Since I Lost My Baby", "Don't Look Back" and "Fading Away" for the Temptations. Now he used that mood and the music Tarplin had given him as the basis for an exploration of his favourite theme: the masks that we use to disguise our true emotions. "People say I'm the life of the party," his new lyric began, " 'cause I tell a joke or two. Although I might be laughing loud and hearty, deep inside I'm blue. So take a good look at my face – you'll see my smile looks out of place . . ." Later he was to re-examine the subject in two more of his finest songs, "The Love I Saw in You Was Just a Mirage", also with music by Tarplin, and his hugely successful collaboration with Stevie Wonder, "The Tears of a Clown".

Released in the US on 23 June 1965, "The Tracks of My Tears" reached No 16 in *Billboard*'s pop chart and No 2 in the rhythm-and-blues list (kept off the top spot by James Brown's "Papa's Got a Brand New Bag"). In Britain, where – despite the Supremes' success – Motown records were still a cult item, it failed to register.

As well as being a record label, Motown was also a publishing company – its boss, Berry Gordy, was quick to see that true prosperity flowed from publishing copyrights rather than record royalties. So the label's artists were often required to fill up their albums with versions of songs owned by the company, which is why the first cover of "The Tracks of My Tears" was by Gladys Knight and the Pips, on a 1968 Motown album entitled *Silk 'n' Soul*. Curiously, Knight ironed a little of the poetry out of the song when she sang "you're the only one" instead of Robinson's "you're the per-ma-nent one" at the end of the second verse, thus eliminating an exquisitely judged use of an essentially unpoetic word.

59

There was a little more character to the next significant version, by Bryan Ferry, who included it on *These Foolish Things* (Island), his first solo album, in 1973. With its exaggerated vocal inflections and clumpy Brit-rock drumming, Ferry's reading now sounds like a camp period piece, betraying the affection he undoubtedly felt for the song – although, strangely, he shared Knight's preference for "only one".

Linda Ronstadt, at the height of her popularity (*Prisoner in Disguise*, Asylum 1975), restored the "permanent" and took the song back into the US charts, but the country-rock arrangement nailed it firmly to the floor, while Ronstadt's inflexible voice suffered by comparison with Robinson's fluid, highly wrought phrasing. Surprisingly, the most successful homage came from the British pop duo Go West, whose respectful treatment reached the Top 20 in 1993 (*Aces and Kings: The Best of Go West*, Chrysalis). Sensitive electronics and sensible blue-eyed soul singing added little, but neither did they take too much away.

No, this always was more than just a great song. It was a great record, its components so interlinked that every reinterpretation has been forced to exist in reference to the original. Singers may not use it as a vehicle for the exploration of their own feelings: in trying to recreate its magic, the best they can hope for is a reminder of how they felt when they first heard it. Unlike the rest of the songs in this book, "The Tracks of My Tears" is not open to negotiation.

Nor was its essence open to duplication, even by its creator. In concert, Robinson treats "The Tracks of My Tears" with special care. But when he tried to make a follow-up in the autumn of 1965, "My Girl Has Gone" – guitar intro and all – seemed no more than a faded carbon-copy.

As for the original, the years have only clarified its qualities. In 1969, it was reissued and reached the British Top 10. In America, it is one of the best-loved and most-played golden oldies. When Oliver Stone, making *Platoon* in 1986, wanted to show us his tragic, brutalised group of American soldiers, stuck amid the degradation of the Vietnam war and trying to lose their conscious minds in opium and dreams of home, he needed a piece of music that was not only in period but would evoke the 95 per cent of all human emotions missing from this particular season in hell.

Briefly silencing the dark beat of the gunship rotors and the crackle of automatic weapons, "The Tracks of My Tears" became, for Stone and for us, the perfect reminder of a better world.

60

MY FAVOURITE THINGS

BY GEOFF DYER

SOME SONGS have a special quality of loyalty: they only come fully alive when played by their composer. Others drift from performer to performer, happily, promiscuously. Sometimes, though, a song can end up being so firmly identified with a particular performer that it becomes theirs, not the composer's. This may take time: Ornette Coleman's "Lonely Woman" is gradually becoming a Charlie Haden song. But "My Favourite Things", well, that's been a Coltrane song for more than 30 years.

American musicians have long found jazz in unpromising sources – as Sonny Rollins did with his swinging-in-the-saddle version of "Wagon Wheels" – but few pieces have travelled as far from their origins as the dainty little tune "My Favourite Things".

★ ★ ★ ★ ★ ★ ★ ★ ★ ★

In this one song, we can hear Coltrane's relentless journey of search, discovery and further searching.

★ ★ ★ ★ ★ ★ ★ ★ ★ ★

It was written by the songwriting factory of Richard Rodgers (music) and Oscar Hammerstein (lyrics) as part of their 1959 stage musical *The Sound of Music*. This harmless piece of entertainment went on to blight the lives of children the world over when, in 1965, it was made into a multiple-Oscar-winning film starring Julie Andrews as Maria, the nun-to-be who finds love and happiness as a governess in the strict household of Baron von Trapp (Christopher Plummer).

Now, the musical, as we all know, is the most worthless cinematic form imaginable and of all the irritating moments from this inherently repulsive genre, none is more nauseating than when Andrews, reassuring the awful Trapp children in the midst of a thunderstorm, embarks on a spontaneous list of her favourite things: "bright copper kettles and warm woollen mittens, brown paper packages tied up with strings, these are a few . . ." The reason it's *so* nauseating is that it's extremely catchy. It has the irresistible inanity of a nursery rhyme.

John Coltrane was drawn to catchy tunes. He recorded "Greensleeves" and "Chim Chim Cheree" from *Mary Poppins* but neither of these captivated him or his listeners like "My Favourite Things". He first recorded it within months of establishing his own regular band, on 21 October 1960 – before the film was made. Three quarters of what would become the greatest quartet in jazz history are present on this recording. Jimmy Garrison soon replaced Steve Davis on bass but the core sound – of Trane plus Elvin Jones on drums and McCoy Tyner on piano – is already there.

Trane never tired of playing "My Favourite Things"; it became almost his signature tune. The last recording I have was made in Japan on 22 July 1966, a year before his death. In between there are more than a dozen recorded performances. In this one song, then, we can hear in microcosm the relentless journey of search, discovery and further searching that characterised Coltrane's most creative period.

Trane had made his name as a tenor player. "My Favourite Things" was one of the first recordings on which he played soprano. From the start his soprano playing had an eastern feel and this became even more pronounced later – to the disgust of Philip Larkin who disparaged his "cobra-coaxing cacophony". Certain characteristics of those subsequent recordings are there on the first one: the pretty melody gradually breaking up into squalls, coils, strangled cries and a piercing morse that summons back the melody. But compared with later versions, it actually lopes along pretty gently. Elvin sets up a relaxed, swinging beat; relative to its full, propulsive power, McCoy's pounding left hand sounds almost restrained here (*My Favourite Things*, Atlantic 1961).

Although by jazz standards, Trane's quartet was a stable unit, there were intermittent changes and additions to the personnel. In a live performance on 23 November 1961 the quartet – with Reggie Workman substituting for Garrison – is augmented by Eric Dolphy on flute (*Coltranology* Vol 1, Affinity 1978). At the Newport Festival in July 1963, Roy Haynes sat in for Elvin (who was undergoing mandatory rehab following drug problems). The quartet sound came to be dominated by ferocious battles between Elvin and Trane; with Haynes behind the traps we hear Trane in a more spacious setting. I can't improve on the distinction in the liner notes: Haynes, for all his intensity, doesn't "*surround* Coltrane with rhythm" as Jones does (*Newport '63*, Impulse 1993).

The more Coltrane played "My Favourite Things" the further it moved from its origins. The increasing familiarity of the refrain enabled him to allude to it more and more briefly and obliquely. It also got longer and longer. In Antibes on 27 July 1965 we hear the classic quartet – Trane, Tyner, Garrison, Jones – at the peak of their form, responding instantaneously to each other's every move, enhancing the lyricism of the tune by the ferocity of their attack on it (*Live in Antibes*, INA 1988).

By the autumn of 1965 Coltrane had pushed the quartet form to the limit. Although he had often embellished his music with extra musicians he now used younger "free" players – like Archie Shepp and Pharoah Sanders – to create a fundamentally different sound. In the increasing musical density – for a while he used two drummers, Elvin and Rashied Ali – Tyner was having trouble making himself heard, but it was actually Elvin who left first, in December 1965. Tyner himself quit three months later.

When Trane appears at the Village Vanguard in May 1966 it is with the band that will mark his final phase: wife Alice on piano, Pharoah, Rashied Ali on drums ("he ain't playin' *shit*," was Elvin's comment), and Garrison, the only member of the quartet to stay with Trane till the end. The wonderful, turbulent assault on "My Favourite Things" (*Live at the Village Vanguard*

Again!, Impulse 1966) begins with a long solo by the bassist. By July, in Tokyo (*Live in Japan*, Impulse 1991), the piece has extended itself to an hour, with Garrison's bass intro alone lasting 15 minutes.

Asked why he tended to use white bassists (like Haden), Ornette Coleman said that "black people haven't taken the string instrument as a part of their high ethnic expression"; strings, in other words, were too securely attached to the white European tradition. In out-chambering, out-reciting anybody who ever picked up the bass in a classical setting, then, Garrison's solo represents a discreetly important moment in the ascendancy of black music. Since then even the cello, in the hands of players like Abdul Wadud, has been able to play its part in the *Coon Bid'ness* (to borrow the title of a Julius Hemphill album that features Wadud to great effect) of serious black music.

In Tokyo, when the band enter after Garrison's solo, Trane is on *alto* sax, an instrument he'd never played in his own bands. Yamaha had given one to both Trane and Pharoah when they arrived in the country and he thought he'd try it out. Within moments we realise it's a completely new sound: Trane's never sounded like this and neither has the alto. He wails and calls and cries for five minutes before we recognise the melody and he's off again, this time taking us even further out before swerving briefly back to the theme. Now he is flying. With Alice playing star-splash piano and Rashied on shimmering, stellar drums he's set free of what Steve Lake has called the "gravitational tug" of Elvin and McCoy. They drove Coltrane; Alice and Rashied *beckon*. It's pretty and then dangerous as he reaches so high the sky blues into the darkness of a space before re-entering, everything burning up around him. Despite its extended length it's a masterpiece of economy, this solo: a whole career on alto compressed into just 11 minutes.

63

In a relay race, the moments of greatest intensity are when the baton changes hands. Same in jazz. When Trane ends his solo and Pharoah, 26 at the time, takes the stand, you sense him handing over the torch. Sanders, after flaring full of grace for a couple of minutes, doesn't know what to do with it, loses his way – by which I mean that *I* don't know what he's doing with it. *I* lose *my* way. It's the same either way: Pharoah and the listener share the same dilemma.

Trane was driving forward so relentlessly that his solos start from the point where, a few months previously, they would have come to a shrieking climax. The pace was such that by late 1965 he was unsure where to go next.

When the other band-members failed to show up on time at the Newport Festival in February 1966 he went on stage with Thelonious Monk and his group. After the set the promoter expressed relief that the band hadn't shown up and Trane confided that he sometimes doubted if he was going in the right direction. Elvin had been in no doubt: all he could hear in his last months with Trane "was a lot of noise".

In this context "My Favourite Things" is like a familiar path through a jungle. We cherish the hope that an artist's last works will be his best but some of Coltrane's – like the duets with Rashied Ali from February 1967 – are frenzied, despairing testaments to the musical impasse to which he drove himself.

Pharoah's problem that night in Japan, then, is the one that jazz has been grappling with ever since this heyday of the avant-garde: if you start with a scream where do you go from there? Or to put it another way, what is there left after Trane? In a sense Pharoah's subsequent career has been dedicated to answering that question, to bearing the torch.

After Pharoah there's an inconclusive duet between Rashied and Alice, lengthy enough to leave us wondering if, deep down, we don't wish it were still Elvin and McCoy there instead. Then it's Trane again, this time on soprano. He seems to be trying to put into this one solo everything he's ever done and ever will do and he's doing it. I begin to think yes, maybe it's his greatest performance ever (this incessant ranking and judging: the critic groping for criteria of rapture) because – the idea is mind-blowing – along with everything else he is *swinging* harder than ever.

And perhaps he even answers the question of what will come after him. Traditionally musicians built up their solos by moving from a theme or melody outwards. Coltrane's last recordings turn this inside out: he works his way towards them, just as, in the quarter century since his death, jazz has worked its way back to tighter, more traditional forms. Shepp has ended up playing the blues; Pharoah's screaming has brought him to the grandeur of what he calls his "cathedral" sound.

And the melody, as Trane plays it for the last time, "free through all he has given up, rejoicing in his mastery", sounds fresher, more beautiful, more full of life than ever. The words are Rilke's, from a poem written four months before his death:

> Ah the ball that we hurled into infinite space,
> doesn't it fill our hand differently with its return:
> heavier by the weight of where it has been.
> Yes, but lighter too!

I sometimes wonder if there is any life left in some popular jazz tunes, like Monk's "Round Midnight" or Coltrane's "Naima". Rather than exhaust "My Favourite Things", though, Trane suggested the opposite: its inexhaustibility.

That's why people still play it. At the Jazz Café in London a few years ago Ahmad Jamal's trio vamped through a wonderful dancing version of the piece. One reason it works so effectively in a trio setting is because there is no horn player to remind us of the power and invention of the absent master.

Most recently, the song crops up, sort of, on Elvis Costello's album *Brutal Youth* (WEA 1994). The song "This is Hell" turns Rodgers and Hammerstein upside down, itemising Costello's least favourite things. It all comes to a head when

> 'My Favourite Things' are playing again and again.
> But it's by Julie Andrews and not by John Coltrane.

64

ERLKÖNIG

BY TIM ROSTRON

TWO FRIENDS call on Franz Schubert, an unknown, 19-year-old composer who lives with his father in Vienna – to find him in a state of high excitement. He is reading aloud a Goethe poem: a horror story with the power of myth, told with great sophistication. He paces for a moment, then goes to his desk (he does not compose at a piano: he does not even own one). In less than two hours he is satisfied. He and his friends rush out to give the song "Erlkönig" its first, otherwise unattended performance.

The anecdote is told by one of those two friends in a memoir. It might even be true. The song's hurtling forward motion, the seemingly subconscious complexities of the music, smack of fevered inspiration. Doubters who point out that merely to transcribe the score would take longer than two hours should reflect on the rest of Schubert's output in his *annus mirabilis* of 1815: more than 150 songs, four operas, two symphonies, two masses and a string quartet. Shall we settle for three hours?

★ ★ ★ ★ ★ ★ ★ ★ ★ ★

Somewhere along the line, "elf king" became "alders' king", and thus one of the most famous songs in all Lieder came to feature the king of catkin-bearing trees that favour moist ground.

★ ★ ★ ★ ★ ★ ★ ★ ★ ★

"Erlkönig" was not an immediate hit. The turning point, both for the song and Schubert's career, came in the winter of 1820, when it was included in a private concert given by a barrister called Ignez Sonnleithner. It brought the house down, and has done ever since.

Schubert had published nothing by 1820, so there was no sheet music to meet the first trickle of demand. Sonnleithner's son Leopold von, another barrister, came up with a plan and some of the funds to publish Schubert's songs privately, and at a subsequent Sonnleithner soirée 100 copies of "Erlkönig" – Schubert's Opus 1 – were sold. (One was sent to Goethe: he did not acknowledge receipt.)

Public performances followed, always to the sound of enthusiastic applause backed up by the equally uplifting sound of money being exchanged for sheet music. The musical establishment of his native Vienna at last embraced Schubert. He died at 31, too soon to enjoy fame. The cause of death remains unknown, but two candidates are typhoid and syphilis. He died poor, thanks to the unscrupulousness of the first company to officially publish his works, and the incompetence of the second.

Schubert was not the originator of German Lieder. Nor, even as the composer of more than 600 songs, was he the most prolific exponent. (That honour probably belongs to J. F. Reichardt, 1752–1814, with 1,500 songs.)

Schubert is, though, the genre's unsurpassed genius. There exist some 50 other settings of Goethe's poem, and a sketch by Beethoven. Only one, composed by Carl Loewe in 1818, has any currency today. It is a fair effort, but this is what it has to compete with:

For the first 15 bars the pianist hammers out triplets. The older and scratchier the recording, the more the listener will be reminded of an accompaniment to a silent film. Not the Keystone Cops, though, because there's obviously something nastier around the corner than custard pies. The approach to Dracula's castle by horse-drawn carriage is more like it.

The voice enters. Like us, the narrator is peering uncertainly into the raging darkness. *Wer retet so spät durch Nacht und Wind?* – "Who is riding so late through the night and wind?" It is the father with his child. And the child is held safely in his father's arms.

For all but the last of its remaining seven verses, the poem consists of dialogue. There are three voices: the reassuring father – "My son, why do you hide your face in fear?"; the terrified son – "Father, don't you see the Erlkönig?"; and the sinisterly reassuring warlock – "Sweet child, come with me. I'll play wonderful games with you". It's just the wind rustling in the withered leaves, claims father.

What manner of creature is it that is now saying, "Won't you come with me, my fine boy? My daughters will wait upon you . . ."? The Erlkönig is worse than a figment of the imagination. He is a figment of mistranslation. Goethe, looking for a subject for an irrelevant ballad to drop into a theatre work of 1782, *Der Fischerin*, came across a Danish legend about the elf king. Or it should have been about the elf king. Somewhere along the line, *ellekönig* became not *Elkönig* but *Erlkönig* – alders' king – and thus one of the most famous songs in all Lieder came to feature the king of catkin-bearing trees that favour moist ground.

Perhaps it is the catkins in a mist that the son now believes to be the Erlkönig's daughters. Father says that they are the just the old willows gleaming.

But now the Erlkönig is heard again – "I love you – your fair form allures me" – and the son's third cry of *Mein Vater, Mein Vater* becomes panic-stricken. "The Erl-King is hurting me!"

The father shudders and makes his horse ride more quickly. We have reached the last verse. The soprano Lotte Lehmann, in her book *More than Singing* (Boosey and Hawkes, 1945), explains how to tackle the final two lines: "Straighten up with an audible indrawn breath as if a sudden shock has made you catch your breath. Sing '*In seinen Armen das Kind* [In his arms the child . . .]' *pianissimo*, with an expression of pain, and end with a whisper lacking in any tone (but distinctly) '*war tot* [was dead]'."

An extreme test of a singer's virtuosity, artistry and intelligence, and of a pianist's wrists, "Erlkönig" is Lieder's four-minute decathlon.

Schubert sets the poem as a continuous melodrama, through which the strophic form of the original can be glimpsed. The texture of the opening

66

bars permeates the song – a tuneless, harmonyless rattle in the right hand, a surging rumble in the left. This conjures up the wind, rain, thunder and galloping hooves, but is disconcerting for purely musical reasons – bass lines usually move in stately fashion and give us our bearings.

The most conventional – and thus comforting – music is that of the Erlkönig. For his verses the piano part replaces the triplet rattle with the oom-pah-pah accompaniment it has been a nightmare parody of, then rippling arpeggios.

The boy's cries strain a semitone above the accompaniment as if he is being wrenched away. For the Erlkönig's final, abrupt verse the comforting tone is abandoned – this is the sound of naked desire. When we arrive at the original key we might assume salvation is in sight. But the bass begins to climb chromatically and for a few vital bars we do not know where we are. The major chord we finally reach is not the home key but a semitone above it – in a physical sense close to the expected goal but in musical terms extremely remote. It is left to the narrator to remind us, drily, how near and yet so far.

The BBC Record Library holds 38 different versions of the song. This seems a little light for such a popular number. It does not include, for example, the one by the Swingle Singers listed, but not held, by the National Sound Archive.

The earliest recordings include that of an elderly Lilli Lehmann (*Schubert Lieder on Record 1898–1952*, EMI 1982, to be reissued in 1997) – heard not at her best, even allowing for 1906-vintage surface noise – and two in French, using an orchestration by Berlioz and a translation that retains more of the power of the original than has ever been managed in English. In one of these Gallic "Erlkönig"s, the tenor Georges Thill is joined by a baritone and boy soprano (*Schubert Lieder on Record*, as above). The result ought to serve as a warning to solo interpreters that any over-characterisation of the song's four voices will turn great storytelling into a mere puppet show. In the event, Thill's mini-opera is tremendous, and hardly kitsch at all. This experiment has remained unrepeatable since 1930.

On the now unavailable LP *The Surprising Soprano Michael Aspinall* (London 1976) the warning is loud and clear. Aspinall, performing live and in a frock, milks "Erlkönig" for laughs without changing a note or a word of the original. It is all a matter of funny voices and – judging by the laughter which is disproportional to the admittedly pretty amusing soundtrack – a deal of mugging.

Schubert wrote the song for tenor and piano (and left four versions: one simplified, two with minor revisions). But is it ideally a man's song? Many women have tackled "Erlkönig"; it can be argued that a woman is distanced by sex from the characters in the song, and so is at less risk of coming over as a ventriloquist.

Lotte Lehmann recorded the song three times officially (live, pirate recordings sometimes appear), and her last, made in 1945 with Paul Ulonovsky, is one of the first things I would grab in the event of a fire. She characterises with exactly the right restraint and – she was 56, but in good voice – comes across like a grandmother reading an irresponsible bedtime story. It is not the most spontaneous rendering, but it is the most frightening. The recording is currently unavailable but it resurfaces periodically on "historic reissues".

Jessye Norman, accompanied by Phillip Moll in 1984 (*Schubert: Lieder*, Philips), is less operatic than might be feared from this singer, who has the range to impersonate the biggest-chested father and the most hysterical child. She just about keeps things in Lieder proportions until the very end, when the listener – who knows as well as she does what is coming – might feel she overreacts to the child's death.

In the 1920s, there was a vogue for singing "Erlkönig" in English. Peter Dawson's is the only one that ever flits back into catalogue (*The Art of Peter Dawson*, HMV 1983). Despite being an Australian, he cannot quite defeat the absurd Britishness that inevitably comes over the poem in translation. As the critic J. B. Steane said of Dawson's record, the "wonderful games" with which the Erlkönig tempts the boy are likely to be rugby and cricket.

But inevitably any "Erlkönig" collection has to start with one of those by the baritone Dietrich Fischer-Dieskau and pianist Gerald Moore, Lieder's A-team. (At the time of writing, DG's 1970 recording is available on a single disc of Schubert songs, *Franz Schubert: Lieder*.) Fischer-Dieskau's achievement is to sound caught up in the thrill of the story. It is his eagerness to convey this excitement that informs his characterisation, rather than an effort to put on a show. Especially treasurable is his bluff good humour as he sets the scene: "Don't worry chaps, the child is safe and warm!" he seems to be saying, and we are on the edge of our seats wanting to tell him things are more serious than that.

Within Schubert's lifetime "Erlkönig" was already popular enough to have inspired spin-off marches and waltzes. Though Schubert took a dim view of these remixes, he was not above giving private performances of the song on the comb.

But "Erlkönig" was not to everyone's taste. In 1817 one of Schubert's champions submitted the song to a publisher in Leipzig. The publisher, who could not believe that it was the work of Franz Schubert – the more famous Franz Schubert the violinist – sent it to him for verification. This other Franz Schubert replied: "With the greatest astonishment I have to say that this cantata was never published by me. I am keeping it in my possession in the hope of discovering the fellow who sent you such trash."

YOU SEND ME

BY NICK HORNBY

SAM COOKE may or may not have been the first soul singer, just as Iggy Pop may or may not have been the first punk, and Joe Turner the first rock'n'roll singer, and "Mouldy Old Dough" by Lieutenant Pigeon the first ambient house record. It doesn't really matter much either way. But Cooke is certainly the first and most uncomplicated example of a gospel singer who went secular to make hits.

This journey from church to chart came to characterise soul music, and several other singers (notably Aretha Franklin) followed Cooke's trail; but Cooke snubbed the Lord in 1957, before any of them. "You Send Me", released that autumn, was his first commercially successful post-gospel record. (It reached No 1 in the US chart, although it only scraped into the Top 30 in Britain.) If anyone wanted to make a case for "You Send Me" as the first popular soul 45 – and these things are important to some people – you would have to have something pretty recherché up your sleeve to rebut the argument.

★ ★ ★ ★ ★ ★ ★ ★ ★

Aretha Franklin, Mavis Staples and Otis Redding were determined to turn it into a great song if it killed them

★ ★ ★ ★ ★ ★ ★ ★ ★

The original version of "You Send Me" does not sound much like a soul 45 now. It has a sugary (white) girl chorus, a hopelessly dated MOR quickstep beat, and it ends with a corny, horrible and hilariously bathetic twangy guitar chord. Pat Boone could have used exactly the same arrangement, and nobody would have accused him of coming over all funky. Art Rupe, owner of the R&B-and-gospel label Specialty, was so appalled by the girly chorus that he refused to put the recording out on his label, and the producer, Bumps Blackwell, had to take it elsewhere. "You Send Me" does have charm, and not all of the period variety: its chaste, dreamy sentiment can transport even the most cynical to a place where heartfelt romantic gesture has meaning. Nobody wants to be grown-up and complicated all the time.

In fact, "You Send Me", a Sam Cooke composition, isn't much of a song at all. Its lyrics consist of just one verse ("At first I thought it was infatuation/ But it's lasted so very long/ And now I find myself wanting/To marry you and take you home"); the rest is an endless repetition of the phrases "You send me", "You thrill me" and "Honest you do". Cooke may have had the original soul voice (only he has managed to combine the sweetness and the grain *simultaneously*), but he didn't give himself much to sing with it.

Yet "You Send Me", like "Cupid", "Only Sixteen", "Wonderful World" and so many other Sam Cooke songs, has enjoyed an extraordinary longevity. After he was shot dead in a Los Angeles motel in 1964, Cooke seemed to acquire a whole new set of meanings for the nascent soul-music community, and it was *de rigueur* for singers to cover at least one Cooke song. (Otis Redding, never a man to do things by halves, had a bash at five.) Cooke assumed an equal, if not identical, importance for those singers who were not black but wished they were: Rod Stewart, Eric Burdon of the Animals and Van Morrison have all shown off their croaks on "Bring It on Home", and Mick Jagger gave "Good Times" a good seeing-to.

It hardly mattered, then, that "You Send Me" was a bit of pop fluff. Aretha Franklin, Mavis Staples and Otis Redding were determined to turn it into a great song even if it killed them, even if they had to rearrange it and rewrite it and slow it down and add lyrics and give it more gravitas than it really deserved.

Redding was the first of this illustrious trio to try his hand, on *Pain in My Heart*, his first album (Atlantic 1964). His version provides a tantalising hint of what might have been if Bumps Blackwell had taken Cooke to see Jerry Wexler of Atlantic Records. ("He only had to pick up the phone," Wexler said years later. "Sam Cooke was our kind of singer.") Redding was backed, not by strings or girly choirs, but by Booker T and the MGs, Atlantic's brilliant house band; what could they have done with Cooke, one wonders? This is "You Send Me" as straight R&B, and only the horn charts have survived from the original. Unsurprisingly, they no longer fit properly.

When Aretha Franklin recorded "You Send Me" in 1968, she was near the beginning of the longest hot streak in the entire history of pop: between 1967 and 1972 she recorded 11 almost flawless albums for Atlantic on the trot. Her version of the song closes the first side of the album *Aretha Now* (Atlantic), and has to follow both "Think" and "I Say a Little Prayer"; that it holds its own in this company is a measure of its success.

Aretha's own, piercingly beautiful, solo piano intro changes everything: ironically, given the genesis of the song (Cooke was, after all, trying to dump God and make himself a few quid when he wrote it), this is "You Send Me" as straight gospel. The Franklin voice swoops over and under Cooke's melody line, she double-tracks herself to thrilling effect, and the chorus is provided by the Sweet Inspirations, who feature on all Aretha's Atlantic work, rather than the wannabe Beverley Sisters who ruined the original; at this point "You Send Me" becomes a great song in spite of itself. Disappointingly, Aretha finds it necessary to tinker with the words: "I want you to marry me/ Please take me home", she begs. And this from the woman with the most intimidating voice in soul history, the woman who sang "Respect".

Mavis Staples of the Staple Singers was not quite in Aretha's league – her deep, rich, treacly voice never allowed her to soar over her material in the same way. But for a while she was the next best thing, and she was lucky enough to record two solo albums for Stax at the end of the sixties, soul's golden age, when the songs had become less generic and the singers were allowed to stretch out. (She was also lucky enough to be produced by Steve Cropper, Booker T and the MGs' guitarist, and by now something of an authority on Sam Cooke cover versions; he must have recorded more Sam Cooke songs than Sam Cooke ever did. He almost certainly would have played on the other two Stax/Atlantic versions of "You Send Me", by Percy Sledge and Solomon Burke.) Staples has "You Send Me" down as an agonised, torchy and unfeasibly sexy ballad; she slows it right down, and finds all sorts of things hidden in its nooks and crannies (reissued on *Don't Change Me Now*, Stax 1988).

Fairground Attraction covered it, prettily but unremarkably, on their bits-and-bobs album *Ay Fond Kiss* (RCA 1990); it also pops up on Steve Miller's *Fly Like an Eagle* (Capitol 1976) as an acoustic throwaway, although we are not allowed to throw it away until Miller has shown us some pretty fancy vocal trills. In the late seventies, Roy Ayers recorded a jazz-funk interpretation (*You Send Me*, Polydor 1978). At seven minutes it's twice as long as any of the others, and everybody, especially vocalist Carla Vaughan, gets to show off. The result is as pleasant and unaffecting as all the other seven-minute late-seventies jazz-funk ballads.

Van Morrison quotes the song – or rather he delegates and lets his deputy, sweet-voiced Brian Kennedy quote it – during a stirring version of his own "In the Garden" on the R&B celebration *A Night in San Francisco* (Polydor 1994). What it's doing in the garden isn't clear, but as usual Morrison comes up smelling of roses.

Only two acts since Aretha have really had anything new to add. The Everly Brothers recorded the song during one of their frequent, brief and usually disastrous reunions (*EB84*, Mercury 1984). They see the song as a mournful, wistful hymn – not unlike "All I Have to Do is Dream", funnily enough – which doesn't make much sense, given the explicit celebration of the song, but sounds terrific anyway.

On his 1974 album *Smiler* (Mercury), Rod Stewart squashed "You Send Me" on to the end of "Bring It on Home", dispensed with its solitary verse, and contented himself with chuckling a lot over a sweeping string arrangement. It works brilliantly; by now, one is used to the idea that this flimsiest of songs, this piece of dated teen-pop corn, can become a raucous, riotous, laddish show-stopper should anyone wish it to be so.

71

YESTERDAY

BY GILES SMITH

EVERYBODY knows about the man who turned down the Beatles. Dick Rowe, the rep from Decca, who heard some of the Fab Four's early recordings and decided that he just couldn't see a future in them, has become a legendary figure of fun. But what about the man who turned down the Beatles' biggest song? Doesn't he deserve a pillorying too? Step up, Billy J. Kramer.

It was Kramer who approached Paul McCartney in 1965 and asked him if he had written anything new that he could have for a single. McCartney played him a little ballad he had written on the guitar, with a lyric on a conventional blues theme – the man whose lover has walked out on him, without quite saying why. The first verse went: "Yesterday/ All my troubles seemed so far away/ Now it looks as though they're here to stay/ Oh, I believe in yesterday." Kramer thought about it for a minute and decided he didn't rate the song.

The rest of the band distanced themselves from the song, and ribbed McCartney mercilessly.

Seven years later, what was not good enough for Billy J. had proved acceptable to 1,186 artists around the world, all of whom had seen fit to make recorded versions of "Yesterday", a song which McCartney had rapidly come to believe was "the most complete thing I've ever written".

For "written", read "dreamt". The tune for "Yesterday" came to McCartney in his sleep. "I woke up one morning in London in Wimpole Street in an attic flat. Just woke up and I had that tune of 'Yesterday' in my head, with no idea where it came from. They gave me an award for it because it's been [broadcast] five million times – and the next song down is three million so it's way out ahead. And I dreamt it, so if that's not magic, what is? Dead jammy."

The lyrics, though, had to be worked for. At first, McCartney simply attached a couple of prototype lines of daft verse to the tune – a common practice for him while he was weighing up a melody and wondering which way to push the song's mood. But in this case, the lines he hit on could have sunk the song for good. Before "Yesterday" was "Yesterday", the words ran "Scrambled eggs/ Oh my darling, you've got lovely legs". When a writer reaches the send-up stage this early in a composition, ordinarily he or she is on the verge of throwing the whole thing away and moving on. But something in the tune's solemn roundedness seems to have called McCartney back from the edge and forced him to take the job seriously.

It was still called "Scrambled Eggs" in January 1964, when he showed it, rather sheepishly, to the Beatles' producer, George Martin. Consider McCartney's predicament: he was 22, at the front of the world's greatest pop group, the writer of mould-breaking snappy teen anthems and heart-melting ballads

– and yet into his lap had dropped a composition which was stately, formal, oddly classical in the way phrase answered to phrase, and about as hip and youthful as a pot of tea. He told Martin that he was looking for a one-word title for the song, that "Yesterday" had come to mind, but he was worried that it was too corny. Martin encouraged him to persist.

The song was not recorded until Monday 14 June 1965. Mark Lewisohn's scholarly guide, *The Complete Beatles Recording Sessions*, informs us that the track was completed in three hours in the evening. McCartney played acoustic guitar and sang, while a classical string quartet accompanied him, filling the track out and plotting its rhythmic direction without need for the heavier certainty of drums. "Yesterday" marks the Beatles' first use of orchestral instruments, and by no means their last. The strings were Martin's idea. As Andy Partridge, the songwriter from XTC, once said: "George Martin is often described as the Fifth Beatle; he may well have been the First."

Whatever, none of the other three contributed to "Yesterday" (though George Harrison was evidently in the studio during the session). This was widely interpreted at the time as rock-solid evidence that the Beatles were on the verge of splitting – but then, in 1965, very few things weren't interpreted that way. And though "Yesterday" appeared on the *Help!* soundtrack album (Parlophone 1965) – if not in the movie itself – and was the title track of an EP, it is certainly true that the rest of the band distanced themselves from the song and ribbed McCartney mercilessly for its fuddy-duddiness. McCartney said, "I remember George saying, 'Blimey, he's always talking about "Yesterday", you'd think he was Beethoven or somebody.' "

73

In fact, there is nothing fancy or ornate about the song's construction. McCartney's opening guitar part sets the tone – one repeated chord, played with downward strokes of the thumb, which is the most basic kind of strumming. The unique thing, when the song moves into the verse, is its cycle of chords. "Yesterday" is built on a set of perfectly common cadences, but as you travel through them, you pass across neat little bridging chords so that the movement of the strings beneath the voice appears subtly interleaved.

George Martin has revealed how McCartney was determined that the string players should keep their vibrato to a minimum, so as not to give the song any cumbersome emotionality. The same principle informs his singing, which maintains an understated warmth, even when it climbs high into the middle section. ("Why she had to go/ I don't know/ She wouldn't say/ I said something wrong/ Now I long for yesterday.") The recording is primitive and partly botched: occasionally you hear the voice double up. Not a deliberate effect, this is simply the trace of an earlier take, spilling out of the headphones in the studio. But the key thing about the basic instrumentation is that there is nothing here to betray the song's age, no particular noise pinning it to its era. This has had a double benefit: it made the song sound like a standard, even when it was freshly minted; and it has since rendered it immune to the passing years.

Hence that slew of cover versions. No one has taken the song to No 1 –

but then, neither did the Beatles. (Released as a single retrospectively, in 1976, "Yesterday" only went as far as No 8.) Most shots at the piece fall into one of two camps. On one hand, there are those who have realised McCartney's worst fears about the song. Many of these use the presence of strings on the original as an excuse to ladle giant, sticky violin sections all over the arrangement, somehow forgetting that there was only a quartet there to begin with and that it played with rasp and edge. If McCartney had somehow been able to hear Richard Clayderman's dizzyingly sugary instrumental version in advance, can we really believe he would have bothered to complete the song?

On the other hand, there are recordings by Ray Charles and Marvin Gaye whose versions amply support McCartney's hunch that, when he wrote "Yesterday", he was creating more than just a bauble to hang on Perry Como's *Take it Easy* album (RCA 1990). Charles's 1967 version (*The Collection*, Castle 1990) replaces the guitar with a piano and inserts a moment of silence before each verse. "Suddenly," he snaps, "I'm not half the man I used to be." It's as if those little gaps are the spaces in which the singer is trying to gather what is left of his strength. On Gaye's version (*That's the Way Love Is*, Motown 1970), a prominent bass drum and cymbal lend the song the slink of a Motown ballad, with Gaye calling out, "People, now I need a place to hide away". For all the song's ostensible English poppiness, you barely have to rub at the surface to reveal something of gospel and soul there.

As a rule of thumb, don't trust anyone who slows the song down. It is easy to underestimate the medium pace at which McCartney's version ticks along. "Yesterday" owes its becoming blitheness, its refusal to wallow, precisely to this. Generally, when people put the brakes on, they are hoping to milk the song for something it cannot give them. This is why the version by the four-woman singing group En Vogue on the *Funky Divas* album (East West 1992) makes a fresh break. They move the tempo up a notch and stuff the track with close-packed harmonies set to a thumping drum machine. In the process they become probably the first act to give the song a defiant swagger.

Better this, certainly, than the decelerated Tom Jones version (*Delilah*, Decca 1968), which is crammed to breaking point with bogus suffering. Jones gives it the big-voice treatment, but, as "Yesterday" is apt to make clear, size isn't everything. Shocking to say, even Elvis Presley, live in Las Vegas (*On Stage*, RCA 1970), exercises more decorum, though a nicely modest vocal delivery is spoilt by the intrusion of backing vocalists, who rather disrupt the song's solitary, confessional thrust. ("Yesterday," sings Elvis: "Yesterday!" coo the singers, in case you misheard the first time.)

And so it goes on: Dionne Warwick gives the song heart (*Unforgettable*, Castle 1987), Diana Ross empties it of content (*I Hear a Symphony*, Motown 1966); Merle Haggard and Willie Nelson lift it effortlessly (*Help Me Make it Through the Night*, RCA 1984), Ray Conniff sits on it, heavily (*Easy Listening Beatles*, CBS 1985). With "Yesterday" it can go either way. McCartney seems to have known this even as he wrote the song. But at least he left us, in the shape of his own version, the instruction manual.

74

HOW LONG HAS THIS BEEN GOING ON?

BY RHODA KOENIG

THE FIRST time I heard "How Long Has This Been Going On?" it made an impression very different from the one George and Ira Gershwin intended. I was listening to the record of Judy Garland's 23 April 1961 appearance at Carnegie Hall, on which her intensity was matched by the hysterical adulation that greeted her comeback tour. I assumed that the song concerned adultery, and that the title was the question of a heartbroken wife – ie, "How long have you been making a fool of me?". The lines "Kiss me once, then once more/What a dunce I was before!" seemed to support this: the wife confusedly asking her faithless husband for comfort, while berating herself for not noticing the obvious signs. Garland's breathiness as she leaned into the "How", and the agony with which she gobbled up the final phrases over the pianist's staccato attack, further convinced me that this was a song about misery and betrayal.

Judy, however, was just being Judy – laying on the singer-on-the-verge-of-a-nervous-breakdown mannerisms that, unfortunately, the fans of her later years encouraged. The original meaning of "How Long Has This Been Going On?" couldn't be more innocent: a girl and a boy discover, with their first kiss, the wonder of love. The Gershwins wrote it for Adele Astaire and Stanley Ridges in the Broadway musical *Funny Face* (1927), but it didn't go down well in the out-of-town try-outs and was dropped from the show. It appeared the next year, rather overpowered, in Florenz Ziegfeld's production of *Rosalie*, described by one critic as "romance in fine feathers and gold and ermine all over everything". The lyrics of the boy's verse exhibited Ira Gershwin's tendency to be, like his idol P.G. Wodehouse, a bit babyish. "As a tot, when I trotted in little velvet panties/I was kissed by my sisters, my cousins and my aunties." Ira ties up this sticky image with the bow of schoolboy literary allusion: "Sad to tell, it was Hell – an inferno worse than Dante's."

In the chorus, the fussy tune and lyrics dissolve into melting simplicity. "I could cry salty tears," goes the confession, followed by a statement so direct it buries the internal rhyme: "Where have I been all these years?". Words and music capture the mood of awestruck bewilderment, with repeated notes suggesting the singer's stupefaction; Alec Wilder, in *American Popular Song* (Oxford, 1972), points out the "curious self-consciousness" of the seventh measure's lead-in to the minor seventh that opens the hesitant question of the title: "Is this really what everyone feels? Why didn't anyone tell me?"

"How Long Has This Been Going On?" remained in the shadows until the early 1940s, when Peggy Lee recorded it with Benny Goodman's band (*Peggy Lee Sings with Benny Goodman*, Columbia 1984). Since then it has become a standard for singers and musicians, especially jazz artists. Lee nicely cushions the "oh" that begins the release, but her interpretation, on the whole, sounds tense. It would be difficult, however, for anyone to establish the intimacy the song requires with a full orchestral backing. This is a number for a piano, bass and a little light work on the drums.

What Lee did, though, with her sultry vocal, was to fix the change in style from the 1920s, when Broadway musicals were still influenced by operetta, stars were tenors and sopranos, and the mood was dainty charm – or, to put it another way, sexless twittering. In the 1930s, popular music got lower and slower; baritones and contraltos, singing in a more robust and knowing manner, took centre stage, and tempi relaxed and opened up. Though marked "moderato", "How Long Has This Been Going On?" has for most of its life been sung very, very slowly. With the transition in tastes, most singers dropped the verse, and added a sensuality which suggested that the sexual act in question was not the first kiss, or the first anything else, but the first one that rang the bell and knocked the ball out of the park. Sarah Vaughan, in her typically lush recording of 1957 (*How Long Has This Been Going On?*, Pablo 1978), starts off dreamily, but on "all these years" suddenly speeds up, as if waking in amazement. Lena Horne (*Stormy Weather*, Music Club 1993) practically softens the wax by stretching out and purring the first line of the release: "Oh, I feel just like I could melt."

★ ★ ★ ★ ★ ★ ★ ★ ★

"Don't be silly," says Fred Astaire. "Everybody wants to be kissed, even philosophers."

★ ★ ★ ★ ★ ★ ★ ★ ★

The sweetness of the Gershwins' original idea still had its adherents. Ella Fitzgerald, on the classic five-record album *The George and Ira Gershwin Song Books* (Verve 1959), tinkled her way through a gentle, bemused version in which she made four, five and six spacey syllables out of "goin'". (Like nearly everyone else, she dropped the final "g".)

The only exception I have come across was the very proper rendition by Audrey Hepburn in the 1957 movie of *Funny Face*. In *My Fair Lady*, Hepburn opened her mouth, and out came the high notes of Marni Nixon, Hollywood's premier dubber; but in the earlier film she used her own small, tentative voice, which suited the shy character she played. (With its pentatonic structure and narrow range, "How Long Has This Been Going On?" has always been a comfortable choice for non-singers.) The star of *Funny Face* (same title and songs as the stage musical, different story) was, as 30 years before, Fred Astaire. Playing a fashion photographer, he barges into a Greenwich Village bookshop with a model and a clutch of squealing stylists and dislodges Hepburn, a little brown mouse whose interests are entirely academic. When the two are alone, and she is standing on a rolling library ladder to replace the fallen books, she explains her enthusiasm for the French philosophy "empathicalism": "You actually feel what the other person is feeling. You put yourself in the other person's place."

Astaire pulls the ladder close and kisses her. "Why did you do that?" she timidly asks.

"Empathy," he replies. "I put myself in your place and I felt that you wanted to be kissed."

"I have no desire to be kissed," she says stiffly, "by you or anyone else."

"Don't be silly," says Astaire. "Everybody wants to be kissed, even philosophers."

Left to herself, Hepburn wonders, in song, if there could be more things than she has dreamt of in her philosophy. She picks up a chiffon-draped hat, twirls giddily around the shop before wistfully, dubiously asking (in a line written for the film by Leonard Gershe), "Can one kiss do all of this?" and, leaving the final line unsung, returns (temporarily, of course) to mousery.

"How Long Has This Been Going On?" has seldom been recorded by men – are they loath to admit they don't know everything? – but a memorable version was cut by Louis Armstrong with the Oscar Peterson Trio Plus One (Louis Bellson on drums; *Louis Armstrong Meets Oscar Peterson*, Verve 1957). Armstrong wades right into the verse, gargling his disgust at soppy childhood kissing and announcing emphatically, "So, my dear, I swore/'Never, never-more!'". In the chorus, he treats the idea that he never knew about all this love stuff as a huge joke on himself. The end of the release ("Don't wake me if I'm asleep/Let me dream that it's true"), sung as a desperate plea by most female vocalists, becomes a chuckling tease, Uncle Louis on Christmas morning.

If I had to choose a supreme recording of "How Long Has This Been Going On?" it would be the one made by Lee Wiley (*Lee Wiley Sings George Gershwin and Cole Porter*, Monmouth-Evergreen 1939). A part-Cherokee from Fort Gibson, Oklahoma, Wiley at 15 was singing with the Leo Reisman Orchestra, and soon afterwards in all the chic Manhattan supper clubs, sounding like a woman twice her age and the most sophisticated one in the house. Though she never became a popular favourite, connoisseurs of jazz and theatre music adored her, and she influenced a generation of better-known singers with her exquisite phrasing and the gently shaded timbre of her rich but delicate contralto: she sings like a sexy ghost. George Gershwin, according to the notes on this recording, "liked the way she sang [his songs] and often said so". I'll bet he did. She brings immense poise to this simple song: the smokiness of her faint Southern accent, the unexpected flattening of the first "on", making the question wryly rhetorical. The back-up group isn't bad either – Fats Waller, Pee Wee Russell, George Wettling, Bud Freeman, Eddie Condon, Max Kaminsky. With Lee Wiley the two interpretations entwine; the song trembles with the sound of innocence meeting experience.

77

AUTUMN LEAVES

BY MARCEL BERLINS

IT APPEARS in 1945, a poem of lost love, memories and regrets. As the dead leaves of autumn pile up, the poet remembers his past lover. They loved each other, lived together. Life was happier then; the sun burned more brightly than today.

> But life separates those who love
> Quietly, without a sound
> And the sea effaces on the sand
> The footprints of parted lovers.

The author of "Les Feuilles Mortes" was Jacques Prévert, poet, screenwriter, dramatist, Left Bank intellectual and a pivotal figure in the fluctuating St-Germain-des-Prés set which included Sartre, de Beauvoir and a dramatically beautiful singer with a smoky voice called Juliette Gréco. Prévert had written the scripts for some of France's finest films of the late thirties and forties, including Marcel Carné's three masterpieces: *Quai des Brumes, Le Jour se lève* and *Les Enfants du Paradis*.

In 1945, in the euphoria of the Liberation, Prévert turned his talent to writing the story for a ballet with a symbolic message, *Le Rendezvous*. Choreography was by Roland Petit, the backdrop tableau by Picasso and music by Joseph Kosma, the Hungarian-born composer. Like Prévert, Kosma had been successful in the cinema; among his compositions was the music for the Jean Renoir classics *La Grande Illusion and La Règle du Jeu*. He also – clandestinely, because he was a Jew and it was 1943 in Nazi-occupied France – composed and arranged the music for *Les Enfants du Paradis*. He had worked with Prévert on other films too, and they wrote songs together.

Le Rendezvous was seen by Carné, who was immediately seduced into making a film of it. It was around that time that Kosma picked up "Les Feuilles Mortes" and, so the story goes, sat down at the piano one day after lunch and idly started picking out the wistful melody for the verse.

> Oh, je voudrais tant que tu te souviennes,
> Des jours heureux où nous étions amis
> (I so much want you to remember
> The happy days when we were friends.)

The song's structure was unusual: 24 bars of introductory verse containing two changes of mood and melody, followed by a 16-bar refrain. It was a "difficult" song; no one thought of it as material for mass appeal.

Carné's film, *Les Portes de la Nuit*, was to star Jean Gabin and Marlene Dietrich. "Les Feuilles Mortes" would appear in the film, but only hummed, wordlessly, by the two lovers, as background to the final scene. When the stars dropped out, Carné, in desperation, hired a young popular singer called Yves Montand to take on the Gabin role: he was known to the French as Edith Piaf's lover, but had no acting experience. To Montand's disappointment, Carné decided that the song in the film should now be sung, still offscreen, by another singer, Fabien Loris. The film, an uneasy mixture of pretentious political realism and fey fantasy, flopped; but Montand started including "Les Feuilles Mortes" in his concert repertoire. Reaction was cool. It had no beat, an over-sophisticated melodic structure and a sad message. Montand persevered; but it took several years for it to become his biggest hit and most requested song.

He recorded it often (for instance on *Singer*, EMI 1993); but his most moving interpretations are the early versions, accompanied by a small, quiet group – piano, guitar, clarinet, drums and accordion. In one, he recites the first 16 bars as a poem, almost reluctantly breaking into song when he reflects on the north wind blowing away dead leaves and memories "in the cold night of oblivion". But he has not forgotten – "tu vois, je n'ai pas oublié".

Montand's voice was still a little rough then, redolent of too many Gitanes, too many glasses of cheap red wine, and with a quality of convincing vulnerability. They said, at the time, that he was singing to Edith Piaf, who had left him. Strangely, or perhaps understandably, Piaf's own over-mannered recordings of the song never quite reach the profundity of feeling achieved by many other French interpreters.

★ ★ ★ ★ ★ ★ ★ ★ ★ ★

When Yves Montand thinks of his loss, he is in anguish; when Nat King Cole does, he suffers a mild sentimental pang.

★ ★ ★ ★ ★ ★ ★ ★ ★ ★

If "Les Feuilles Mortes" belongs primarily to Montand, part of it should be remembered for Juliette Gréco – Little Miss Existentialist – black-clad, black-maned, still in her early twenties but already a near-legendary figure around the cafés and dives of St-Germain-des-Prés. Gréco, too, is better in her earlier recordings, not least because some of the later ones are spoilt by insensitively intrusive string backings. At her best, she turns "Les Feuilles Mortes" into an erotic hymn, a tribute to lost sexuality. She will never again, we know, love so intensely.

The conversion of "Les Feuilles Mortes" into American, in the mid-fifties, was dramatic. Only a part of the opening verse was retained and even that is rarely, if ever, played or sung. As performed and recorded, "Autumn Leaves" is only the 16 bars of the refrain of the French original. Sixty per cent of the song has been jettisoned.

The English lyrics, by the fecund and occasionally inspired Johnny Mercer ("Moon River", "That Old Black Magic", "One for My Baby", "Blues in the Night"), captured only a tiny whiff of the original. What they have in common is the memory of a past love, evoked by the season.

The falling leaves drift by the window,
The autumn leaves of red and gold.
I see your lips, the summer kisses,
The sunburned hands I used to hold.
Since you went away the days grow long
And soon I'll hear Old Winter's song.
But I miss you most of all, my darling
When autumn leaves start to fall.

But where Prévert's words suggest a deep but doomed passion, the most consuming of the singer's life, Mercer's could be about a passing attachment, possibly unconsummated, over a summer holiday. We feel that the French performer – whoever it is – has lived a tormented emotional existence since the end of the affair; his or her American counterpart married a nice girl (or boy) and has two lovely children and a secure suburban life. When Yves Montand thinks of his loss, he is in anguish; when Nat King Cole does (*Greatest Love Songs*, Capitol 1982), he suffers a mild sentimental pang.

That is not to say that the American versions are always inferior. The lush cascading strings that preface Cole's entrance have an atmosphere of uneasy nostalgia that never fails to entice. His satin voice makes you believe in his regret; but it is a shallow regret none the less.

"Autumn Leaves" has been sung by scores of excellent artists, Streisand, Sarah Vaughan, Bing Crosby, Eartha Kitt and Billy Daniels among them. I have not heard all the recordings, but of those I know, there is a Frank Sinatra which must, I think, be the slowest of them all. There is not even time for the customary repeat of the refrain. Yet it is a brilliant performance, Sinatra in his best three-o'clock-in-the-morning-and-I'm-all-alone mood, extracting heartache from every clearly and lengthily enunciated syllable. (*Where Are You?*, Capitol 1957.)

The jazzmen, too, have taken to the song: Stan Getz, Erroll Garner, Bill Evans, Keith Jarrett (with a wonderful coda), Oscar Peterson and dozens more. Yehudi Menuhin has attempted it, in one of his sessions with Stephane Grappelli. Most have turned it into an upbeat number, far from the mood of the original.

It is Miles Davis who delivers the sorrow, especially in his 1958 recording with "Cannonball" Adderley (*Miles in Berlin*, CBS 1987). This is Miles searching into his heart, blowing with quiet desperation. Every note penetrates the hidden emotions we do not want to surface. The track may be entitled "Autumn Leaves", but Miles is playing and feeling "Les Feuilles Mortes". And that is how it should be; for Miles Davis first heard it in Paris, sung by the love of his life, Juliette Gréco.

"It's a song that resembles us/ You who loved me/ I who loved you," the refrain begins. It ends with inevitable parting. Prévert could have written it for them. But then it could have been about anyone. "Les Feuilles Mortes" is the truest anthem to loss and regret ever put to music.

80

SATISFACTION

BY JASPER REES

"(*I CAN'T* Get No) Satisfaction" was a first, and not just thanks to those brashly placed brackets. It begins more memorably than any pop song before or since. Just two notes of a guitar phrase that sounds like someone haring up a short step-ladder and tumbling down again, and you know what you're listening to – the definitive yell of youth, the original rock'n'roll sneer.

For the first time the electric guitar spoke not in the exhilarated language of pop, nor in the weeping tones of the blues, but with a darker purpose. The opening riff, the mother and father of all riffs (and nowadays the grandparent), howled of menace, threat, real rebellion. Here, at last, the Rolling Stones found a sound to match their fury. It was the first great burst of music, and perhaps still the greatest, to emanate from the songwriting pair known as Jagger-Richards.

★ ★ ★ ★ ★ ★ ★ ★ ★ ★ ★

Richards worried that "the song was basic as the hills, and the fuzz-guitar thing was a bit of a gimmick."

★ ★ ★ ★ ★ ★ ★ ★ ★ ★ ★

It's all ancient history now – the flouting of authority that caused such dyspeptic outrage – and nearly 30 years down the line, the ceasefire long in place, it can all look a bit twee. But the impact of "Satisfaction" is as fresh as the day it was recorded. Of the many artists who have invited the song to shine a little light on them, even Samantha Fox, idiotically singing "I can't get no girlie action", couldn't destroy it utterly.

The song's birth was preceded by a brief but troubled labour. On 6 May 1965, during their third American tour, the Stones were staying in a motel in Clearwater, Florida. The increasingly unstable Brian Jones had just administered a beating to his date and was paid back that morning by one of the band's entourage. "Brian was given two cracked ribs," recalls Bill Wyman in his autobiography, *Stone Alone*, "to the satisfaction of everyone." Trust Wyman to use that word so unknowingly.

The same day Keith Richards played a riff to Mick Jagger and said, "The words that go with this are 'I can't get no satisfaction'." He had put it on tape in the middle of the night. "I dreamt this riff," Richards recalled later. "That was the first time it had happened to me. I just woke up, picked up the guitar and – 'I can't get no – satisfaction'. On the tape you can hear me drop the pick [the plectrum] and the rest of the tape is me snoring." It would not be the last time Richards fell asleep in mid-performance.

Jagger sketched out some lyrics, but by the time the band reached the Chess studio in Chicago on 10 May – the place where Chuck Berry, Keith Richards' deepest influence, had recorded his hits – the song had grown on neither of its composers, who saw it as an album-filler. It must be stressed that the fame of the Stones at this stage had virtually nothing to do with songwriting. It was based on their looks, their attitude, and their interpretation of rhythm-and-blues classics penned by black Americans – Berry, Bobby Womack, Willie Dixon. "The Last Time" and Marianne Faithfull's "As Tears Go By" were the only hits on which they had a writing credit.

At the Chess session the song didn't take wing. The Stones flew to Los Angeles to continue work on their album *Out of Our Heads*. They booked into RCA's studio in Hollywood and, according to Wyman, "the song just gelled". The difference was down partly to Charlie Watts finding a tempo he was happy with, partly to Wyman delivering a quirky, jumping bass line, but mainly to the fuzzbox Richards used to give his playing that distinctive shimmering leer. Blending in Jagger's seductive, breathy vocal, which rapidly mutated into a declamatory howl, this was suddenly a song to get excited about.

Unless you were Mick Jagger or Keith Richards. The rest of the band, plus keyboard player Ian Stewart, manager Andrew Loog Oldham and engineer Dave Hassinger, thought it should be their next single. Jagger and Richards thought otherwise. It was put to the vote, the men who wrote the song lost and it was released in the US on 5 June, less than a month after Richards had nodded off in mid-composition. It went to No 1 and stayed there for four weeks, the Stones' first US chart-topper. In Britain, it was released on 20 August and spent three weeks at No 1.

"In later years," recalled the ever-neutral Wyman, "Mick always said that only Keith was doubtful about it." Sure enough, Jagger confided to the Stones' biographer Philip Norman that "doing 'Satisfaction' was the only real time we ever had a disagreement".

Richards worried that "the song was basic as the hills, and I thought the fuzz-guitar thing was a bit of a gimmick". He also fretted that his intro bore too close a resemblance to Martha and the Vandellas' "Dancing in the Street". In fact "Satisfaction" was the Stones' debut as a band with their own sound, rather than one pastiched from the swamps of Mississippi. It was, to all intents and purposes, the first rock song, as opposed to rock'n'roll.

It was also one of the first songs, if not the first, about the rock lifestyle. Though the title is Richards', the words are Jagger's. Richards later described it as "just a working title. It could just as well have been 'Auntie Millie's Caught Her Left Tit in the Mangle'." For Jagger, however, the phrase was fortuitous: it provided a launchpad for an inspired moan about the protected, pampered life on the road, about "drivin' round the world, and doin' this and signin' that, and tryin' to make some girl".

This was the first sophomore lyric, written not in pursuit of stardom but on the crest of it, on the road, in a faraway hotel room. The defining song of the 1960s did not celebrate the libertine age to come; it lamented the cynicism of the media, the coerciveness of advertising:

**When I'm watching my TV
And a man come on and tells me
How white my shirts should be.**

82

"That's what I say," sings Jagger, and to let you know that he means it he drops into the chorus almost as soon as the song starts. "I can't get no," he screams three times, and thanks to the brief repetition of the title that is more of a preamble than a first verse, you already know what it is he can't get. Then comes the verse proper, delivered, almost shouted, on all but one note:

When I'm driving in my car
And a man comes on the radio
He's telling me more and more
About some useless information
Supposed to drive my imagination
I can't get no . . .
No no no.

It is at this point that most people switch on to the song's lyrical content, to hear if not to listen, and that is why most assume that is exclusively about sex: they certainly thought so on *The Ed Sullivan Show*, bleeping out the line "trying to make some girl". The lyrical core tends to disappear in the frenzy of the atmosphere in which it is usually heard – parties, discos, Stones concerts. It is a song about personal experience that has been co-opted as an anthem for the herd mentality. Most herds tend to miss the nuances in the verses and pick up on the hook in the chorus. "Girlie action" is only a small part of the picture: Jagger doesn't get round to mentioning it until the last third of the song. A classic can rarely have been so misinterpreted.

There would never be another version like it. With a song so umbilically linked to the playing of the guitarist who came up with the tune, you half-expect there to be no versions at all, but all the baggage that "Satisfaction" carries with it has proved too great a temptation for soul deities and talentless starlets alike.

The carcass was still warm when the instrumentalists ripped into it. The cover most faithful to Richards' guitar came that same year, from the rock'n'roll drummer Sandy Nelson (*Drums A Go Go*, Liberty). A parping saxophone fills in for the lyrics, Nelson's bashing is mechanical and already the song has lost some of its sheen. In the same year a much better instrumental came from David Rose, the veteran composer of "The Stripper", and his orchestra. This was the other side of the sixties coin – sassy and hedonistic, with foxy, swinging strings that are lush but just a bit sinister. The Stones' first brush with a big band yielded a hugely sympathetic reinterpretation.

Richards' tune was still there but its perfect fit, Jagger's lyrics, had been lost. Oddly, things hardly changed when a major singer tackled "Satisfaction" the following year. For all their fame, Otis Redding had not heard of the Rolling Stones when Steve Cropper of Booker T and the MGs played him the song in 1966. He liked it and promptly recorded it in the Stax studios (*The Dock of the Bay*, Stax 1968). It was only appropriate that the next person to have a hit with the song should be not a pale English imitator but an artist

83

who sprang from the tradition that had first seduced the Stones into music.

Redding's version has overwhelming internal energy, with furious, belting horns and a speeding bass line. So overwhelming that two days after his death in December 1967 a journalist alleged it had been a Redding original all along, that the Stones had bought it from him in Memphis and that they owed him $50,000 in unpaid royalties. Not only did the Stones first visit Memphis six months after they recorded the song, but Cropper has said that he copied down what he thought were the lyrics from the record and gave them to Redding. So it might not just be the frenzied pace of the rendition that makes some of Redding's vocals difficult to unravel. This is the closest a Jagger lyric ever came to scat.

The Stones' concert albums being universally dismal, the version on *Otis Redding in Person at the Whisky A Go Go* (Stax 1968) is probably the best live recording of the song, unless you count Aretha Franklin's on *Aretha in Paris* (Atlantic 1968), another frenetic affair in which Franklin's backing singers have to hurry to keep up.

Franklin's studio version from 1967 (double A-side single with "Chain of Fools", Atlantic), which was the song's third incarnation as a hit single, is a typical Aretha cover. The queen of soul, who was also a daughter of gospel, flies around the melody as only she can, offering something that is at once wild and yet utterly under control, a meshing of vocal fervour and technical discipline – which is a fair definition of gospel. More than any other, this version shows you where the Stones got it all from, even more, perhaps, than Buddy Guy's live version at the Chicago Blues Festival (which the sleeve, intriguingly, dates 1964), a raunchy busk that slows the whole thing down (*Original Blues Brothers Live*, Vanguard 1983).

From here on, "Satisfaction" became less satisfying. Herbie Goins and the Nightimers (*No. 1 in Your Heart*, Parlophone 1967) and Mac & Katie Kissoon brought solid soul versions of the song to Britain. The Shadows had a go in 1970 (*Shades of Rock*, Columbia), adding a tricky organ intro before letting Hank Marvin loose, but it isn't a song for musical virtuosity, as the big-band Latin inflections and twirly flutes of José Feliciano's version from the same year (*Fireworks*, RCA) also suggested.

It required a rocker even older and more sexually threatening than the Rolling Stones to put the intimidating scowl back on the face of the song. In 1973 (*The Session*, Mercury) Jerry Lee Lewis slowed it down and swathed it in swirling blues tones – crashing cymbals, fingers slinging their way down the piano keys, nasty guitars – but whatever dash of humour belonged to the original was buried.

In 1975 the re-formed Troggs gave the song a psychedelic intro and mixed Reg Presley's wild Andover burr to the forefront (*Wild Things*, See For Miles). A much more innovative version gave Devo, Ohio's premier New Wavers, an early hit. They changed the title to "(I Can't Get Me No) Satisfaction" and delivered the song in their trademark dippy, robotic style (on *Q: Are We Not Men? A: We Are Devo*, Warner 1978). The riff, transferred to a synthesiser,

ABOVE: Ask people what they think of when they think of Simon and Garfunkel and they will say "Bridge over Troubled Water". It's a real party piece. Ironic, then, that Paul Simon wrote it as a "humble little gospel hymn".

LEFT: Smokey Robinson's "The Tracks of My Tears", which he recorded in 1965, is one of the most affecting of all pop records. His swooning falsetto is a sound overloaded with regret, hope and lamentation.

★ ★ ★ ★ ★ ★ ★ ★ ★ ★ ★ ★ ★

CENTRE: *In 1965, Paul McCartney played a little ballad he had written on the guitar to Billy J. Kramer, who didn't rate the song. Seven years later "Yesterday" had proved acceptable to 1,186 artists around the world.*

FAR LEFT: *"The Dark End of the Street" was sung originally by Memphis deep-soul man James Carr in 1966. At least part of the song's haunting power derives from the enigma of Carr himself, variously described as "a reserved, religious-type person" and "almost narcoleptic".*

ABOVE: *The original, Screamin' Jay Hawkins, recording of "I Put A Spell on You" was a masterpiece of tortuous simplicity. Nina Simone's version in 1965 was opulent and seductive, the kind of song – in her words – that "no one could ignore".*

BELOW: *"Ev'ry Time We Say Goodbye" was written by Cole Porter in 1944 for a Broadway revue. The show failed but the song lived on. In 1987 Mick Hucknell, with Simply Red, became the only man to make the song a hit.*

LEFT: *"Twist and Shout", the song that the Beatles chose to close most of their concerts, has remained a popular closing number, notably by Bruce Springsteen, Peter Gabriel and Sting on their Amnesty International tour of 1988.*

BELOW LEFT: *"Fever" was brought to a mainstream audience in 1958 by Peggy Lee, but it is its original adults-only content that has attracted dozens of cover versions, including one from Madonna.*

BELOW: *"Take Me to the River" was recorded in 1981 by a relatively unknown art-school quartet called "Talking Heads". It was their breakthrough record, and it is their version, rather than Al Green's original, that is the standard by which other versions will be judged.*

★ ★ ★ ★ ★ ★ ★ ★

RIGHT: There is a long history of American musicians finding jazz in unpromising sources. John Coltrane first recorded Rodgers and Hammerstein's "My Favourite Things" in 1960. He never tired of playing it, recording it at least a dozen times; it became almost his signature tune.

BELOW RIGHT: "September Song" was conjured up in 1938 especially for Walter Huston, the gruff-but-gentle star of Knickerbocker Holiday *– a Broadway show remembered only as the vehicle that carried a sly old man's musical lament for the passing of youth.*

BELOW: Written by Iggy Pop in the late 1960s, "No Fun" was to become the first and last breath of punk. In 1978, it was the last song of the Sex Pistols' final gig, at San Francisco's Winterland Ballroom. Three days later the band went their separate ways.

★ ★ ★ ★ ★ ★

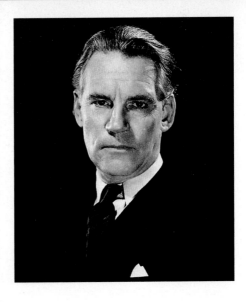

ABOVE: Aretha Franklin recorded her version of "You Send Me" in 1968, with a beautiful, solo piano intro, swooping voice and gospel chorus.

RIGHT: The late Kurt Cobain of Nirvana took the British pop charts by storm in 1991 with "Smells Like Teen Spirit" which appealed to indie fans and heavy-metal lovers alike.

★ ★ ★ ★ ★ ★ ★ ★ ★ ★ ★

ABOVE: *Stevie Wonder had just turned twenty when he wrote "You Are the Sunshine of My Life", a song now very much associated with late-night Radio 2 programmes.*

RIGHT: *"Autumn Leaves", written by Jacques Prévert in 1945, belongs primarily to the young Yves Montand. At that time known mainly as Edith Piaf's lover, he added it to his repertoire after starring in* Les Portes de la Nuit. *It eventually became his biggest hit. People said that he was singing to Piaf, who had left him.*

★ ★ ★ ★ ★ ★

LEFT: "Send in the Clowns" was recorded by Barbra Streisand in 1985. It brought out the best in her: no trace of histrionics, and with an orchestration closely resembling the original, which was composed by Stephen Sondheim for the musical A Little Night Music.

BELOW: Ewan MacColl, who wrote "The First Time Ever I Saw Your Face" in 1957, was a communist folk singer living in Beckenham, a working-class hero who didn't approve of pop music or showbusiness. The song earned him a Grammy, an Ivor Novello award and a lot of money.

only crops up just before the fade. In spirit, if not in sound, this is as close to the original version as anyone gets — frenetic, irreverent, novel, but rather wittier.

In the song's dotage, the wrong people have got hold of it. None was more wrong than Jonathan King, who had a hit with it in 1974 under the name Bubblerock. It was one of his more apposite pseudonyms (*King Size King*, PRT 1982). The instrumentation — acoustic guitar and strings — gives the song a country flavour, but King's laid-back vocal is indistinguishable from boredom. In Jagger's phrase, his best song was "on a loser's streak".

It is one of those songs minor artists sing to earn kudos by association. Samantha Fox's tediously sultry version (*Samantha Fox*, Jive 1987) fails to change the sex of the line "trying to make some girl", unlike Aretha or Tania Maria (*Bela Vista*, World Pacific 1990), who delivers a slow salsa in a sub-Nina Simone tenor. Tom Jones mines the past more thoughtfully, but this was his Art of Noise phase and his version is over-produced and colourless (*At this Moment*, Jive 1989). It's probably best to draw a veil over Vanilla Ice's reading (*Extremely Live*, SBK 1991), however much his view of the opposite sex may resemble Jagger's at the same age. "Oh yeah, remember this one?" he drawls. Not the way that he does.

All the best songs end up as advertising jingles, a fate which has not escaped the song that rubbished "all that useless information". That, and the sampled massacre perpetrated by Ice, brought the song full circle. An artist who is no more than a product of hype covered a tune about the cynicism of hype. You suspect the irony was lost on him, just as the real intentions of the lyrics are masked from most of the song's admirers, who are too busy losing themselves to listen in. In the end, the greatness of "(I Can't Get No) Satisfaction" is down to the genius of Keith Richards, visited in a dream by two phrases: a musical one to play on the guitar, and a vocal one, to sing along to it. The durability of the song proves that nothing else in it matters. Has rock ever been so simple?

85

★

THE FIRST TIME EVER I SAW YOUR FACE

BY JUSTINE PICARDIE

LIKE MANY people, I didn't hear "The First Time Ever I Saw Your Face" until 1972, 15 years after it was written, when Roberta Flack had a worldwide hit with her version of the song. I was 11, and I had never fallen in love with anyone – not even David Essex or Marc Bolan – but I thought it was a tremendous record. It had a sort of theatrical understatement – like a stage whisper – and the words seemed like pure poetry to me. There was a beginning ("The first time ever I saw your face/ I thought the sun rose in your eyes/ And the moon and stars were the gift you gave/ To the dark and empty skies, my love"); there was a middle ("The first time ever I kissed your mouth/ I felt the earth move in my hand/ Like the trembling heart of a captive bird/ That was there at my command, my love"); and a very exciting end ("The first time ever I lay with you/ And felt your heart beat over mine/ I thought our joy would fill the earth/ And last 'til the end of time, my love"). And that was it. Three verses, no chorus, but it told you everything you'd ever wanted to know about love and sex and yearning.

Yet were it not for Clint Eastwood, the song would never have been a hit. Roberta Flack, a former nightclub singer and classically trained pianist, had recorded it on an album (*First Take*) for Atlantic Records in 1969, but no one had taken much notice until 1972, when Clint included "The First Time Ever" in his soundtrack for *Play Misty for Me*. This is a very scary film about a maniacal woman who becomes obsessed with a disc jockey, played by our hero, Eastwood. Luckily, "The First Time Ever I Saw Your Face" is not used as a signature tune for the crazy lady, but as a pastoral soundtrack for the scene in which Clint frolics in the woods with his own true love.

Lots of people saw the film and liked the song, so Atlantic put it out again, and it became the best-selling single of the year. The man who wrote the song, Ewan MacColl, won a Grammy for it, and an Ivor Novello award, and made a lot of money. All of which was quite pleasing for him, of course, but also a bit embarrassing, because he was a communist folk singer living in Beckenham, a working-class hero who didn't approve of pop music or Hollywood or showbusiness.

MacColl had written "The First Time Ever I Saw Your Face" in 1957 for Peggy Seeger, an American folk singer who was to become his third wife. There are two versions of the story of its origins. MacColl, who died in 1989, used to say that he had sung it down the telephone to Peggy, who was on tour at the time in America. He had been forced to stay behind in England because the US authorities believed he was too dangerous a subversive to be given a visa, and he claimed to have composed it off the cuff when Peggy said she needed a two-and-a-half-minute song to fill a gap in her show.

I am inclined to believe Peggy Seeger's account, however, for MacColl was a wonderful storyteller who occasionally reinvented his own history. She had met MacColl in 1956; she was 20, he was 40 and married – for the second time – with a young son. They started an affair, and at the beginning of 1957 Seeger returned to her father's house in California. "Things were so confused between me and Ewan that I went home," she says. "He used to send me tapes with him talking on them, and one of them had him singing 'The First Time Ever' on it . . . The intensity of it quite frightened me."

She returned to London six months later. By 1959 Ewan had left his wife for Peggy, and she started including the song in their concerts together. But Ewan never sang it again. "Maybe he felt self-conscious," says Peggy. "He didn't like baring his emotions on stage. He felt they were nobody else's business, and of no interest to anyone else. But I think he liked to hear those sentiments in my mouth . . . When I first started singing it, I felt almost stripped naked on stage."

It took a few years before other people recorded the song. In 1965 the Kingston Trio did a sanitised version ("The first time ever I held you near . . ."), with jolly three-part harmonies, befitting their role as the acceptable face of the American folk revival. They wore matching stripey shirts and had short hair and

★ ★ ★ ★ ★ ★ ★ ★ ★ ★

Ewan MacColl was appalled. He had a special section in his record collection for these versions, entitled "The Chamber of Horrors".

★ ★ ★ ★ ★ ★ ★ ★ ★ ★

smiled a lot. They were followed by the Brothers Four, who were very like the Kingston Trio except that they had one more clean-cut white boy in the group, and replaced that tricky line in the third verse with "The first time ever I held you close".

Then there were the Smothers Brothers, Tom and Dick – "The Wonderful Brothers Smothers", according to their album notes. They included the song on their 1966 album *Play It Straight,* on which they avoided doing the comedy routines that had made them popular. The album cover shows them looking selfconscious in suits and black ties and polished shoes, as if they are on their way to a job interview. They are both studiously ignoring the white chicken pecking grain on the ground next to them. Dick sings the song, complete with a pseudo-harpsichord backing. It is awful, but at least he includes the line "The first time ever I lay with you", delivering it with a manful determination.

The song soon became a smooth standard for the more commercial end of the American folk market (although almost everyone who did it left out the traditional folk grace notes of the original). Harry Belafonte included it on a 1967 album, *Belafonte on Campus* (RCA), complete with a background chorus of male crooners. And Peter, Paul and Mary did it in a swirly, girly, breathy sort of way.

Apart from fans of Peggy Seeger's version, no one in England seemed to take very much notice of "The First Time Ever I Saw Your Face" during the sixties, although the Scottish folk musician Bert Jansch did a lively instrumental version in 1966, on an album called *Jack Orion* (Vanguard). In his autobiography, *Journeyman*, Ewan MacColl wrote that the sixties covers "made singularly little impression on me . . . I had lots of other things on my mind, not least of which was the need to make a living". He had four children to support by then, and the royalties from the song were "a pittance, not enough for luxuries like food".

By 1972, when Roberta Flack had her massive hit with his song, "I was in my mid-fifties and had lived hand to mouth for almost all of my life . . . I had survived without making compromises." Suddenly, everything changed. It wasn't that he had gone out on the cabaret circuit singing his song, but it seemed as if everyone else had. Val Doonican did it, Engelbert Humperdinck did, too; and so did the Geoff Love Singers and Mantovani and the London Symphony Orchestra. It was crooned in Las Vegas and Atlantic City and Scunthorpe and Wolverhampton. It was everywhere. Elvis did it. Elvis! He released it as a single in 1972, and on the cover he wore a white sequined jumpsuit with a big flappy collar (*Rare Elvis Vol 1*, RCA 1983). He doesn't sing the bit about sex; he just repeats "The first time ever I kissed your mouth", and ends with a big flourish of brass and swelling strings and drums.

In the same year, there were three albums on Columbia alone entitled *The First Time Ever (I Saw Your Face)*. It's unclear why the brackets crept in, or what they signify. Johnny Mathis made one of these albums, and Vikki Carr did another, and so did Peter Nero, with an instrumental piano version. Andy Williams introduced a slight variation by calling it "The First Time (Ever I Saw Your Face)" on his eponymous 1972 album for Columbia. Other than that, they're all the same. Big strings, big voices, big hair, big collars.

Ewan MacColl was appalled. He hated them all. He had a special section in his record collection for them, entitled "The Chamber of Horrors". He said that the Elvis version was like Romeo at the bottom of the Post Office Tower singing up to Juliet. And the other versions, he thought, were travesties: bludgeoning, histrionic, and completely lacking in grace.

He didn't like the Temptations' attempt, either (on a 1972 Tamla Motown album, *All Directions*); or Isaac Hayes's version in 1973 (*Live at the Sahara Tahoe*, Stax). They were too long, too overproduced, too melodramatic.

After the early seventies, things went a bit quiet, though the song remained a cabaret standard. Julian Lloyd Webber did a predictable neo-classical version (*Pieces*, Polydor 1985); the Irish folk singer Christy Moore covered it too (*Voyage*, WEA 1989). It turned up in an Oil of Ulay advertisement, and there was an ill-fated dance version in 1990 by Joanna Law (*Now Dance 902*, EMI).

But it is still a wonderful song. It has survived all the treacle applied to it, all the false sentiment. Peggy Seeger has not sung it since Ewan MacColl died. But I still hear it as his love song for her, a ballad written by a man who was happier singing about politics than his own passion, yet who quietly adored her for more than 30 years.

YOU ARE THE SUNSHINE OF MY LIFE

BY GILES SMITH

THERE'S a party piece that Stevie Wonder does, if egged on by the people around him. It's an impression of himself 20 years from now, in his early sixties, washed up in some Las Vegas casino, churning out the hits for the supper-club crowd. Just for a few seconds before he cracks up laughing, he becomes a caricature crooner, clicking his fingers, corny as hell. And what he sings is this: "Yooo-arrrr the sunshine of my life – yeah! That's why I'll alwaaaaays be arouuunnnnd." Wonder has a fat songbook to pick from, but this is the number he chooses to ruin for a laugh, ahead of the day when he may have to ruin it for a living.

If that time comes, he won't be the first to take "You are the Sunshine of My Life" and leave it a quivering wreck of misplaced accents and duff ad-libs. He'll just be going where light entertainment's elder statespeople have gone before. Frank Sinatra, Liza Minnelli, Perry Como – they've all been tempted to have a shot at this song. And every time, the gun jammed. Stevie Wonder makes it work: Johnny Mathis makes it hard work. What can you say about a number that even Ella Fitzgerald can't cover, without covering herself in embarrassment? What is it about this song, that only its writer can crack it?

So much has "You are the Sunshine of My Life" become the stuff of becalmed late-night Radio 2 programmes, it's easy to forget that it was written by a man who had just turned 20. The song first came out in November 1972, the opening track on the *Talking Book* album (Motown). Some say Wonder had composed it two years earlier for Gloria Barley, a back-up singer with whom he was in love, but that tact prevented him from putting it on his previous album, *Music of My Mind*: he was still married to Syreeta Wright. Come *Talking Book*, though, Wonder and Wright were divorced and Barley got to sing back-ups on the song she inspired.

It's a mid-tempo ballad, tuneful and direct – the kind of song singers would be eager to lift for their repertoires. Like the best Wonder numbers, it nails a sentiment that people might have trouble expressing for themselves, while using the words they would have chosen if they could. True, the lyrics are largely untroubled by technical matters, like rhyme; but maybe this just brings them closer to home. "You are the sunshine of my life/ That's why I'll always be around/ You are the apple of my eye/ Forever you'll stay in my heart."

But despite the best efforts of the Geoff Love Singers and Shirley Bassey, only Wonder has turned those words into a hit: it went to No 1 in America

89

and to No 7 in Britain, and it still follows him around. Keith Harris, his co-manager, says: "When Stevie walks into the piano bar in hotels, invariably it's the tune the piano-player strikes up."

In 1972, people were not necessarily expecting Stevie Wonder to come up with something cocktail pianists would lean towards. On his 21st birthday the previous year, Wonder's contract had been rewritten, making him one of the first Motown artists to call his own shots. The albums he would record in the next six years changed the shape of rhythm and blues and pioneered the use of synthesisers in pop. *Talking Book* also included the mighty "Superstition", the opening bars of which virtually defined the term "funky". Curiously, Vince Hill and Andy Williams passed that one by. But they pounced on "You are the Sunshine of My Life" – and failed miserably with it, like everyone else. Wonder created a paradoxical thing here: a standard that nobody else can do anything with – the model of the uncoverable song.

Almost without exception, covers of "You are the Sunshine" deploy full orchestras, as if there were something grand about it, when there are only four instruments on Wonder's version (drums, electric piano, congas and a bass guitar) and they all come in straight away. Doing most of the work is the electric piano, a Wurlitzer, made furry by mild distortion, and then made woozy by a chorusing device – an electronic effect that makes the sound appear to wash in and out.

★ ★ ★ ★ ★ ★ ★ ★ ★ ★

Sinatra's version is a sin. It don't mean a thing if you give it that swing.

★ ★ ★ ★ ★ ★ ★ ★ ★ ★

Any cover worth its salt will try to pay tribute to this noise – from a toytown chink for Johnny Mathis to a dirty rasp for Engelbert Humperdinck. But it only shows how that sound is poised on the boundary of good taste. Tamper with it, and you go directly to the land of the cheesey home-organ.

Wonder is also on the drums. He is by no means a conventional percussionist, though in the early seventies Eric Clapton described him as "the best drummer in the world", which may only be a slight exaggeration. There's something random about his playing which particularly pays off here. The bass drum is consistent, falling on one and four to create that racing heartbeat which drives a samba. But the clicks on the rim of the snare are scattered, because Wonder keeps leaping off to the cymbals to beat the rhythm out there. In place of a solid, direct beat, we get pattering congas, up high in the mix. Rather than taking a direct route, the song rolls and tumbles forward.

Contrast Frank Sinatra's version, arranged as a swing number by Don Costa on the 1974 album, *Some Nice Things I've Missed* (Reprise). This may be the worst sin Sinatra ever committed while a tape was rolling. As on Wonder's recording, the song shifts up a key into the final choruses – an old pop trick: the key-change as a new lease of life for the tune. But where Wonder sings an ad-lib melody across the divide to waft himself higher, Sinatra negotiates the key change with all the elegance of a train derailing. It was perhaps a bad move to hold the word "you" at this point – "How could so much love be inside of you?". It sounds as if someone has goosed him.

Elsewhere, Sinatra's showbiz emphases are not really his fault. "You are the sunshine of my life," he sings. "You are the apple of my eye." The words are made to float, but the arrangement's accents – the punches of the horns and drums – force him to bring them slap up against the beat, where they sound absurd. It don't mean a thing if you give it that swing.

A similar fault cracks Ella Fitzgerald's version of the song on the concert recording *With the Tommy Flanagan Trio* (Pablo 1977), which at least avoids the orchestra trap. And in the ad-libs at the end, Fitzgerald works in two lines from "You are My Sunshine" (written in 1942 by Jimmy Davis and Charles Mitchell) to remind us where Wonder picked up his motif. But for the rest of the time, she is constrained to make the lyric match a strict samba, where it can only seem impersonal, jerky and unaffecting.

On the other hand, the song won't withstand a relaxed approach either. Perry Como, who has built a career out of a singing style which doesn't seem to involve breathing, includes the song on his collection *Take it Easy* (RCA 1990). He is, the sleeve-note informs us, "the man who invented the word easy". But unfortunately for Perry, Stevie Wonder is the songwriter who invented the word troublesome. It takes more than a murmur to carry the line "I feel like this is the beginning". In concert, Wonder usually plays the song when the set is on the rise and runs it into "Superstition". It is easy listening – but not that easy. Get lazy with it, and it falls asleep.

Then again, there's no need to shake it to keep it awake. The problem with the Humperdinck rendition (on *Close to You – 20 Classic Songs of Love*, MFP 1991) is a problem which has dogged Engelbert throughout his career – the desire to make every song mimetic of the sexual act. The rhythm sets off conventionally, but at the verse, it drops into a kind of pelvic thrust. If a song could sue a singer for sexual harassment, this would be an open and shut case. Humperdinck's version is also a rich source of the amazing ad-libs which accompany every attempt at this number – the toe-curling wo-wo-wos, the wince-inducing yeah!s and baby!s. It reminds you how adept Wonder's singing is here. Of the five Grammy Awards he won in 1974, he gave four away and kept one – the trophy for Best Pop Vocal Performance on "You are the Sunshine of My Life". His is not the first voice you hear. The first chorus is performed as a male/female duet – Jim Gilstrap in the right speaker answered by Lani Groves in the left. Wonder doesn't come in until the first verse: "I feel like this is the beginning/ Though I've loved you for a million years." And from then on, he's busy punctuating the lines with pieces of inarticulate noise. But the point about Wonder's ad-libs is that they are not stuck on – they become part of the lyric. The "hmm-hmm, yeah-yeah" halfway through the chorus, second time through, is a response to the rhythm, an expression of delight in it which appears to occur to him as he sings. And what he does at the end of the word "rescue" defies transcription. It also defies imitation, as any one of the cover versions reveals. You can re-do the song's poppiness, its froth, you can render it as light entertainment, but in the end it comes down to soul and you can't fake that – unless you are Stevie Wonder, playing it for laughs.

91

DARK END OF THE STREET

By Barney Hoskyns

"*THIS IS* probably one of the greatest songs that's ever come out of black American music," announces Ricky Ross over the piano intro to Deacon Blue's live version of "The Dark End of the Street" (*Love and Regret*, EP, CBS 1991). "I first heard it done by Gram Parsons, and then by a guy called Ry Cooder . . ."

Strange, considering that neither Parsons nor Cooder could be described as black Americans. But that's really the point about "The Dark End of the Street", an archetypal "cheatin'" soul ballad which has been interpreted in almost every musical style from country to folk to blues and back to deep southern soul. There is something about the song that sets it apart from your run-of-the-mill cheatin' number, a quality of dread and foreboding allied to an urgent sense of time and place:

92

> At the dark end of the street,
> That's where we always meet,
> Hiding in shadows where we don't belong,
> Living in darkness to hide our wrong.
> You and me, at the dark end of the street,
> You and me . . .

From the ominous descending chords to its central image – bringing the transgression so close while obscuring it in the penumbra of shame – the song is as stark and joyless as cheatin gets. On the original version, recorded by Memphis deep-soul man James Carr in late 1966 (reissued on *At the Dark End of the Street*, Blue Side 1987), the chorus – "You and me, at the dark end of the street/ You and me" – is at once tender and terrified, with Carr supported by the hushed voice of the beloved. With each successive chorus, moreover, the two voices become ever more furtive, the final one reading

> Tonight we'll meet, at the dark end of the street
> *Mmmmmmm . . .*

Haunted by their guilt, these adulterers "know time's gonna take its toll/ We have to pay for the love we stole": in the bridge section, Carr simply wails "They're gonna find us!" three times over a blast of horns and a death-rattling electric guitar.

The song was written by Dan Penn and Lincoln "Chips" Moman, Southern whites with a deep love for black soul music who'd met during a Wilson

Pickett session in Muscle Shoals, Alabama. One of the biggest hits to come out of the Shoals had been Jimmy Hughes' "Steal Away" (1964), virtually a prototype for the whole cheatin' genre. "I'd been wantin' to write another 'Steal Away' for two years," says Penn, "and when I came to Memphis to work with Chips, I still wanted to write that great cheatin' song."

One night in the late summer of 1966, Penn and Moman were attending a country-music DJs' convention at the Anchor Motel in Nashville – "poppin' pills and playin' poker," as Quinton Claunch, James Carr's producer at Gold-wax Records, recalled. Claunch says that when the two men decided to take a break from the game in order to write a song, they asked if they could use his room. "I said: 'Boys, you can use it on one condition, which is that you give me the song for James Carr,' and they said I'd got me a deal."

Dan Penn isn't too clear as to the exact sequence of events that night, but he does recall trading an acoustic guitar back and forth with Moman. "We were only in there for about 30 minutes," he says. "I guess 'Dark End of the Street' was the culmination of two or three years of thinkin' about cheatin'."

He thinks he may have heard the phrase "the dark end of the street" from Moman's partner Don Crews, and that it had lodged in his mind. Certainly the greater part of the lyric was his.

Only a few weeks later, Chips Moman engineered James Carr's "Dark End of the Street" session in Memphis. His own studio was being refitted that week, so the session was moved to Willie Mitchell's Hi studio, where Al Green later cut his string of blockbusting hits. For

★ ☆ ★ ☆ ★ ☆ ★ ☆ ★

Through the doors come the three chords of "Dark End of the Street", and Jagger says "That's my favourite fucking song in the world!"

★ ☆ ★ ☆ ★ ☆ ★ ☆ ★

both Moman and Penn, Carr remains the greatest male singer of sixties soul, and working with him on the song still counts as one of the highlights of their careers. "He had an emotional power that really stirred me up," Moman says. "I could have sat and listened to him all day." There is no doubt that at least part of the haunting power of "The Dark End of the Street" derives from the tragic enigma of James Carr himself, a man recalled by Quinton Claunch as "a very reserved, religious-type person", but by others as "withdrawn" and "almost narcoleptic".

After Carr's "Dark End of the Street" made the R&B Top 10 in February 1967, several soul versions of the song followed in quick succession – none of them a patch on the original. Percy Sledge managed a respectable stab in April that year, but lacked the essential gravitas to pull it off (*Any Day Now*, Charly 1984). Chips Moman engineered a preposterously over-the-top rendition by Oscar Toney Jr, complete with sweeping strings and thunderous drums that all but buried the singer's harsh gospel tenor (*Papa Don's Preacher*, Charly 1988). The version by Roy Hamilton on Moman's own GP label was less bombastic, and certainly better than Joe Tex's lazy, ragged reading on his 1968 *Stone Soul Country* album (Charly).

The most significant cover by a male soul artist was Clarence Carter's 1969 reworking of the song, entitled "Making Love (At the Dark End of the Street)" (*Soul Deep*, Edsel 1984). Carter hardly bothered with Penn's lyric, using "Dark End" instead as an excuse to ham it up as a country preacher, proffering a leery sermonette about the birds'n'the bees over what could almost be the intro to the Wailers' live version of "No Woman, No Cry". According to Jim Dickinson (another legendary "redneck with a black soul"), Carter's "Dark End" was a favourite record of Mick Jagger's. "I was having dinner in Miami with Jerry Wexler, Tom Dowd, Mick and Bianca, and Clarence was playing at the hotel," Dickinson remembers. "Through the doors come the three chords of 'Dark End of the Street', and Jagger pulls everyone back and says, 'That's my favourite fucking song in the world!' Turned out he could recite the entire spoken intro."

Aretha Franklin's treatment of the song on her 1970 album *This Girl's in Love with You* (Atlantic) has become something of a litmus-test for aficionados of her genius. Is it "a brilliant, near-transcendent" reading, as the soul historian Peter Guralnick has claimed, or is it a typical example of her tendency to show off, riding roughshod over Penn's lyric? Whichever way you look at it, it's a long way from the sublime understatement of her "Do Right Woman – Do Right Man", the other classic song Penn and Moman wrote in 1966, and perilously close to what Franklin's own producer Jerry Wexler called "oversouling". (The other notable female version, on Dorothy Moore's 1976 album *Misty Blue*, on Malaco, takes the risk of funking the song up in a somewhat jarring arrangement by New Orleans maestro Wardell Quezergue.)

Written by white country boys for a black soul singer, "The Dark End of the Street" was soon being tackled as a straight country song. This should hardly have been surprising, given the prevalence of adultery in both soul and country music, but it took that cosmic drugstore cowboy Gram Parsons to attempt a version which was soulful *and* countrified. Actually, the version on *The Gilded Palace of Sin* (A&M 1969) by Parsons' Flying Burrito Brothers was all but ruined by Jon Corneal's neanderthal stomp of a drum track, but Parsons' wavering twang intuitively caught the sombre fatalism at the heart of the song.

By the seventies, even respectable country artists were covering the song. Accompanied by her original mentor Porter Wagoner, the 25-year-old Dolly Parton lent "Dark End" her spookiest Smoky Mountain tremor of a soprano: no dark dread here, but major Appalachian guilt, backed by softly strummed guitars, tinkling piano fills, and the wistful sigh of Pete Drake's pedal-steel (*Just the Two of Us*, RCA 1969). It took the Kendalls, a father-and-daughter duo no less, to push the country-duet treatment of the song to its logical guilt-ridden conclusion – not that there wasn't an implicit incest in all the other cheatin' songs they recorded (*Movin' Train*, Mercury 1983).

Compared with the Kendalls, Linda Ronstadt's crisp country-rock rendition on her 1974 album *Heart Like a Wheel* (Capitol) was as bland as her innumerable other covers. A Los Angeleno who got much closer to the brooding spirit of Dan Penn was Ry Cooder. On *Boomer's Story* (Reprise

94

1972), recorded at Muscle Shoals, Cooder managed to capture all the song's fear and loathing in a totally instrumental slide-guitar version. "Cooder was fascinated by Penn, though for understandable reasons Dan wasn't too happy with our version," says Jim Dickinson, who co-produced *Boomer's Story*. The lyrics were included, however, when Cooder revisited "Dark End" on the live album *Show Time* (Warner Bros 1977); indeed, they were all but torn apart over the course of six-and-a-half minutes by the wonderful vocal trio of Bobby King, Terry Evans and Eldridge King. (It was even longer, and just as good, when Bobby and Terry, accompanied again by Cooder, returned to the song on their 1988 album *Live and Let Live*, Special Delivery 1988.)

As it had affected Parsons and Cooder, so "Dark End" touched something in English musicians at the time when every pub-rocker in London wanted to be J.J. Cale. If Chris "Motorbikin'" Spedding's version on his 1972 solo album *The Only Lick I Know* was dire (See For Miles 1985), the song was more successfully rendered as a folk ballad during Richard and Linda Thompson's 1975 performance at London's Queen Elizabeth Hall, when Richard strummed his trusty Martin 00018 and Linda sounded for all the world like Natalie Merchant's big sister. It's strange to hear this classic song of infidelity sung by a married couple, but then the Thompsons' marriage was always rumoured to have been a stormy affair. A decade later, reformed pub-rocker Elvis Costello was performing angrily impassioned versions of the song which sounded like something off the live Albert Hall bootleg by Dylan and the Hawks. (Of course, there are problems of Anglo-American translation here. Just as romantic travel songs are hard to carry off in parochial, claustro-phobic Britain, so the dark end of the street, enunciated in a British accent, merely suggests some dingy suburban cul-de-sac.)

95

If it's downhome authenticity you want, look no further than three late-eighties versions by R&B veterans Lazy Lester, James "Thunderbird" Davis, and Artie "Blues Boy" White – all providing somewhat mumbled treatments, with indifferent lounge-band backing. James Davis hadn't recorded in 20 years when the New Orleans Black Top label tracked him down and matched him with their All-Stars band. His "Dark End", the closing track on *Check Out Time* (1989), bore the grainy, toothless influence of the late O.V. Wright, with whom Davis had toured in the seventies – heavy on gospel vibrato, strong on impending remorse.

The song's appeal for celtic soul merchants – from Deacon Blue to the Commitments, whose Andrew Strong turned it into a piece of Joe Cocker breastbeating (*The Commitments*, MCA 1991) – is obvious, since Catholics are suckers for black guilt. Less obvious is its appeal to Cincinnati's Afghan Whigs, who commenced their career on the Sub Pop label, original home of grunge. But then the Whigs, who were regularly playing "Dark End of the Street" in concert in 1993, have a penchant for "tearing the guts" out of soul classics like Al Green's "Beware" and Percy Sledge's "True Love Travels on a Gravel Road". "You can achieve so much more by not covering these songs in an obviously 'soulful' way," says big Whig Greg Dulli.

"I really don't know why so many people have done the song," says Dan Penn, who has finally got round to recording his own version of "The Dark End of the Street" for *Do Right Man* (Sire/Blue Horizon), which at the time of writing was eagerly awaited. "See, cheatin' was big-time back in the sixties, whereas now people know that cheatin' isn't necessarily too healthy. The song kinda glorifies cheatin', but there's some redemption goin' on in there too. I'm a James Carr fan myself. The other versions, I'm glad they cut 'em and God bless 'em for it, but compared to James Carr's, there are no other versions." Penn seems to approach his own version with trepidation: it's as if he's afraid of the song.

"It's a song that transcends all barriers," says Jim Dickinson, whose own highly entertaining version can be found on an album by his band Mudboy & the Neutrons (*Negro Streets at Dawn*, New Rose 1993). "It's been sung by men to women, women to men, men to men, and women to women. Dan says it's the ultimate cheatin' song, but I finally decided in my old age that it's about politics. It's about keepin' things secret – like, no matter what you get up to in the daylight, the real action takes place in the dark."

96

FEVER

By Richard Williams

ONE DAY Antigonus was told his son was ill, and went to see him. At the door, he met some young beauty. He went in, sat down by the bed and took his son's pulse.

"The fever," said Demetrius, "has just left me."

"Oh yes," the father replied. "I met it going out at the door."

Plutarch may have told a good story, but it took a poet to write "Fever": Otis Blackwell, one of the early poets of rock'n'roll. The author of "Return to Sender" and "Great Balls of Fire" knew how to pluck a metaphor from everyday life. And when he and his collaborator, Eddie Cooley, picked on the idea of using "Fever" to express sexual tension, they created a climate of eroticism more explicit than anyone had previously managed in a song that could also be played on the radio.

★ ★ ★ ★ ★ ★ ★ ★ ★ ★ ★

Alvin Robinson's version is the best Ray Charles record that Ray Charles never made

★ ★ ★ ★ ★ ★ ★ ★ ★ ★ ★

Most people associate the song with Peggy Lee, who brought it to a mainstream audience in 1958 and whose version provided the template for perhaps 95 per cent of the subsequent attempts. But she was not the first. The song had made its debut two years earlier, recorded by Little Willie John, a significant figure in the transition from rhythm-and-blues to soul music.

Bobby Schiffman, the manager of the Apollo Theatre in Harlem, called him "the best male singer I ever heard" – quite a compliment from a man whose theatre featured the likes of Sam Cooke, Clyde McPhatter and Jackie Wilson.

Today, however, Little Willie John is remembered only by aficionados. He was born William John Woods in Camden, Arkansas, in 1937, and moved to Detroit in childhood. Discovered by the bandleader Johnny Otis at a talent contest in 1951, he sang with Duke Ellington and Count Basie in his mid-teens. His first solo record was "Mommy What Happened to the Christmas Tree?", and he recorded for a variety of small labels before signing a contract in 1955 with Syd Nathan of King Records. His producer, Henry Glover, found the right formula straight away. The hits began with "All Around the World", and didn't stop for six years.

Apparently he didn't think much of "Fever" when it was presented to him; at least that's what he wrote to Syd Nathan from prison a decade later, when he was trying to remind the company boss of what might be owed to him. But when it came out, in the summer of 1956, 18-year-old Little Willie John was hot, and the song swept up the charts.

In its initial form (reissued on *Free at Last*, King 1976), "Fever" was an appealing record, but not an entirely exceptional one. A lightly swinging small-band arrangement featuring plaintive guitar, subdued saxophones, wire brushes slapping on a snare drum and a sympathetically ooh-aahing male chorus left plenty of room for the singer's amorous reverie: "You'll never know how much I love you/ Never know how much I care/ When you put your arms around me/ I get a feelin' that's so hard to bear/ You give me fever . . ."

In 1966, five years after his last hit, Little Willie John got caught up in a drunken scuffle in a Seattle bar. A man was stabbed to death with his knife, and he was convicted of manslaughter. On 27 May 1968, in the Washington State Penitentiary, he died of pneumonia, aged 30. James Brown was among those who carried his legacy into a new generation, often citing his influence. Another was his sister, Mabel John, whose records for the Stax label in the mid-Sixties included "Your Good Thing (Is About to End)", which ranks alongside Lorraine Ellison's "Stay with Me" and Aretha Franklin's "I Never Loved a Man" among the finest of all deep-soul ballads.

It was the finest of all white jazz singers who revived the fortunes of "Fever" and turned it into a standard. Norma Delores Egstrom had changed her name to Peggy Lee before she left Jamestown, North Dakota, for Hollywood at the age of 17 in 1937. A year later, she entered the big time with the orchestra of Benny Goodman, the King of Swing. By 1958, the year she recorded "Fever", she was one of America's top singers, acknowledged as one of Billie Holiday's most faithful and gifted disciples. What she added to Little Willie John's version were two new verses and a novel arrangement. "I remember the day I demonstrated it to Sammy Cahn," she later wrote in her autobiography, *Miss Peggy Lee*, "and told him I wanted to use just bass, drums and finger-snapping . . ." The string bass played two-to-the-bar, the fingers clicked on the backbeat, and the drums erupted in sudden and unpredictable punctuation. Peggy Lee sang quietly, almost in a whisper, suggesting much but holding it all back.

Her two new verses added another dimension – narratives involving two pairs of famous lovers. "Romeo loved Juliet/ Juliet she felt the same/ When he put his arms around her/ He said, Julie baby, you're my flame/ Thou givest fever/ When we kisseth . . ." Captain Smith and Pocahontas were the other celebrated sufferers from the maladie d'amour whom she took into the Top 10 (and on to many compilations, including *All Time Greatest Hits*, Curb 1990).

But the best version of "Fever" was yet to come. And, like so many other minor classics of the sixties, it was hidden away on a B-side. Alvin Robinson was an unknown New Orleans singer and guitarist when he recorded a Leiber and Stoller song called "Down Home Girl" for the Red Bird label in 1964, under the supervision of Joe Jones, another New Orleans native who had done well with his own recording of "You Talk Too Much" and with the Dixie Cups' "Chapel of Love". "Down Home Girl" earned a measure of celebrity when the Rolling Stones covered it on their second album (the one with the David Bailey sleeve), but "Fever" is the side that stands up today. This was the best Ray Charles record that Ray Charles never made, Robinson's aching voice and a much slower tempo giving it a richer, sweatier, funkier ambience. In Wardell Quezergue's arrangement, a chorus of barping saxophones, stabbing trumpets and a slow-rocking double bass painted a picture of a hot night under a mosquito net in a small cabin deep in a Southern swamp; ringing single notes from a vibraharp were like an ice cube on overheated skin. The underrated Robinson, who later played on Dr John's wonderful *Gumbo* album, died back home in New Orleans in 1989, aged 51.

By contrast, the next significant version of "Fever" removed it from the world of grown-up sex to that of teenage crushes. The McCoys were a four-piece group from Union City, Indiana, typical of young white Americans affected by the Beatles and the Stones. In 1965 their record of "Hang on Sloopy", a cover version of a far superior rhythm-and-blues original by the Vibrations, shot to No 1. For the follow-up (Immediate 1965), they chose "Fever", fitting it to the simplified harmonic movement and crashing dance beat of "Sloopy". Sadly, the McCoys turned out to be one-hit wonders. A year after "Fever" failed to repeat the success of its predecessor, they had gone psychedelic.

But it is the original adults-only content of "Fever" that has attracted dozens of cover versions by singers and groups from Elvis Presley to Freddie Starr, from Helen Shapiro to Chaka Khan, from Madonna to the Cramps. The song mapped an emotional territory whose frontiers were later explored on the one extreme by Doris Day with the pyjama-party promises of "Move Over Darling" and on the other by Etta James's sulphurous "Let's Burn Down the Cornfield". Bruce Springsteen, indeed, took the song and turned it into a complete sub-genre of his own work, creating three fine variations: "Fire" for the Pointer Sisters, "The Fever" for Southside Johnny and "I'm on Fire" for himself. No cure for Demetrius's complaint, it seems, has yet been found.

99

BLOWIN' IN THE WIND

By Jasper Rees

BOB DYLAN was not the first singer to perform "Blowin' in the Wind"; nor has he ever had a hit with it. For a while there was doubt that he was even its author. The first of many cranks to dog Dylan's steps was a New Jersey economics teacher, who claimed that a pupil of his called Lorre Wyatt had penned the song at the age of 15, and that Dylan had bought it with a $1,000 donation to charity. Wyatt soon admitted that Dylan's song resembled his own "Freedom is Blowing in the Wind" in name only, then waited until 1974 before confessing that no such song ever existed.

★ ★ ★ ★ ★ ★ ★ ★ ★ ★

"Jesus, Bobby," Dave van Ronk told him, "what an incredibly dumb song! I mean, what the hell is blowing in the wind?"

★ ★ ★ ★ ★ ★ ★ ★ ★ ★

No one denied the simple folk melody owed something to a spiritual entitled "No More Auction Block for Me", but the words were Dylan's own, jotted down on 16 April 1962 in a Greenwich Village coffee house, the Commons. He was 20, and still unknown outside the Village; his debut album had been released a month earlier. He tried the song out on fellow folkie Gil Turner, who was so blown over he included it in his set that night at Gerde's Folk City. With a lyric sheet on his mike stand, Turner became the first in a long line to pose that lilting litany of metaphorical questions starting with

How many roads must a man walk down
Before you call him a man?

Riotous applause told Dylan, if he didn't know it already, that "Blowin' in the Wind" was his first classic. The next day Dave van Ronk, who had been working the Village scene far longer, begged to differ. "Jesus, Bobby," he later recalled telling him, "what an incredibly dumb song! I mean, what the hell is blowing in the wind?" A few weeks later he had the answer. "I was walking through Washington Square Park and heard a kid singing, 'How much wood could a woodchuck chuck if a woodchuck could chuck wood/ The answer my friend is blowin' in the wind'. At that point I knew Bobby had a smash on his hands."

Bob Spitz, one of Dylan's biographers, claims that "Blowin' in the Wind" may be the only song from the 1960s that will be remembered a hundred years from now. If so, it will be because it was built to outlast its context. As the civil rights movement gathered pace, some sniped that this so-called protest song was too like the breeze of which it sings, an insubstantial offering which held back from actually saying anything. But this missed the point.

"Blowin' in the Wind" was Dylan's shot across the bows. Its very lack of polemic, its mere hint of ire, is what made it so popular – that, and a sweet tooth of a tune. It led a double life as an angry anthem and a pretty pop bauble. Anyone could render it – folk singers, country acts, gospel groups, cabaret chanteuses, beat combos, guitar heroes, orchestras, even the New Seekers – and practically everyone did.

Like many folk ditties that call for just a voice, a guitar and a passing acquaintance with three major chords, it could have been written yesterday, or some time in the first century. The lines "How many times must cannon-balls fly/ Before they're forever banned?" may have voiced a modern concern at the nuclear threat, but you'd never guess from Dylan's antiquated imagery that hi-tech weapons had even been invented, let alone recently deployed on the island of Cuba.

"Cannonballs" is one of the song's tiny handful of polysyllables. Few songs that pack such a literary punch use so many short words. The three verses and their echoing refrain are a model of brevity. Couplets like "How many deaths will it take till he knows/ That too many people have died?" trip along with a fleet-footed simplicity that has a mesmerising power.

In May 1962, the lyrics were published in *Broadside* magazine. Dylan himself recorded the song on 9 July. Dry, deadpan, almost downhearted, his version would not just overshadow most others but leave them looking like a misreading. The treatment, like the song, was a case of less being more: just him, his acoustic guitar and his harmonica. It's verse, refrain, solo, verse, refrain, solo, verse, refrain, solo; no bridge, no middle eight, no climax. The solos are more like fills – brief, almost brusque. The vocal is done with the minimum of fuss, and no variation in dynamics: Dylan sings the nine questions as if they'd just occurred to him, with a casual "Yes and" before the second and third one in each verse. He sounds not remotely uplifted. Amazing, when you listen to just about everybody following behind.

Even before Dylan gave his own version to posterity, the song had become a Village anthem: someone somewhere was performing it every night, and its popularity so dispirited Dylan that he considered leaving it off his second album, *The Freewheelin' Bob Dylan* (CBS 1963). He relented, but only on the insistence of his veteran producer John Hammond who, after Dylan's critically reviled debut LP, needed something to justify his faith.

By this time the song was already famous, thanks to Albert Grossman, Dylan's manager, who farmed it out to another of his clients, Peter, Paul and Mary. The smiley trio, fresh from a hit with "Puff the Magic Dragon", took a honeyed version of the song into the upper echelons of the chart, adding harmonies, bolstering the instrumentation and passing the lead vocal around the group (*In the Wind*, Warner Bros 1963). It may have taken away a harsh edge but it persuaded a million people to buy the single. As Grossman calculated, the song opened doors for Dylan – the doors that led from the small, sophisticated subculture of Greenwich Village to the wide open spaces of middle America, where Dylan had come from.

By the end of 1964 the song had been recorded by a good 60 acts, from Joan Baez to Sam Cooke, Bobby Darin to Marlene Dietrich. It was open season on "Blowin' in the Wind".

Cooke's recording was a live one, made in 1964, the year he died (*The Songs of Bob Dylan*, RCA). He did it as a chain-gang spiritual, with a chugging guitar, cheery horn section, chiming cymbals, and a beautiful, easy swing that paved the way for the song's rebirth as a feel-good R&B love tune. That's how it was done by the young Stevie Wonder (*For Once in My Life*, Motown) who in 1968 became the only act other than Peter, Paul and Mary to have a hit with it, and in 1992 sang it at the 30th-anniversary Dylan tribute concert at Madison Square Garden.

The exception to the rule that the lusher the instrumentation, the softer the punch, is Marlene Dietrich (*Best of Marlene Dietrich*). This was probably because she first recorded the song in German. As with "Where Have All the Flowers Gone?", her first success with a protest song, Dietrich soon cut the song in English, but "Die Antwort Weiss Ganz Allein Der Wind" is the stronger version. Her deep, haunted voice, backed by Burt Bacharach's jaunty orchestration captured the song's weary resignation in a way that Bacharach's other muse, Dionne Warwick, was unable to match.

Marianne Faithfull recorded it in only her second stint in a studio, as a follow-up to "As Tears Go By" (*Come My Way*, Decca 1965). Hers is the only version with a fade-out, which doesn't come soon enough. It would be good to hear her do it now that her voice has, as it were, broken. She might wrench something apocalyptic out of the song as no one has yet managed, not even a direly howling six-minute version by Neil Young, captured for evermore on the festival-of-feedback live album, *Weld* (Reprise 1991).

The Hollies gave it the "He Ain't Heavy" treatment, big, booming and hollow (*The Hollies Sing Dylan*, Parlophone 1969). The Brothers Four, and many others, turned it into a country thigh-slapper (*This Land is Your Land*, MFP 1981). Diana Ross and the Supremes recorded it in 1969, close to the end of their tether (*Let the Sunshine In*, Motown), and reduced it to just another product on the Motown conveyor belt – a tinny, percussive version which did no justice to the lyrics. The Ray Conniff Singers (*Always in My Heart*, CBS 1988) turned it into lift muzak. But no one plumbed the depths quite like the New Seekers (*Best of the New Seekers* Vol 2, Polydor 1982). Their version, elaborating on the more restrained example of the Seekers, is a happy-clappy sing-along with a ghastly lead guitar break.

For a song whose bite is in its lyrics, there is a surprising array of instrumental versions. Duke Ellington, Duane Eddy and Chet Atkins all came up with accounts of the melody that sound just as you'd expect them to. The London Philharmonic Orchestra, meanwhile, passed the parcel between the prettier instruments before letting a funereal choir in on the act (*Opus One*, Philips 1980). How many times must a song be sung, before its spell starts to wane?

ONLY LOVE CAN BREAK YOUR HEART

BY BEN THOMPSON

NEIL YOUNG'S *After the Goldrush* is one of those records that have no right to be any good. Why else should it be so easy to find in second-hand shops? The cover's not too promising either; an unprepossessing monochrome with a hint of hippie remnant about it. But once the music has become familiar it's hard to imagine what, apart from the call of the bailiffs, could make anyone want to part with it.

Some of Young's most famous songs are on this 1970 album (Reprise). There's the title number, a justly notorious piece of dope-addled whimsy, and also the spikily regionalist "Southern Man', which riled the hell out of Lynyrd Skynyrd. But the one it's hardest to get out of your head is sandwiched between these.

"Only Love Can Break Your Heart" is an absurdly simple little tune. It's in waltz time, and the structure and instrumentation are sparse to the point of minimalism. Piano, guitar, bass and drums strike up gently and plod along together, happily oblivious to the fact that there don't seem to be any off-beats.

"When you were young and on your own," Young inquires, "how did it feel to be alone?" That trademark quaver has an even more distinctive wobble in it than usual. He answers his own question, gently pulling the words out: "I was always thinking of games that I was playing, trying to make the best of my time."

The chorus follows, sung to the same tune as the first bit of the verse but with subtly different emphasis. "Only love can break your heart, try to be sure right from the start. Yes only love can break your heart, but if your world should fall apart . . ." And then, well, basically, that's it. The second verse follows the same pattern. The words shade in some of the echoing space between those three dots, but not much. "I have a friend I've never seen, he hides his head inside a dream." The heart of the matter seems to be that Young has a mate who needs cheering up: "Someone should call him and see if he can come out — try to lose the down that he's found". There's another chorus, and then the first two lines of the second verse are repeated, melting into "Only love can break your heart", which repeats to fade.

On the page, this doesn't seem like earth-shattering stuff. It verges on the banal even, but there's a warmth in Young's voice that lasts long after the tune is over. It's a brief, wistful song — like Elvis's lovely "Wooden Heart" without

103

the clogs – but there's real strength in it. The effect of "Only Love Can Break Your Heart" is affirmative, not maudlin; as if anything that can make you so miserable must also have a powerful upside. The beauty of the song is such that even the possibility that the backing vocalist is Nils Lofgren cannot diminish its power.

Asked about it now, more than 20 years later, Neil Young is as endearingly grizzly as his legend decrees. "I usually try not to get too into what my songs are about," he informs the crestfalling interviewer. "They're like thoughts; if you analyse them, they lose their value." Please say something about it – anything. "Well, it was written for somebody – I think it was Graham Nash" – the Blackpool-born ex-Hollie who became one of his partners in the ever-divergent close-harmony quartet Crosby Stills Nash & Young, at whose periodic reunions throughout the seventies and eighties the song would sometimes be performed – "he'd just broken up with Joni Mitchell". The author won't be drawn any further on the subject of this song, except to say that "it endures", and that he still plays it occasionally – at the memorial concert for the legendary promoter Bill Graham, at the periodic benefit shows he does for the special school run by his wife Pegi.

★ ★ ★ ★ ★ ★ ★ ★ ★ ★

"I usually try not to get too into what my songs are about," Young informs the crestfalling interviewer.

★ ★ ★ ★ ★ ★ ★ ★ ★ ★

Since leaving his care, the song has had a strange life which fits in with the unique balance of continuity and switch-back that has been Young's artistic life. When it came out as a single in America, "Only Love Can Break Your Heart" was a hit, something Young has had amazingly few of. Its impact was sufficient to inspire a quick cover. Jackie DeShannon, the country-rock stalwart and pioneering female singer-songwriter responsible for "Needles and Pins" and, later, "Bette Davis Eyes", slipped a version of it on to her 1972 album *Jackie*. It's nicely sung, in a Karen-Carpenter-meets-Lisa-Stansfield kind of way, but the simplicity of the song seems to have been an invitation to tinker. You get a bizarre switch in time signature halfway through, from waltz-time to a less lilting 4/4, and a gratuitous pop-gospel climax. Arif Mardin's accordion is nice, though.

The rest, it seemed, was silence. If ever there was an example of a great song going into hibernation, this was it. Young's career went every which way – drunken wakes, raging polemics, heroic reaffirmations, bizarre genre-hops – and "Only Love Can Break Your Heart" stayed where it was. Until 1984, that is. In this year of ill-omen, with Young about to enter his least appealing phase, as a Reagan apologist, his erstwhile guitar foil Stephen Stills (the man who put the S in CSNY) decided to teach the world how not to do a cover version.

His "Only Love Can Break Your Heart" appears on the misleadingly titled album *Right by You*. It's clear from the credits that all is not well: the first thanks go to Stills' powerboat-racing team. A nightmarish fairground organ leads the speed-loving guitar-slinger and his backing vocalists, including, poignantly, Graham Nash, through a cod-reggae interpretation so horrible it's a wonder the song survived.

From here, the only way was up. In the late eighties, Young's prolonged period of battery-recharging finally started to pay off – with the inspiringly noisy "Eldorado EP", a prophetic requiem for a doomed soap opera, and then the album *Freedom*, which saw him firmly back on the crest of the Zeitgeist. And his influence on the generations that had followed him was at last starting to be acknowledged. An album of his songs done by other people, *The Bridge* (1989), was recorded before that phenomenon had switched from novelty to curse.

This was not the "embalming" experience Young had nervously expected. It contained, he was later driven to admit, "some pretty wild stuff". Among the wildest was "Only Love Can Break Your Heart", as seen through the crusted eyes of Genesis P. Orridge. This veteran shaman and folk-devil, now relocated to California to escape the tabloid press, slowed the song down still further and drenched it in violins. His voice too is saturated; languid and woozy, and by the time he and his band Psychic TV had finished tinkering with it, the song was up and running again.

Less than a year later, it got an audacious re-spray, in a dazzling high-art dance treatment by Croydon debutants Saint Etienne (Heavenly, single). What made these self-conscious students of Brit-pop cool pick the work of an ageing Canadian longhair for their first essay in recorded sound? "We'd always wanted to do a song by Neil Young," says chief theoretician Bob Stanley, "because he never takes any notice of what anyone else thinks. At first we were going to do 'Ambulance Blues', but it would have taken too much effort." There was nothing lackadaisical about their approach to the song. They took the whole thing out of waltz time, changed the chords slightly to make them more melancholic, and added a big shuffling mystery drum sample, a clanking keyboard off-beat, a resonantly thin female vocal and something that certainly sounds like Augustus Pablo's melodica, even if it isn't. "What I liked about the original," Stanley says, "was that it's very cyclical, repetitive – almost mantra-like." These were the qualities Saint Etienne emphasised, but the spirit of the original was still in place, and if anything almost intensified – even if the words did seem to have been changed from "down that he's found" to "gown that he's found".

"Only Love Can Break Your Heart" has certainly haunted Saint Etienne – they've never been able to write anything as timeless themselves. But what did the author think of the audacious rejig? "I thought it was interesting," he says warmly. "It had a good beat."

105

SEPTEMBER SONG

BY ROBIN STUMMER

OCTOBER 1938. Hitler's sixth year of power. That autumn the drift to war was beginning to seem as inevitable as the change of seasons. A bleak note had begun to sound on Broadway. The previous 18 months had produced a clutch of songs that spoke of love lost, imperfect or against the odds. Irving Berlin's "Let's Face the Music and Dance" augured

> There may be trouble ahead
> But while there's moonlight and music and love and romance
> Let's face the music and dance.

Rodgers and Hart had produced the bittersweet "My Funny Valentine", and in Dubin and Warren's "September in the Rain"

> My dreams lie buried in autumn leaves
> They're covered with autumn rain.

106

The songs were sophisticated creations, products of a craft that was nearing its apogee, yet the most poignant of these "problem" ballads wasn't born, as the others had been, of a long, considered collaboration. "September Song" was the surprise child of a show that was itself something of a freak. Its parentage was odd too.

Though Broadway lost no time in hailing the number as one of its finest achievements, "September Song" sounds as European as rain and romance, a melancholy tour from present to past and back. Like most great numbers, it wields a power beyond words and music, yet its heart remains obscure. Should we laugh or cry at life? Or both? And where does it belong? The lilting, semi-spoken introduction, a major-key "confessional" of sexual conquests, and the hypnotic major/minor phrasing of the main theme place it not on Broadway, but among the small, intimate theatres of thirties *Mitteleuropa*. And in the hands of their greatest songwriter.

One of the new faces on the New York musical scene in 1938 was Kurt Weill, a 38-year-old composer who had arrived, after brief stays in Paris and London, in September 1935. His Berlin collaborations with Bertolt Brecht, most famously *The Threepenny Opera*, had carried his name across the Atlantic. The popularity of their work had been phenomenal, and *Threepenny Opera*'s lurid opening number "Mack the Knife" became the 20th century's blackest hit.

But Broadway wasn't Berlin. In the two years since he arrived in

America Weill had enjoyed only modest success. What he needed was an American Brecht, someone who could tap in to popular consciousness yet provide a libretto taut enough to carry an elaborate musical theme. In Maxwell Anderson, an acclaimed left-leaning playwright, Weill found something close.

For some time Anderson had been toying with the idea of a historical drama based on the early history of New York, originally the Dutch colony of New Amsterdam. The starting point was to be Washington Irving's *Father Knickerbocker's History of New York,* but the theme would be the dangers of dictatorship. The kind of tyranny the liberal playwright had in mind was not the European variety, but that of President Roosevelt, at that time wielding immense powers under the New Deal. Accordingly, Anderson chose as his bullying leader Pieter Stuyvesant, New Amsterdam's peg-legged, pig-headed governor.

In April 1938 Weill and his wife, the singer Lotte Lenya, spent a weekend at Anderson's country home. When they left, *Knickerbocker Holiday* had been conceived. Anderson had never worked on a musical before, nor had Weill worked the American way, where music is written before, not after, the lyrics. Accordingly, Joshua Logan, a young director who had been working with Rodgers and Hart, was brought in to guide the show to the stage.

Work on *Knickerbocker Holiday* progressed through that spring and summer. The score included some fine Broadway-type songs but Logan soon realised that the show was seriously flawed. It was too heavy, the Stuyvesant character was underwritten and why, anyway, did a heartless tyrant feature in what was supposed to be a "musical comedy"? Logan's solution was to bring in a star. For the Stuyvesant role he wanted Walter Huston, the gruff-but-gentle 54-year-old vaudevillian who had made a name in Hollywood (and would later make another as the first of a cinema dynasty). Logan visited Huston in California. He accepted the part, but on his own terms: "Couldn't this old bastard make love to that pretty young girl a bit? . . . she could even consider him for a fraction of second when she hears his song."

★ ★ ★ ★ ★ ★ ★ ★ ★ ★

Huston accepted the part, but on his own terms: "Couldn't this old bastard make love to that pretty young girl?"

★ ★ ★ ★ ★ ★ ★ ★ ★ ★

"Song?" Logan replied, wondering if he'd heard correctly.

"Sure. Something nice I could sing to her . . . a moment for the old son of a bitch to be charming."

Logan couldn't afford to refuse.

Back on the East Coast, Weill and Anderson conjured up the number their show's dictator wanted in a couple of hours. Neither had any idea what Huston's vocal talents were, if any. Still less did they know if he could keep time, or remember lyrics. They played safe, keeping the words simple and cyclical and the vocal line tied firmly to the accompaniment. The next day they rang Huston and played him "September Song" for the first time.

> When I was a young man chasing the girls,
> I played me a waiting game,
> If a maid refused me with tossing curls,
> I'd let the old earth take a couple of whirls,
> While I plied her with tears in place of pearls,
> And as time came around she came my way,
> As time came around she came . . .

Huston was overjoyed. He sang it back to them over the tinny, long-distance line the only way he knew how – bumptious and semi-spoken, like a grandfather doing a turn at a family reunion.

> But it's a long long while,
> From May to December,
> And the days grow short,
> When you reach September . . .

After another run-through, he had mastered it.

> The autumn weather
> Turns the leaves to flame,
> And I haven't got time
> For the waiting game.

108

Knickerbocker Holiday opened on 19 October 1938 and closed the following April, destined to be remembered only as the vehicle that carried a sly old man's musical lament for the passing of youth. A decade later Weill and Anderson would collaborate on *Lost in the Stars*, this time to great acclaim, but by then their hurried offering to Huston would have taken on a life of its own.

Bing Crosby recorded the song twice. Its gentle lilt and soporific phrasing suited his croon perfectly. His December 1943 recording, one of his earliest hits, is the first to omit the introduction and treat it as a straightforward wooing number. It's no longer about ageing, it's about seducing. Bing returned to "September Song" on his last recording, the *Seasons* album (Polydor), a month before he died in 1977. It's an ageing song once more, a ponderous, lush, heavily reverbed farewell.

Ella Fitzgerald and Sarah Vaughan seized on its torch-song qualities. Pared down to a languid Paul Smith piano accompaniment and stripped of its second refrain, Fitzgerald's 1960 version is one of her most sensuous moments (*Let No Man Write My Epitaph*, HMV). She stretches "The days dwindle down/ To a precious few,/ September, November" to a pained eternity, and ends "these precious days" with the solemnity of a hymn. Vaughan's version has become a jazz classic (*Sarah Vaughan*, EmArcy 1955). After a laid-back Herbie Mann flute intro, she falls into a sultry, Billie Holidayesque "But it's a long, long while," sandwiching an intricate double-time middle section featuring Clifford Brown's trumpet as well as Mann's flute before adding her own "not January, February, June or July" coda.

In the midst of a flurry of fifties jazz versions, Lotte Lenya made her only recording of her husband's song. Her "September Song" (*American Theater Songs*, CBS 1957) is over-orchestrated, and her craggy, flat voice, perfect in the spartan recordings she had made of Brecht/Weill compositions, wanders off at a tangent to the strings and harps. Hers is not the only version of the day that is too soft, but Sinatra (*Point of No Return*, Capitol 1962), Nat King Cole (*Nat King Cole Sings/George Shearing Plays*, Capitol 1962) and Eartha Kitt (*The Romantic Eartha*, HMV 1962) manage to climb out of their eiderdown accompaniments to offer languid interpretations that make the most of the ennui, even if they miss out the sex. The three backing tracks are virtually indistinguishable.

Dion and the Belmonts (*Wish upon a Star*, Laurie 1960) gave the song a preppy facelift and the Impressions (*The Never Ending Impressions*, ABC 1964) made it a joke, with a Curtis Mayfield "higher and higher" falsetto ending. Lou Reed, invited by Hal Willner to join in the Weill tribute album *Lost in the Stars* (A&M 1985), chose "September Song", and mined the menace in the lyric. His treatment pushes it off the stage and on to the street. Reed snarls and sneers through his four minutes, soiling the song in a splendid high-*Transformer* drawl (". . . and those days/ I'd like to spend 'em/ wichoo"). You feel cornered, not charmed. A year earlier, Ian McCulloch took time out from Echo and the Bunnymen to offer a dark, accordion-and-piano single (Korova, worth a fortune if you can find it) with a leering string section, arranged by David Bedford, that took Huston's song into the realm of "I am the Walrus".

The nineties have seen "September Song" once more as nostalgia. Jeff Lynne gave it the good-time treatment on his 1990 album *Armchair Theatre* (Reprise), lubricated with a George Harrison slide-guitar line, and most recently it appeared, inevitably, as the theme to the BBC sitcom *May to December*. (Though, less inevitably, it was not the theme to the BBC sitcom *September Song*, starring Russ Abbot.)

As with most great numbers, the heart of the song remains elusive. In 1928 "Mack the Knife" had been a last-minute addition to *The Threepenny Opera*. Before he died in 1950, Weill had the peculiar pleasure of knowing that his other great popular hit, the song that would make his name live, was also one that had come out of nowhere.

With acknowledgments to 'The Days Grow Short: The Life and Music of Kurt Weill' by Ronald Sanders (Holt, Rinehart, and Winston, New York, 1980; reissued Silman-James Press, 1991).

EV'RY TIME WE SAY GOODBYE

BY GILES SMITH

COLE PORTER, ingenious and effusive as a lyricist, was often restrained almost to the point of austerity as a composer. His attitude frequently seems to have been: why use two notes where one will do? Think of "Night and Day", with its introductory verse entirely on a single note and the little strings of repeated notes the melody keeps returning to. Or think of "Miss Otis Regrets" and the long run on the same note in its opening line ("Miss Otis regrets she's unable to lunch today").

Or think of "Ev'ry Time We Say Goodbye". The song opens: "Ev'ry time we say goodbye, I die a little," and, amazingly, the first eight notes you hear are the same. The next line begins a few tones higher up, but again a note is held, on this occasion repeating seven times: "Ev'ry time we say goodbye, I wonder why a little." After that it gets more complicated, as the melody starts to turn its slow, melancholy pirouettes. But it's a mark of the song's genius that it should seize the opportunity offered by monotony.

★ ★ ★ ★ ★ ★ ★ ★ ★ ★

Porter's publisher told him this was "a heavenly beautiful song. It is not less a gem than any immortal song of a Schubert or Schumann".

★ ★ ★ ★ ★ ★ ★ ★ ★ ★

Monotony has one obvious advantage for the composer of popular songs: it bestows instant familiarity. There's also a kind of one-note writing which can assist a poor singer. When the question is not "can you hold a tune?" but "can you hold a note?", there's a lot more of us with our hands in the air. But can you hold the note at the start of "Ev'ry Time We Say Goodbye"? Distinguished performers have risen to the challenge – from Ella Fitzgerald through Julie London to Mick Hucknall – with varying degrees of success. When Burt Bacharach wrote "This Guy's in Love" for Herb Alpert, he got around the problem of Alpert's extremely limited range by devising a tune whose hook stuck determinedly to one note. But the tactic would have failed had Bacharach not also thoughtfully provided another prop in the form of a consistent beat on which to punch the words home. In "Ev'ry Time We Say Goodbye", the series of identical notes strings out across a long, open space, making complicated demands on a singer's ability to hold and pull away from a note and enforcing all kinds of decisions about phrasing and shaping. And many have come and many have fallen.

"Ev'ry Time" was written in 1944 for a Broadway revue called *Seven Lively Arts*. Since the Broadway show *Leave it to Me* in 1938, Porter's capacity to write hits had appeared to be on the wane. After *Something for the Boys* (1943) the drama critic George Freedley had written in the *Morning Telegraph*: "[the show had] none of the tunes that you go out of the theater whistling. . . In that respect, Cole Porter has fallen down in all his latest shows." And following *Mexican Hayride*, which opened on Broadway in 1944, the same paper suggested that Porter's gift had "very nearly reached vanishing point". Porter himself had grown depressed and irritable.

Seven Lively Arts was conceived by its big-time producer, Billy Rose, as an extravaganza ranging right across the arts. There were songs and sketches from a cast featuring Beatrice Lillie and Bert Lahr. Benny Goodman played jazz clarinet and the dancer Alicia Markova performed to a 15-minute ballet suite, *Scènes de Ballet*, specially commissioned from Igor Stravinsky. A show so ambitiously mixed was clearly flirting with disaster, but on the day of the opening at the Ziegfeld Theatre, Porter received an encouraging letter from Dr Albert Sirmay, his music editor at Chappell publishing.

Sirmay wrote: "I myself have a personal affair with your song 'Ev'ry Time We Say Goodbye'. It chokes me whenever I hear it, it moves me to tears. This song is one of the greatest songs you ever wrote. It is a dithyramb to love, a hymn to youth, a heavenly beautiful song. It is not less a gem than any immortal song of a Schubert or Schumann . . . This song is a classic and will live forever as many others of your songs." These were overblown words, maybe, but they were prescient. *Seven Lively Arts* was attacked by the critics for its pomposity and died after 183 performances. But "Ev'ry Time" endured.

It's a simple tune and it sounds easy in the right hands, but its tone can prove hard to hit. The song is in the voice of a standard romantic type – the lover who cannot bear to part – but it dusts that old cliché down by thinking not in terms of some cataclysmic, final separation, but of the regular to-ings and fro-ings of a life. The word "little" goes a long way here. In the urbane world of Porter's lyric, to "die a little" and to "wonder why a little" carry the same disenchanted but quietly resolute force.

Elaborate conceits arch winningly through these lines, the singer wondering "why the gods above me/ Who must be in the know/ Think so little of me/ They allow you to go". We are not on the edge here: despair is tempered by charm and the song closes with a musical joke, the chords modulating with the lyric:

111

> When you're near there's such an air
> Of spring about it
> I can hear a lark somewhere
> Begin to sing about it
> There's no love song finer
> But how strange the change
> From major to minor
> Ev'ry time we say goodbye.

Porter famously said: "writing lyrics is like doing a crossword puzzle". His internal rhyme schemes could turn a lyric into a cunningly calculated, tightly locked grid. The small cluster of internal rhymes here ("I die", "I wonder why", "begin to sing", "how strange the change") serve to brighten the lyric, and set a current running contrary to the expected mood. Whatever the sentimental burden here, it is manageable, though many singers would try and convince you otherwise. In doing so, they miss the point. In "Ev'ry Time", Porter produced a song embedded in the circumstances of everyday life. There's no reason why this song might not occur to you daily.

It was Ella Fitzgerald who sent it round the world. She recorded the song in 1956 at the start of her systematic assault on the great American songs and it appears on the album *Ella Fitzgerald Sings the Cole Porter Songbook* (Verve). The band arrangement is simple, lightly strung, not much interested in counter-melodies or distractions, and Fitzgerald opens up in the space granted her and sings like a clarinet, as if her throat were made of polished wood. Critics of Fitzgerald often centre their reservations on this very smoothness, hearing no personal drama in her delivery, no gritty autobiography crackling between the lines as there is with Billie Holiday. But this is a song in which the uncluttered dispassion of her approach clicks a light on over the song's wit. "Ev'ry time we say goodbye, I die a little," she sings, and her control, her lack of insistence, does remarkable justice to that little death. Her delivery is a miracle of mildness.

"Ev'ry Time" became Fitzgerald's most popular song with British audiences. In the late 1950s, radio programmers were deeply reluctant to broadcast jazz: it was as if "scat" were short for "scatalogical". So Fitzgerald's exposure was brief during perhaps her most vital years. "Ev'ry Time", though, nipped under the wire, becoming a request-show staple, particularly on Forces Radio. During the 1960s and 1970s, barely an edition of Sunday lunchtime's *Two-Way Family Favourites* would pass without someone on a posting to Germany requesting it for their beloved back home, or vice-versa. The song, in Fitzgerald's honeyed version, became, as Stuart Nicholson wrote in the biography *Ella Fitzgerald* (Gollancz 1993), "a 'We'll Meet Again' for the Cold War generation". Cometh the hour, cometh the song. The strident and billowy optimism of Vera Lynn bolstered those about to go before the guns and those who watched them leave. Something less intense, something which dealt with its sentiments more coolly, seemed to fit those parted by a non-war and serving in a stasis.

Ray Charles reached the song in 1961 on the album he made with the jazz singer Betty Carter, *Ray Charles and Betty Carter* (ABC-Paramount). Hard to think of anything more potentially disruptive of the song's easeful play of mind than a duet. In fact, their voices do not meet, except to croon a reprise of the title by way of a closing flourish. Charles sings the song right through and then drops back to concentrate on the piano while Carter gets her turn. It's a useful exercise in contrasts. Carter sings like a sax taking a break, angling in and out on jazzy paths, but it's what Charles does that stays in the mind. The calm poise of his phrasing answers to the refinement of the lyric and he paces himself like someone with a sense of the whole shape, rather than snapping the song into fragments of skill, which is rather Sarah Vaughan's approach on the album *After Hours* (Mercury), recorded the same year.

Jazz instrumentalists have gone to the song for the neat shifting of its chords, which makes a plush bed for soloing, and for the challenge of that single-note start. The saxophonist Sonny Rollins put a version on *The Sound of Sonny* (Prestige) in the summer of 1957, where it is apparent that the mood of the lyric interests him not a jot. The song whips along at a breezy up-tempo swing and still holds together. Rollins also cracks a gag with the melody's monotony, rattling off some 20 staccato notes at the top of the second verse, as if trying to blow a hole in it. John Coltrane's saxophone takes it easier on *The Paris Concert* album, recorded in 1962 (Pablo), scooping deep into the tune in search of disenchantment and pulling it out in handfuls.

The trumpeter and singer Chet Baker was in a position to come at the song from both sides, instrumentally and vocally. (A version is on the sound-track to the film about Baker's last days, *Chet Baker Sings and Plays from the Film 'Let's Get Lost'*, Novus 1989.) The solo is exquisitely pained, but the vocal manages to eclipse it – a quiet, resigned sigh, as of someone slowly exhaling cigarette smoke. This seems perfectly in tune with the song's mood and helps explain why Nina Simone makes a good singer of the song while a showman like Sammy Davis Jr does not. On *The Best of Nina Simone* (RCA 1970), Simone's melancholy bell of a voice deliberately lacks attack, never pushes for extremes, and the song favours those undramatic virtues.

Mick Hucknall understood this. In 1987 with Simply Red, he became the only man to make the song a hit, hoisting it to No 11 in Britain. (The single was taken from the album *Men and Women*, Elektra.) Elsewhere, his voice is the epitome of lustful, throaty exertion, but he tempered it for the occasion to produce a vocal which sits patiently in the arrangement, coming over all level and engaging. Less successful versions will normally wrench the song away from its domestic root. The torch singer Julie London may be thought to have started something on her album *All Through the Night* (London) as early as 1959. Backed by the Bud Shank Quintet and drenched in studio reverb and self-pity, she seems to be whispering down an air vent. It is possibly the first use of "Ev'ry Time" purely as a vehicle for a star's sensibility – a notion which Annie Lennox picked up in 1990, when she recorded it for the 1990 *Red Hot and Blue* charity album (Chrysalis), a tribute to Porter by contemporary pop stars.

Lennox's delivery is effortful, encouraging you to acknowledge its graft. It works fine if what you're after is a frenzy of hand-wringing, but it seems to issue from somewhere other than the lyric or the melody. The subtext appears to be: "Ev'ry time we say goodbye, I permit myself three minutes of self-flagellation". The song is smaller than that, and greater.

113

BODY AND SOUL

BY PHIL JOHNSON

IN THE film *Round Midnight* (1986), Bertrand Tavernier's romantic homage to classic American jazz, the song "Body and Soul" carries an awful lot of narrative weight. It's played in one of the many nightclub scenes by Dexter Gordon, who impersonates the fictional saxophonist hero, Dale Gordon, an alcoholic wreck washed up in Paris in the late 1950s. As Gordon begins to play, the film cuts between his slumped body and blank, bleary expression to the suddenly animated faces of the audience and the rapt profile of Francis, his French acolyte and protector, who is watching the scene on the home movies he has taken at the club. All of life, the film seems to say, is here in this song; a tailor listens as he repairs a jacket, the musicians smile knowingly to each other and a pair of lovers exchange meaningful glances. Gordon finishes his solo and stretches out a hand for the drink resting on the piano, which the pianist moves out of his grasp. Denied this solace, he turns back to the tune and delivers a moving coda, as the lovers walk off into the night and Francis stares into space with passionate intensity. At the end of the scene, Gordon steals the tip left by the lovers, goes on a bender and ends up in hospital, rescued once more by the faithful Francis.

★ ★ ★ ★ ★ ★ ★ ★ ★ ★ ★

To play it, you have to show you can feel, and, as Pharoah Sanders says, "not just honk your horn".

★ ★ ★ ★ ★ ★ ★ ★ ★ ★ ★

Pain and loss, darkness and death, love and life gone sour: this then, is the subtext to the song – at least in the film, which puts a doomy French spin on the dreamy cadences of the tune. And this is largely what "Body and Soul" has come to mean for us today, even without the lovelorn lyric. Incarnated by Billie Holiday, Abbey Lincoln or Betty Carter and too many instrumentalists to mention, "Body and Soul" has become the iconic reduction of all those late-night crying-into-your-beer jazz ballads. It's a standard for all saxophonists not because it tests their technical skills but because it challenges their powers of emotional expression. To play "Body and Soul" – and even the title is indicative of a powerful duality – you have to show you can feel, and, as the saxophonist Pharoah Sanders says, "not just honk your horn".

Since it first became popular in the early thirties, "Body and Soul" has provoked some of the most important jazz performances of the century, and left its obscure origins far behind. Surprisingly, it began as a jaunty ballad, even as dance music. When Louis Armstrong cut the first jazz version in 1930, it rocked along at 120 beats per minute; when Freddie Hubbard recorded it in 1981 the tempo was down to 48 bpm. Even Coleman Hawkins's landmark version of 1939 (*Body and Soul*, Charly) – which more or less confirmed the tenor saxophone as the most expressive instrument in jazz – is a canter rather than a crawl. It's as if the tempo has slowed, and the intensity deepened, as the innocence of the original tune and lyric has been gradually corrupted by the tragedies of modern jazz experience.

This process can be seen most clearly in the many performances of the song by Billie Holiday. It's the tune which, according to jazz legend, she performed as an audition for her first job in New York in 1930. Trailing the bars of 133rd St for work, she told the owner of Pod and Jerry's that she could dance. He had the pianist play something for her, and when it became evident that she was no dancer he asked her to sing. When she started "Body and Soul" it is said that the patrons began weeping openly. Nevertheless, her recorded version of the tune from 1940 remains relatively sunny (*Strange Fruit*, Giants of Jazz 1991); but by the time of her Carnegie Hall concert of 1956, the song has become a threnody, the tempo slowed to a hip dirge, her cracked voice halting on the syllables in what we read today as a moving testament to the rigours of the jazz life (*The Essential Billie Holiday: Carnegie Hall Concert*, Verve reissued 1989).

"Body and Soul" is one of those songs that appear in retrospect to have been written by committee, the list of composers recalling nothing so much as a firm of solicitors. Originally credited to Johnny Green, the song didn't really take off until it appeared in the show *Broadway Follies*, gaining in the process the names of three lyricists, Heyman, Sour and Eyton. The words come as standard (though Holiday rarely sang it exactly as written), but the feeling of the song is changed greatly according to the gender of the singer. With Louis Armstrong (*Satchmo's Classic Vocals*, Classic Jazz on Charly) or Henry "Red" Allen (*Original 1933–41 Recordings*, Classics), "My heart is sad and lonely, for you I sigh, for you dear, only. Why haven't you seen it? I'm all for you, body and soul" is delivered with an élan that suggests the singer is hardly down for the count. With Holiday, the confession of undying love sounds more like masochism; in the sleeve-notes to *Carnegie Hall Concert* – released shortly after her death in July 1959 – she is described by the critic Gilbert Millstein, borrowing Aldous Huxley's phrase, as "a born murderee".

There's even a politically correct version of the song on a recent album by the David Murray Quartet (*Body and Soul*, Black Saint 1993), where vocalist Taana Running rewrites the lyrics because, she says, "They're kind of masochistic and it's just next to impossible for me to sing lyrics that I have a problem with poetically or politically". The contemporary jazz singer Cassandra Wilson, who has recorded the song twice (*Live*, JMT 1991; *She Who Weeps*, JMT 1991), says: "I can understand that approach because the way you empower yourself is to rewrite the words; you have to change the way you look at a song to step outside the victim persona. But I think the words of 'Body and Soul' are beautiful and I think it's about submission, and that has no gender. It's a kind of falling back into darkness and I don't care what you say, it's like 'boom, I'm in love', and that's a real human emotion."

Betty Carter, who performed perhaps the slowest and most languorous of all versions on her Village Vanguard live album of 1970, gets around the

115

problem of the words by turning them into a vocal version of a saxophone solo: the lyric comes across as deadpan while the melody lingers on (*Betty Carter at the Village Vanguard,* Verve reissued 1993).

It's as an instrumental, however, that "Body and Soul" has proved most influential. Hawkins' version of 1939 signals the beginning of modern jazz; it's one long saxophone solo lasting two complete choruses of the song, and played with a trembling vibrato. He opens with a fairly close paraphrase of the melody and then doubles the tempo, playing with the original chord sequence by substituting new fingerings for the conventional shapes, in a method which anticipated the bop experiments that were to follow. It was, for jazz, a big hit. "I'll never know why it became such a classic," he said. "I was just making the notes all the way and I wasn't making a melody. I just played it like I play everything else."

The following year, Duke Ellington and his bassist Jimmy Blanton recorded three takes of the tune that have re-surfaced on a wonderful CD (*Duke Ellington: Solos, Duets and Trios,* Bluebird 1990). With Blanton taking the melody line as first a bowed, and then a plucked solo, the performances are suffused with a deep melancholy, accentuated by the ungainliness of the big bass fiddle, which had never been played with such freedom before. Though the tempo veers between slow and comatose, the feeling perfectly encompasses the darkness of desire expressed in the song. It's the essence of jazz: improvisation on a shopworn theme that transforms popular song into an art as dense and brooding as Baudelaire. It also anticipates the keening sax of Dexter Gordon, weeping his heart out through his horn as the world goes on about its business all around him: "My life a wreck you're making, you know I'm yours for just the taking; I'd gladly surrender myself for you, body and soul."

116

YOU'LL NEVER WALK ALONE

BY ROBERT BUTLER

THE OTHER day I was talking to a man who supports Liverpool Football Club. He has relatives who are members of a local amateur dramatic society, so he went along to see a production they were doing of *Carousel*. In the second act some New Englanders return from a clam-bake party, only to discover that the hero, a ne'er-do-well called Billy, has stabbed himself. His wife, Julie, runs to him, and Billy dies in her arms. Julie sobs, "What am I going to do?"

It's a tough question, but her cousin Nettie has the answer. "Why, you're going to stay here with me." she says, "Main thing is to keep on living. Keep on caring what's going to happen. Remember the sample you gave me. Remember what it says."

And Julie, who's in tears, with her dead husband in her arms, and the village standing round, remembers what the sample says:

> **When you walk through a storm**
> **Keep your head up high**
> **And don't be afraid of the dark**

They're tender words, but to a Liverpool supporter watching the show, they come as a bit of a shock. "I couldn't figure it out ," he said, "I didn't know what it was doing there."

CAROUSEL, a musical by Rodgers and Hammerstein, opened at the Majestic Theatre on Broadway in 1945, just across the street from *Oklahoma!*, their hit of 1943. *Carousel* was a smash too, running on Broadway for 890 performances. There are a dozen good songs in the show, but only one became so famous that it left its roots way behind.

On the original-cast recording (MCA), Christine Johnson, playing Nettie sings "You'll Never Walk Alone" with a slow, urgent vibrato reminiscent of kids in a playground swirling rubber tubes. It's a simple song, with big open vowels, and Johnson brings plenty of sombre colour to the "dark" in the first verse, which then turns, in the second, to the delicate promise of the "lark".

To get from the dark to the lark, what you have to do is walk: first through the wind, then through the rain. The repetitions drive the song on towards the catchphrase title which, like any good catchphrase, you get twice. The second time it's cranked up so the message leaps out in the boldest type. Or seems to, except halfway through Johnson sounds unsure and fades away. She needs the assurance of the others.

The New England villagers rally round. The chorus is a quieter, broader wave of sentiment that builds again, but this time, finding strength in numbers, they give the title a big finish. It's an anthem of hope that works best as a faltering journey out of despair.

The song was recorded that same year by the young showbiz veteran Judy Garland (reissued on *The One and Only*, Capitol 1991). There's a heavenly choir to keep her company, but Garland defies the soft-pastel backdrop. Yes, you think, she's been through the storm, she's been through the rain, and she got *drenched*.

Compare her version to the more overtly inspirational or even perspirational ones. In *Cilla Black with Barry Manilow* (Columbia 1993) the message turns triumphalist: you'll never walk alone because Cilla and Barry will always be there too. When Max Bygraves suggests you "walk on" through all this rotten weather (*Fifty Golden Years*, Braveworld 1993) it comes over like friendly advice: remember to take a mac, son, it's raining out there.

But Garland chews up the words with an anxiety that reverberates right through a word like *storrrrmmmm*. When she lingers over the final "alone", she goes very small. Loneliness, you feel, is a good deal worse than a bad cold.

It's one reason that, well before Liverpool, people liked to sing this song in a crowd. In the late fifties Louis Armstrong was on the road with the All-Stars, taking his trumpet version of "You'll Never Walk Alone" to Savannah, Georgia, and giving it a strict New Orleans beat that never failed to get everyone up and dancing. The recorded version (*Chicago Concert 1956*, CBS 1984) doesn't have any words, but in Savannah the audience, who are all black, supply them. Armstrong goes through two choruses and the audience won't stop singing. They want the song again. "Most touching damn thing I ever saw," Armstrong told the reporter David Halberstam, "I almost started crying right there on stage. We really hit something inside each person there."

★ ★ ★ ★ ★ ★ ★ ★ ★ ★

Liverpool did their own version in 1977. You wouldn't know that they had distinguished themselves as a team.

★ ★ ★ ★ ★ ★ ★ ★ ★ ★

Six years later the song crossed the Atlantic and took the ferry across the Mersey. In October 1963 Gerry and the Pacemakers took it to the top of the British charts: it was their third release, and their third No 1 – a record that has never been bettered (Columbia, reissued on several compilations). "*Waaaaalk arrnn!*" goes the 21-year-old Gerry Marsden. His mouth is so close to the microphone the saliva sounds as if it's part of George Martin's orchestral arrangement. It's – slow – stuff – this – with – big – breaths: an unembarrassed slice of schmaltz. Six weeks later someone sang it on the terraces of Anfield. "Well, if there was one person," says Marsden in the book *The Kop* (Stephen F. Kelly, Mandarin 1993), "I'd like to shake his hand."

"*WALK ON!*" they go. Then there's a gap. "Walk on!" Then another gap. They sound asthmatic: it's as if 14,000 Liverpool supporters are climbing the 100 steps of the Kop. They're standing there, arms outstretched, scarves aloft, swaying. It's something they've done for 30 years, but this afternoon's game against Newcastle is the second-last time they'll be able to do it standing up.

Next season, following the recommendations of the Taylor Report – commissioned after 95 Liverpool fans had been crushed to death at Hillsborough in 1989 – Anfield becomes an all-seater stadium.

"Walk on!" they go, with renewed urgency. They are one-nil down. The crowd bellow out Rodgers and Hammerstein in short phrases that rise and fall like the revving of an engine. Maybe that's why Gerry and the Pacemakers' version caught on. It offers so many places to draw breath.

It's a shame the crowd limit themselves to the last verse. You don't get to hear the Kop going all soft over the sweet silver song of the lark. It's spring, and the sun is shining, but it's not hard for the fans to imagine wind and rain: their team is a shadow of its former self, and one of the players who made it so good then, Peter Beardsley, is on the other side today, running rings round Liverpool.

The crowd on the Kop is way down from the 25,000 who packed in there in the late sixties. But they still say the Kop is always worth a goal. Today it's worth two. Both scored by Newcastle, whose supporters, standing at the other end from the Kop, cheekily pick up the song and give it Cilla and Barry's upbeat treatment.

The Liverpool team did their own version ("We Can Do It", State Records) for the Cup Final in 1977. Kevin Keegan's bouffant helmet haircut on the sleeve fixes the year firmly in the mind. You wouldn't know from the single that here were 11 people who had distinguished themselves as a team. When that high note arrives (*"neeeeaaaarrr-vaaaarrrr"*), they lunge after it like a late tackle. They lost the Cup Final, too.

You can hear the crowd themselves, more movingly, more eerily, at the end of "Fearless" on Pink Floyd's 1971 album *Meddle* (Harvest). There's a soft, diffuse quality, as it spreads out across the stadium, joining the triple-claps, the whistles and the *Liverpool-Liverpool!*s in this low, almost mournful, surge of loyalty.

Mourning brought the song back into the charts. After the Bradford City fire in 1985, Gerry Marsden got together an all-star group of singers, called them The Crowd, and took a charity version back to No 1. Four years later came Hillsborough. At the Cup Final that year, between Liverpool and Everton, 80,000 people stood and sang the song, led again by Marsden (whose autobiography is entitled *I'll Never Walk Alone*). The song can mean as much the occasion demands. You know it means very little when Slade put it back to back with "Auld Lang Syne" on *The Christmas Party Album*.

In 1992 the National Theatre put on a major revival of *Carousel* which later transferred to the West End and Broadway, and the song returned to its source. Patricia Routledge, who played Nettie, told me, "When everything is at its darkest, she is the voice of hope. Keep going, she says, just keep going." Messages don't get any simpler. Hammerstein said he was more at home with characters who didn't have a big vocabulary. "You find people who are primitive in their education – they're more likely, I think, to say what they mean."

Rodgers' music sounds deceptively simple too. It's a song that everyone thinks they can sing. But be warned. "It's so simple," says Routledge, "It's like a Bach chorale or a piece of Schubert. And they, of course, are very difficult."

119

I'LL BE YOUR BABY TONIGHT

BY Allegra Huston

ODD THAT it should be Bob Dylan, revered by two generations of literary critics and street revolutionaries, who wrote the plainest of plain country songs. *John Wesley Harding* (Columbia 1968), recorded in Nashville in late 1967, was Dylan's first album to be released after his near-mythical motorcycle crash. Gone is the florid jangle of *Blonde on Blonde* (1966); in its place is brimstone biblical imagery, echoing the itinerant preachers of an ageless past, who invoked the presence of God in everyday life.

"I'll Be Your Baby Tonight" is the last track on *John Wesley Harding*, and very different from the rest of the album. It was one of only two songs which emerged fully formed, words and music together. Though it is gentle where most of the album is fierce, a private rather than a public speech, it shares the same ethos: it catches the promise of understanding in a very ordinary moment.

★ ★ ★ ★ ★ ★ ★ ★ ★ ★

"Let's just lay here and listen to the music," Adam Faith says to his potential lover, who must already be disconcerted by the presence of a third person in the room.

★ ★ ★ ★ ★ ★ ★ ★ ★ ★

This directness, both spiritual and emotional, couldn't be conveyed in Dylan's signature whirl of symbol. The poet Allen Ginsberg recalled Dylan "telling me how he was writing shorter lines . . . there was to be no wasted language, no wasted breath. All the imagery was to be functional rather than ornamental".

Dylan sketches a scene in words that are few and simple enough to be those of someone who has never been to school. Three verses consist of three extremely short lines followed by the refrain:

> Close your eyes
> Close the door
> You don't have to worry any more
> I'll be your baby tonight.

Then there is a central verse in a different key, more rollicking and even more defiantly unsophisticated. The music has a sound untouched by the decades – easy, rolling pedal-steel guitar with a snatch of harmonica as the only decoration.

From the first line ("Close your eyes") the outside world falls away. The scene is a room – it could be any room – with a bird singing outside and a clear night sky, and two people, one slightly fearful, the other easy and reassuring. There is a bottle of liquor, and a shade at the window. That's all.

The timelessness of the picture is partly owing to the scarcity of detail, and partly to the central verse. "That mockingbird's gonna sail away": rural America, unchanged for generations. "That big old moon's gonna shine like a spoon": the traditional rhyme for inarticulate passion, straight from an age of sentimental valentines. Though Dylan pokes gentle fun at the downhome images of country music, the emotional integrity of the song is beyond question. The words are no less true for being store-bought.

But what is the fear? Maybe the girl is afraid of falling in love. Maybe it's just a coy tentativeness that a few swigs from the bottle will release. Here is the delicacy of the song: the singer is the seducer, the persuader, but threat and pressure are taken away. Not "Be my baby tonight", but "I'll be yours".

This is the feminine mode of seduction, and on the whole, women sing the song better. As Dylan performs it, it's a song of contentment, and he embraces its clichés with the joy of a city boy released into the countryside. The song has been covered many times, but a curious number of singers seem to lose confidence in it. Either they're embarrassed by the hokey central verse and bluster through it, or, like Graham Bonnet shouting "I'm gonna be your lover baby!" at the end of his hard-rock version (c 1978, reissued on *The Rock Singers Anthology*, Vertigo 1990), they try to push the song to a sexy climax that clashes with the careful tenderness of the lyrics.

Unlike Bonnet, Adam Faith doesn't try to turn the song into something that it's not, but still his country-flavoured version is a template of disaster (*Midnight Postcards*, Polygram 1993). Obviously worried at the gaping holes that his gravelly growl leaves between the words, he's added a "shadow vocal" which soon runs off with the melody. Faith flails chaotically in its wake, and it seems to be a great relief when the instrumental break comes. "Let's just lay here and listen to the music," he says to his potential lover, who must already be disconcerted by the presence of a third person in the room. Now a saxophone player pops up as well.

Dylan's bare, precise details are like the fine threads of a net holding the song together. They can expand to accommodate styles other than country, but if the intimacy is broken, the song falls apart.

The boppy reggae beat provided by UB40 on Robert Palmer's 1990 version (*Don't Explain*, EMI) is so natural that the song might have been written that way. It's still an uncomplicated evening, but now we're in the Caribbean – a warm night, a bamboo shade, a bottle of Jamaican beer. The moon shines with a tropical brilliance. But suddenly, the spell is broken. Into this idyll lollops a whole troupe of backing singers, chorusing "Be your baby" like a gang of schoolgirls mocking some tongue-tied teenage Romeo. Even after they've shut up, you feel as if they're still loitering round, watching for shadow-patterns on the windowshade.

This is an intrusion, but for sheer absurdity imagine 50 people at once offering to be your baby tonight, as on the gospel version by the Brothers and Sisters. Gospel covers traditionally demand imaginative indulgence – the line "Kick your shoes off" being addressed to the Lord Jesus would be the prob-

121

lem here – but, perhaps nervous of blasphemy, the Brothers and Sisters hold back from giving Dylan's song the full devotional treatment. The soaring call of ecstasy isn't there, so the "you" is firmly mortal. Even if the "you" were Don Juan, he would blanch.

These are all later covers. At first, it was the country chanteuses who picked up the song, and within two years five versions were recorded. Unlike the men, they felt no need to fill in the silences, but swoop and glide on the long-held notes. Emmylou Harris provides the most unashamedly country version (*The Legendary 'Gliding Bird' Album*, Jubilee 1969) – surprisingly, since it was recorded in New York before she moved to Nashville. Though she begins with the sound of heartbreak catching in her voice, she is the most declarative, as if she herself takes heart from the words "Do not fear". Linda Ronstadt (*Hand Sewn, Home Grown*, Capitol 1969), like Rita Coolidge, is more seductive. But where Coolidge's version (*The Lady's Not for Sale*, A&M 1972) sports a racy ragtime piano intro, Ronstadt brings the tempo down to a mesmerising slowness. She too seems uncomfortable with the central verse. A crude striptease drumbeat cuts into her lingering phrasing, and suddenly the pressure is on, the tenderness lost.

The other two come to grief with the bottle. Anne Murray (*Snowbird*, Capitol 1970) has to drag her wholesome voice along the river-bottom to make it sound as if the bottle contains anything stronger than milk. Maria Muldaur (remember "Midnight at the Oasis"?) has the opposite problem, slithering around the melody so uncontrollably that it sounds as if she has already downed most of her bottle (*Pottery Pie*, Carthage 1970). With her pleading little-girl voice and distracted "la-la-la"s at the end, she could be Blanche Dubois in *A Streetcar Named Desire*.

For me, only one recorded cover can stand beside the original. Marianne Faithfull released *Faithless* in 1978 (reissued in Britain in 1988, on Castle Classics). She almost had to make a country album just to use the title. It was her first album since the sixties, and her pretty voice sounds as if it has been grated through rusty iron; tattered and torn, it holds knowingness, frail hope and a longing for shattered illusions.

This splendidly ravaged voice belongs to no backwoods sweetheart. On "I'll Be Your Baby Tonight", it suggests an anonymous motel room at the edge of some rural town, and two people blotting out the time with a bottle of bourbon and each other. "Do not fear," Faithfull cajoles, as if her man might be married and afraid she won't let him go in the morning. This is a woman aware that she can do no more than carve one night of companionship out of the scorched earth of her heart. Behind her, the upbeat rhythm sounds slightly forced, like someone smiling bravely through pain.

There is one terrific unrecorded version as well. In the 1980s the actor Harry Dean Stanton toured California with a small band. They appeared live on a Los Angeles radio station, KCRW, and played "I'll Be Your Baby Tonight". Again the contrast between a sad, wistful voice and the cheery bounce of the music haunts the song. Stanton is backed only by two guitarists, who stop playing at the start of the refrain and sing close harmonies. For once other voices aren't an intrusion. The three come together, slow and *a capella*, like one sweet voice, and on the next line Stanton's solo vocal sounds like its yearning shadow. I hope one day he will record this. My bootleg tape is almost worn away.

SEND IN THE CLOWNS

By Robert Cushman

VICTORIA WOOD once wrote a musical called *Good Fun* whose heroine, at a point of emotional catastrophe, sang out approximately as follows: "This isn't going to be a song about clowns; I hate bloody clowns." I know how she felt. However, the song to which she was implicitly referring isn't about clowns either.

The story goes that Harold Prince, directing *A Little Night Music* on Broadway, summoned Stephen Sondheim, author of the music and lyrics, to rehearsals to watch how Glynis Johns, the leading lady, was playing a particular scene. The show is based on Ingmar Bergman's *Smiles of a Summer Night*; Johns played an actress who tries to lure her ex-lover, a lawyer, away from his unresponsive young wife. He feels the tug but cannot break free. Johns was bringing such intensity to the scene that a song seemed called for, an expression of her pent-up feelings. And so, impromptu, a song was born: not Sondheim's best song, not even his best ballad (I prefer "Not a Day Goes By", a real heartbreaker from *Merrily We Roll Along*), but easily his best-known.

★ ★ ★ ★ ★ ★ ★ ★ ★ ★

Singers tend to feel that the one Broadway standard of the last 20 years deserves the grand manner, or can be knocked about a bit, or both

★ ★ ★ ★ ★ ★ ★ ★ ★ ★

The tale has always puzzled me. "Send in the Clowns" is Johns's only song in the musical's second act, and her only solo anywhere. Weren't they intending to give her one? The show would certainly have been unsatisfying without; in a musical songs are how we get to know people, and she is the heroine. In the event, "Send in the Clowns" not only evened the balance; it centred the show.

I found this out in stages. *Night Music* opened in 1973; I first saw it the following year in Toronto: the road-company version with Jean Simmons playing Desiree, the actress. I admired its elegance and I liked the music, but I was unmoved. The next week in New York I was persuaded to see it again. To begin with, the show and I kept our accustomed distance from one another. But Glynis Johns's husky humanity warmed me from her first entrance, and when she got to the song she transformed the evening. *Night Music* is a parade of lovers, most of them poignantly or hilariously mismatched; the pattern was clear but not very involving. Johns's song – about the acceptance of heartbreak – not only brought her own situation to life; it illuminated the complications and resolutions that were to follow and – in some not quite explicable way – made sense of what had gone before. It was as if a frieze had come to life.

The entire *Night Music* score is composed in waltz time, though the lilt is often disguised. "Send in the Clowns" is a sober, cold-light-of-dawn variation on the theme. It begins with a chaste woodwind statement of the melody, taken up – still soberly – by the strings. Then the voice comes in: "Isn't it rich, are we a pair . . ." The lines are short, and they could conceivably be bitter, but the tone is maturely ironic: if there is any anger she's directing it at herself and saving it up for later. This man has been chasing her and now, when she's ready to give herself, he's unavailable: "Me here at last on the ground, You in mid-air . . ." The images are economically exact if you know the story, tantalising if you don't. Sondheim habitually deals in half-truths and unconscious self-betrayals, but here Desiree is singing exactly what she feels. The greatest irony is that her partner isn't listening.

Since she is an actress, her vocabulary is theatrical. "Send in the clowns" – the phrase that, with variations, ends every section of the main strain – is the traditional command when something goes embarrassingly wrong in a circus or vaudeville and the audience has to be distracted: a kind of desperate shrug. Towards the end Desiree ruefully recognises the image's reference to herself – "Don't bother, they're here" – but she isn't indulging in Pagliacci self-pity.

The song is divided into the pop song's traditional four sections, AABA; and one of the lovely things about it is the ease with which the A section, the main strain, flows into the B. This bridge begins in very similar vein – same rhythm, same sawn-off lines – "Just when I'd stopped/ Opening doors" – and then stretches itself, gets more open and voluble – "Finally knowing the one that I wanted was yours/ Making my entrance again with my usual flair" – before returning to cryptic defeat – "Sure of my lines/ No one is there".

125

We are back in the mood and metre of the main melody, so the second transition is as tight and logical as the first. At the end, when her lover has gone, Desiree sings an extra A section: an instant reprise. The short phrases were written to accommodate Johns's limited voice, which also accounts for the song's truncated range. It's meant to be acted. But it's also meant to be sung, and it's notable that Johns sang nearly every note.

The glory of Sondheim's lyrics is their conversational quality, but this point is lost when people start speaking them. After all, anyone can talk conversationally.

Matter-of-fact, gently sardonic, temperamental but vulnerable, Johns's performance – of the song and the role – remains definitive (on the Broadway cast album, Columbia 1973). How much so was revealed in London when Jean Simmons resumed the part, and was beautiful but bland. (Elizabeth Taylor in the film was blank.) However, by the time of the West End opening, *Night Music* was able to advertise itself as "the 'Send in the Clowns' musical". The song had become a hit.

This was odd. Plenty of good theatre songs, including Sondheim's own, have been ignored by the pop world; and, out of its context, this one is hard to understand. But paradoxically that may have helped it. The seventies were the time of the singer-songwriter, when the favoured style was the sensitive-obscure. "Clowns" must have seemed to fit right in with Joni Mitchell; certainly it did in Judy Collins's best-selling and totally uninflected performance (recorded 1973; on *Judith*, Elektra 1975). Listeners could make of it what they wished; and I swear that most of them thought it was a Pagliacci song. So did some performers. I remember a Manhattan club singer furiously embellishing the lyric: "Where are the clowns? You promised me clowns." It didn't work.

Other singers were more thoughtful. Cleo Laine, one of the first to adopt it (*Live at Carnegie Hall*, RCA 1973), appreciated the drama; she was actively sad, bristlingly ironic, sometimes coming close to milking pathos but stopping in time. Some tried to explain it. Bing Crosby, singing it in concert, provided an outline of the plot, adding that he was surprised more singers hadn't taken the song up. (Where had he been? It was inescapable.) Late Bing made any song a pleasure to hear, but his mellow style hardly suited this one (*That's What Life is All About*, UA 1975).

Frank Sinatra was another story. Most unusually, he provided a spoken introduction on record (Reprise 1976, reissued on *The Sinatra Collection*) as well as in person: an edited but acceptable version of the facts. "This is about a couple of adult people . . . it's a break-up." His voice is at its gravest and most gravelly, and so it is in the song itself. He starts with world-weariness – the opening is slightly dismissive – then opens up, emotionally and technically, with virtuoso extended vowels – "you in mid-a-a-air, one who can't mo-o-ove" – to activate the rhythm. The accompaniment is solo piano, and there are seconds of troubled silence. "Just when I'd stopped opening doors" is harsh and abrupt, "making my entrance again with my usual flair" speeds up lightly for self-mockery, "sure of my lines . . . – no one is there" gets one of those haunted pauses. It's one of his finest, most compassionate performances; the fastidious separation of consonants on "don't you love farce" is trademark Sinatra – though this time Glynis Johns got there before him – the insistent definition giving both performances a signal authority.

The song also brought out the best in Barbra Streisand, who tackles it on *The Broadway Album* (CBS 1985) without a trace of histrionics and with an orchestration closely resembling the original. She claimed never to have understood the lyric, and Sondheim obliged with a second B section that spells everything out: "What a surprise!/ Who could foresee/ I'd come to feel about you/ What you feel about me?" I doubt that it improves the song, but it gives it a more orthodox shape.

The song has undergone other kinds of expansion from singers who feel that the one Broadway standard of the last 20 years deserves the grand manner, or can be knocked about a bit, or both. From the first it was a fixture in New York supper clubs. Mabel Mercer, the Queen Mother of cabaret, was in her seventies when it came out, and sang it on a rising arc of passionate regret. Her successive readings of the recurring title-phrase – beginning nonchalant, ending up fierce – epitomised her fastidious fanaticism about lyrics. (I once heard her get the pronouns in the opening lines the wrong way

126

round. She stopped, apologised and started again.) She also insisted, more firmly than any other performer, on the song's identity as a waltz (*Echoes of My Life*, Audiophile 1980). Mel Tormé made it an explosive jazz waltz, with a Stan Kenton-ish big band and a roguish introduction to the effect that he hoped the composer never got to hear about it; the lyric comes out neutral, but an all-out sarcastic whiplash approach at this tempo might be very effective (*Tormé – A New Album*, Rhapsody 1980).

In 1977 the song went disco, courtesy of Grace Jones (on *Portfolio*, Polydor 1977), with a calliope-carousel intro to show that nobody was afraid of the obvious. Jones sings the words clearly, but they could be any words; though "making my entrance with my usual flair" is an idea she seems to relish. This is her Broadway medley; "Send in the Clowns" segues into "What I Did for Love" and thence into "Tomorrow" – with both of which she seems to have more empathy, and in both of which the beat makes more sense.

Perhaps the furthest stretch from the song's original economy was Sarah Vaughan's use of it as a showpiece encore, doubling the number of octaves the author first thought of and making all the dramas strictly technical. "She holds the word 'my'," wrote the American jazz critic Gary Giddins, "longer than you can hold your breath, and then plummets into 'career'." Whatever she was losing, it wasn't her timing (*Send in the Clowns*, Pablo 1980).

The song, or its title, has also long served as a headline for any story involving comedians; and I once appropriated it myself to deplore some lacklustre comedy in a Shakespeare production at Stratford. "Where are the clowns? There ought to be clowns. Well, maybe next year." Unfortunately, my editor lopped off the last phrase, and I've waited all these years to reinstate it.

This kind of use, or misuse, has probably made the song over-familiar; as has the fact that it has been recorded by just about everybody. (The only notable hold-out seems to be Ella Fitzgerald; apparently her manager, Norman Granz, wouldn't let her sing anything by Sondheim at any price.) But "Send in the Clowns" keeps coming back to life. It did in the show. At the final curtain, happy ending secured, it surges up full-bodied in the strings to feed the starved romantic in all of us. It's just as well he went to that rehearsal.

127

I FALL TO PIECES

BY JASPER REES

THERE is a pivotal figure in the life of most great songs. So it is with "I Fall to Pieces", but he neither wrote the song nor sang it.

In 1960 Owen Bradley was 45 years old, had been Decca's musical director in Nashville for 11 years and head of A&R for two. As a producer he was already associated with several of the biggest names in the country-music capital – Ernest Tubb, Buddy Holly, Brenda Lee, Gene Vincent, Kitty Wells. His association with Patsy Cline had begun in 1955, but her only big hit to date had come in early 1957 with "Walkin' After Midnight", which smouldered and swung its hips at a tempo Cline was used to working with. Although she switched from the small 4 Star label to Decca, for contractual reasons the material that came her way was inferior hand-me-down stuff that yielded flop after flop.

At that time Harlan Howard and Hank Cochran were fresh in town from California. At 26, Cochran's main claim to fame had been as half of a country duo with Eddie Cochran (no relation). Howard, six years older, had already hinted at the phenomenal songwriting success he was to enjoy in and beyond Nashville.

* * * * * * * * * * *

Cline falls spine-chillingly to the F on "fall". It is perhaps the most potent note in her entire career

* * * * * * * * * * *

"Hank was the one that brought me the first two or three lines with the title of "I Fall to Pieces", recalls Bradley, now a crackly-voiced 79-year-old. "I did something else he had and said: 'When you've finished this bring it back: I like it.'" Cochran duly completed the song with Howard and resubmitted a demo sung by Howard's new wife Jan Howard, who was shortly to become a country star in her own right. Bradley touted the song around the label, in the way that songs still are in Nashville, but it was turned down by heart-throb Roy Drusky.

"The thing I remember most about the song," Cline's second husband Charlie Dick has said, "was that it had been turned down by a lot of people, and that didn't particularly tickle Patsy: 'If they turned it down, why would I want it?'" Her reluctance was partly down to her discomfort with slow-burning ballads; all her success so far had been with up-tempo western swingers. Also, Bradley recalls, "She liked to really let it all hang out when she sang and that song didn't show off everything."

But Bradley persuaded her. On 16 November between 2.30 and 5.30 a heavily pregnant Cline entered Bradley's studio with three guitarists (electric, rhythm and steel), a pianist, an electric bass (Bradley's brother Harold), a drummer and the ubiquitous vocal quartet the Jordanaires to cut her first three Decca tracks – Cochran's "Shoes", Freddie Hart's "Lovin' in Vain" and the song that was to transform her career.

"We probably worked on it 45 minutes to an hour," says Bradley, "because we felt like we weren't doing very much if we didn't get at least three done." The backing that he came up with subtly transformed the prevailing country style. The rhythm section laid down a shuffle beat that Bradley had never used before, while Hank Garland on electric guitar had "a little gadget – a slapback thing – that you could hook onto the guitar and make it reverberate real crazy. That was the first record I tried that on." The effect was to offer a chugging locomotive backdrop to a vocal melody that on its own would sound slow and laborious.

The structure of the song couldn't be simpler – two verses that subdivide into three pairs of lines, each of which trades on internal repetition:

> I fall to pieces each time I see you again.
> I fall to pieces, how can I be just your friend?
> You want me to act like we've never kissed.
> You want me to forget, pretend we've never met.
> And I've tried, and I've tried, but I haven't yet.
> You walk by and I fall to pieces.

Each verse threatens to build towards a climax but tails away before getting there. The words are about failing to accept rejection; the melody, setting an example of stoicism, refuses to get carried away.

Cline kicks off on a low F, "the lowest she could sing", says Bradley, as if to suggest a low ebb. The melody doesn't test the upper range of her voice, so the expression is mostly in the delivery of the words rather than the notes. It's hard to pin down the precise source of the dignified beauty of her rendition, but part of it is in the diction. For a country singer, Cline's enunciation is extraordinarily crisp. The elision of the words "see you" into "sioux" is about the only deviation from what is more or less textbook BBC elocution. The overall effect, as she swoops up to "pieces" and glides through the "you walk by"s and the "and I've tried"s, is to suggest emotional control through technical control.

The song comes full circle when the last line is repeated and Cline falls spine-chillingly to the F on "fall". It is perhaps the most potent note in her entire career.

Cline always preferred "Lovin' in Vain", but that was to be the B-side while "I Fall to Pieces" was the A. The single was released on 30 January 1961, a week after she gave birth to a boy. It entered the country charts in April and hit the top on 7 August. In September it also reached No 12 in the pop charts. By that time, though, Cline was recovering from a premonitory car crash that almost killed her.

"She came up to my office one day," remembers Bradley, "and stuck her head in the door – this is just as she was recouping; she hadn't started singing again – and she said she never wanted to record any more. 'I just want to enjoy this one because it took so long.' I said: 'You're just kidding', and she said yes."

129

"I Fall to Pieces" cleared a path for "Crazy", "She's Got You" and "Sweet Dreams", the three other ballads on which Cline's reputation principally rests. On 5 March 1963 she was killed in a plane crash.

When Drusky rejected "I Fall to Pieces", it was because it was a lady's song; boys don't fall to pieces, he reckoned, or they don't admit to it. Nevertheless, the first cover was done by Jim Reeves in June 1961. Reeves' pioneering success in the crossover market was down to an easy-listening voice and a realisation that the rest of America didn't want to listen to fiddles and steel guitars. His version comes in on a saxophone intro and, in that vocal style that allowed male country vocalists to be at once strong and sensitive, the melody comes straight out of his boots. They both died in plane crashes, they were the first two to record "I Fall to Pieces", but Cline's voice has lasted a lot better than Reeves'. Posterity has unpredictable taste.

The first good cover was by the Wilburn Brothers (the first bad one was by Johnny Tillotson, the workaday Nashville crooner, on *Poetry in Motion*, Cadence 1962). The Wilburns were a classic vocal duo who in the early 1960s had their own syndicated TV show that helped to launch the likes of Loretta Lynn. In 1962 they recorded a standard harmonised arrangement (*City Limits,* Decca). In the Everlys country/pop idiom, it is soft and sweetly confessional and nothing like as heartwringing as the original. But then no cover is.

Of the other real men to sing it, Faron Young let his deep smooth rhinestone voice loose on it (*The Sheriff,* Allegiance 1984). He sings the first line, rising up to "pieces" like a bat swooping up out of the basement. By some quirk of accent – Young was born in Louisiana – he pronouces "I" and "by" as "oy" and "boy", but the principal vocal mannerism is a crooning style that isn't far short of lugubriousness. Slim Whitman, who recorded the song in 1967 (*Country Classics,* Liberty), sang it in that tremorous yodelling tenor of his which is neither manly nor womanly. His vowels in "you used to do" and "new" are embarrassingly prim, and he ends on a harmonised "woooo" that manages to be both traditional and tasteless. Perhaps Drusky was right after all.

The best male versions of the song are both done by younger, less reverential acts. Michael Nesmith is familiar to most as the Monkee with talent, but the First National Band was his own country-rock creation (*Country Classics Vol 6*, BMG 1970). He gave the song a bit more bar-band swing and a little less seriousness. Greg Kihn, the cult seventies rocker, revised the song (*Kihnspiracy,* Beserkley 1983) with an up-tempo reading replete with thudding, practically punk, bass line. Kihn's vocal is deliberately unvarying, almost sullen: Cochran's lyrics have plainly become irrelevant.

Whether it's because the song lends itself to gender stereotyping or not, female vocalists have had rather more success with the song. Most of the men piled in in the 1960s. The women waited. In 1976 Billie Jo Spears weighed in with a painfully slow version in which the instrumental backing swings like a gaudy movie soundtrack of the time (*What I've Got in Mind,* EMI). Spears' voice is cracked and haunted, hinting at real emotional identification

130

with the lyrics. But better was to come.

When the pioneering female singer-songwriter Loretta Lynn recorded a tribute album of Cline standards in 1977, Owen Bradley was the producer. "Loretta came on the scene just before Patsy died and they became friends," he remembers. "Patsy was pretty well established and she helped Loretta and Loretta thought so much of her." A very different arrangement, with steel guitar to the fore, chimes in with Lynn's much twangier voice. She sings slowly, yearningly, and for the first time since the original you really believe the singer has lived the lyrics. It is no coincidence, after all, that Lynn and Cline are the two country chanteuses whose lives were deemed dramatic enough to be turned into biopics. In *Sweet Dreams* Jessica Lange lipsynched along to an overdubbed Cline soundtrack, but in *Coal Miner's Daughter* (Decca 1980) Sissy Spacek acquitted herself bravely. Her version of "I Fall to Pieces" was also produced by Bradley, and if anything it's even twangier than Lynn's ("again" becomes "agin"). She is filmed singing it live in a declamatory, almost jaunty style. If she cannot carry the title phrase through in one breath, this is still a decided improvement on the versions by most male professionals.

All sorts of dire Scottish and Irish pastiches have emanated from the Celtic country circuit. The only presentable version from this side of the Atlantic is by Everything But The Girl, recorded for the B-side of "Come On Home" (Blanco y Negro) in 1986 when the duo were using orchestral arrangements. Tracey Thorn's plangent voice, with its narrow, low range, is ideal. She gives it a muscular but breathy interpretation, inserting those mannered country hiccups for extra authenticity. There have been two more recent versions. Crystal Gayle (*Best Always*, Ritz 1992) separates the "I fall"s into short, sharp syllables, probably just for the sake of veering away from Cline's definitive version, but otherwise her underrated, rich and mournful voice acquits itself impressively. With its violin and banjo, this was probably the most interesting version instrumentally until Don Was got to grips with the song on the MCA album of crossover duets *Rhythm, Country and Blues* (1994). "I Fall to Pieces" is sung by a yodelling Trisha Yearwood, who is as close to a Patsy Cline descendant as the newly renascent Nashville has to offer, and the ethereal New Orleans soul singer Aaron Neville. Was slows the song almost to a standstill and throws in some shimmering ambient guitar. It is a bravura, almost self-regarding performance, but it does have the virtue of being the first radical reinterpretation of the song in 33 years.

The other duet is the spooky one by Cline and Reeves, posthumously assembled by Owen Bradley in 1981, nearly two decades after their deaths. "Mary Reeves, Jim's widow, had already determined that they sang the song in the same key and approximately the same tempo," Bradley recalls. "It would be much easier now because of the equipment that's available, but we did it the hard way with a razor blade and just plain old tape machine. We made history all round the world." They had never sung together in life, but they duetted in death. It was as if they'd never kissed, they'd never met, but the pieces fell together.

131

THE GIRL FROM IPANEMA

BY JAMES WOODALL

ONE DAY in the winter of 1962, the composer Antonio Carlos ("Tom") Jobim was sitting in a bar in Ipanema, a suburban beach in Rio de Janeiro's south zone, with a diplomat and poet, Vinícius de Moraes. They saw a girl go by, in jacket and tie, on her way to school, and then, later, in a swimsuit on the beach.

They watched her every day, for days on end. She went to her dressmaker; she went to her dentist. She had green eyes, black hair, and golden skin. She was Brazilian, 15 years old, and she was beautiful.

★ ★ ★ ★ ★ ★ ★ ★ ★ ★

"I didn't want to know her, I was a married man; and Vinícius, well, he'd been married about ten times. But we did eventually all become friends. When she got married, I was best man."

★ ★ ★ ★ ★ ★ ★ ★ ★ ★

Jobim had long admired Vinicius. Although they didn't meet until 1956, they were distant cousins. They first worked together on the music for Marcel Camus' film, *Orfeo Negro*, in the late fifties. Vinícius was already famous as a writer; he had published his first volume of poetry in 1933, aged 20. In his forties he began writing lyrics for a new Brazilian sound called "bossa nova"; its roots were in Rio and to a lesser extent São Paulo. Vinícius had no idea, he later observed, that he was giving "this young composer from Ipanema [Jobim] a signal to begin a new movement in Brazilian music".

The name of the bar the two men frequented was Veloso. The girl used to come in to buy cigarettes for her mother. Jobim picks up the story: "When we saw the girl, we'd stop drinking. This was important, a universal thing – a road worker, for example, sees a girl and stops digging his tarmac, he watches, he stares.

"So we just looked at her. I didn't want to know her, I was a married man; and Vinícius, well, he'd been married about ten times. But we did eventually all become friends. She was called Heloísa Eneida Pinto, Helô for short. When she got married, three years later, I was best man."

Before friendship, of course, came the song. The two men did not, contrary to popular belief, write it together in the bar, but separately: Jobim carefully worked out the melody at his piano; Vinícius, up in his mountain retreat in the colonial city of Petropolis, began writing words about a man deep in the blues who suddenly sees this girl "full of swaying". By August of that year the lyrics had been pared down and the song had its première in a Rio restaurant called the Bon Gourmet, with Jobim at the piano and a guitarist, João Gilberto, singing the words – in Portuguese – in a light, lyrical voice. There was also a crooning backing group, Os Cariocas (literally, the Rio de Janeirans). Only now did a title emerge: "Garota de Ipanema", the girl from Ipanema.

In January 1963, Jobim and Vinícius's catchy number was recorded by the Tamba Trio for Philips, and by a singer called Pery Ribeiro for the Odeon label – versions which not even Jobim recalls, and which seem lost to posterity. A year later, thanks to American saxophonist Stan Getz's passion for bossa nova, Jobim and Gilberto agreed to record in New York. The lyricist Norman Gimbel put English words to the song and it became "The Girl from Ipanema". "With Norman," Jobim continues, "I had big fights. I was trying to describe the girl to him in a cab. It was freezing in New York and I was wearing only Rio clothing. Norman said, 'You can't use "Ipanema", this word does not exist.' Even the cab driver agreed. I thought, 'Oh Jesus, Ipanema is going to disappear, these people just don't understand it's a beach' – so I said, 'I want to put the name of the beach in, maybe one day everyone will know about it'."

He was right; they do – and even if "Ipanema" is a bit of a mouthful, the song's lilting opening bars, a cool jazz line promising tropical warmth, are hummed the world over. Brazil has not produced a more universal song, nor a more apparently summery one.

Apparently, because although it sounds soft, sophisticated and beach-like, the song is actually about yearning, unattainability, the painful distance between erotic longing and youthful indifference.

133

> **Oh, but he watches so sadly**
> **How can he tell her he loves her?**
> **Yes, he would give his heart gladly . . .**

These lines, sung in a series of rising minor key changes against the song's dominant major, help stir a wonderful mix of bright feeling and melancholic regret, a brew special to the bossa nova: rhythmically upbeat but never brash, touching but never sentimental. There's a word for it in Portuguese: *saudade* – sorrow, longing, nostalgia, hope, all rolled into one. This is what caught the ear of the world when the song was released in 1964. What may have sounded just sweet was in fact a subtle hybrid, full of nuances.

Like the song itself, the story of its first recording comes in more than one version. Myth has it that Astrud Gilberto, João's wife, and supposedly a vocal novice, happened to be hanging around the studio, and that Getz wanted her to try the song in English – mainly because João's was so bad. In fact, Astrud had already sung with her husband in quite a few bossa nova shows over the previous two or three years, and Jobim approved of her talent. Now was her chance to record professionally, and she insisted she sing. Getz didn't care one way or the other, so it was left to the producer, Creed Taylor, to decide.

He reckoned the song would come to no harm in a language less exotic than Portuguese, but João would open:

Olha que coisa mais linda,
mais cheia de graça,
é ela menina, que vem e que passa
num doce balanço a caminho do mar ...
(Look, what could be lovelier,
more full of grace,
than this girl whom I've seen going by
swinging so sweetly along the seashore ...)

After two minutes of João's sibilant Portugese, Astrud, in a clean, tremble-free soprano – although momentarily flat on the first note – sings the rest of the song alone:

Tall and tan and young and lovely
The girl from Ipanema goes walking
And when she passes
Each one she passes goes, Aaaah ...

The English is a slack approximation of the compactly musical Portuguese, but no matter: released in the States on the Verve label, the song went to No 5 in the *Billboard* charts in 1964, sold two million copies, and won the Grammy Award for Best Song – this in the year the Beatles hit America.

The record has charm, not least in Astrud's slightly strained vowels, it has style, and a bit of sex: "When she walks, she's like a samba/ That swings so cool and sways so gently ...". It does what all good songs should do – evoke a scene through a memorable riff. It's as if João and Astrud are right there on the beach, inviting us to join them in the water – and probably drink a few *caipirinhas* too.

It made an overnight star of Astrud. Getz was clearly taken with more than her voice and her English: she and João divorced soon after, and Astrud and Getz have been together ever since. Astrud carved a decent career in America, but she has always remained the girl from ."The Girl from Ipanema". An attempted comeback in the States in 1983 was greeted by the *New York Post* critic with a sour "Ipanema is not forever". In April 1994, she could again be found playing New York, billed as "The Girl from Ipanema – Astrud Gilberto". Meanwhile, her and João's daughter Bebel has become a singing star in Brazil.

That New York critic was right, in one sense, but wrong in another. The song was and still lives as the vehicle that brought world attention to the bossa nova and the way jazz could use it. Until then, bossa nova was cool, sophisticated club music, confined to select nightspots in Copacabana, Rio's most fashionable beach, then unspoilt. A few American musicians knew about it, such as Charlie Byrd and Benny Goodman, who had toured Brazil together in the early sixties. When Stan Getz added his sassy sax solo to "The Girl from Ipanema", Brazil and the US began a successful musical partnership.

134

Within two years, over 40 cover versions of the song had been made. In the men's department Sinatra, Nat King Cole and Sammy Davis Jnr (with Duke Ellington) distinguished themselves, particularly Sinatra, who duetted with João Gilberto (on voice and guitar) in a big-band version in 1967 (*Francis Albert Sinatra and Antonio Carlos Jobim*, Reprise) which somehow retained the song's intimacy. Nat King Cole's warm voice is matched by a big-hearted orchestral accompaniment, which becomes almost chummy when the trumpets harmonise with him – his "Ah" when the girl passes is so genial, you feel he could be her father. Sammy Davis (*Our Shining Hour*, Verve 1965), by contrast, clicks his tongue, and goes "Hnnn!" when the girl goes by – "she's walking on the beach, you see"; this is a Broadway version, with Ellington's band stamping the girl off the beach and onto the stage in no uncertain terms.

With the ladies – Ella Fitzgerald, Lena Horne, Peggy Lee – "Girl" became "Boy", which makes a nonsense of the lyric. Lee (*In the Name of Love*, Capitol 1964) embellished on the theme of disdain, singing that the "boy" was "so cool, calm, collected, makes a girl feel neglected". Ella, meanwhile, belted the song out in 1965 (*Ella Fitzgerald*, reissued on Walkman Jazz) at a furious lick, as if she were about to explode with impatience: "That boy from Ipanema, no no no no no," she roars at the end. In the original, the girl "just doesn't see", gently but conclusively.

This is not a song that survives a sex change. Female vocalists were perhaps thrown by the idea of a woman singing about another woman. If so, they also missed the point of the original: Astrud's seraphic voice is really an echo of the man's sad desire. Pop versions have included one by the Four Tops (*Live!*, Motown 1966), replete with whistles and interjections such as "Did anyone see that girl walking by?". In the same year, Cliff Richard, perhaps hung up on summer holidays, got stuck on the name of the beach, which he calls "Ipaneeema"; the syncopation also defeated him (*Kinda Latin*, Columbia). More recently, the B-52s sang something called "Girl from Ipanema Goes to Greenland" (*Bouncing off the Satellites*, Warner 1986) whose lyrics – "Witchdoctors are screaming/ Nymphs are dreaming/ This girl's lost someone/ Who is that someone?" – are a decidedly post-punk gloss on the original. The melody is not within earshot.

Instrumental covers, at their best, show off the skills of the arranger: Oscar Peterson is predictably brilliant on solo piano in his 1965 swing version (*We Get Requests*, Pablo 1975), developing a complex theme and variations from the original tune. Charlie Byrd, who knew Brazil well from his tours with Goodman, recorded a flicky guitar solo of the song, backed by strings, in 1966 (*The Bossa Nova Years*, Concord 1991), but he misses that essential bossa smoothness.

The downside of instrumentation has been a tidal wave of piped versions, which now flood into hotel lifts and cocktail lounges at all corners of the globe. In 1990, it was the fifth most-played song in the world, performed three million times. About this, Tom Jobim remains rueful: "There's too much music everywhere – I usually ask my wife to turn off the radio when she puts it on in the car. There are too many versions of this song, too. I've written 400 songs, and just one became a hit, or more of a hit than the others."

Aged 67 and twice married, how does Jobim feel about it today? "I still have an affection for it, as I do for all my children. One is not better than the other."

The bar where he and Vinícius were inspired has become the Garota de Ipanema. The Girl married a man named Pinheiro and has four children. Ipanema, once a parochial paradise, has become a sybaritic, built-up, and relatively safe stretch of Rio beach.

Jobim is a national institution. A shambling, droll figure, he lunches every day at the Plataforma, a famous steak-house in Leblon. A large bottle of whisky is brought to him, with notches on it to mark his tab. In the year of the song's 30th anniversary, he still has one worry: "I'm terrified about a 'Girl from Ipanema' beauty contest on the beach," he snorts. "Any sign of this, and I grab my glasses and my cane, and run away."

SMELLS LIKE TEEN SPIRIT

BY DAVID CAVANAGH

IT WAS almost the end of 1991. Freddie Mercury had died on 24 November and the year was all set for solemn foreclosure. Nobody expected a full-scale rock phenomenon to squeeze in through the little aperture between St Andrew's Day and Christmas. But on 30 November, the new singles chart had an extraordinary tale to tell: at No 9, straight in from nowhere, was "Smells Like Teen Spirit" by Nirvana. A trio of miscreants from America's flaky underbelly had hit serious oil.

Not that it didn't make sense. Nirvana, who were touring Britain at the time, had proved themselves to be just about the most exciting live rock band of their generation. Their 1989 debut album, *Bleach*, was revered as an underground, hardcore classic. By combining heavy rock drums and guitars with often poignant melodies, they achieved the much-envied "crossover", the commercial coup of appealing equally to two famously warring demographics: "indie" fans and heavy-metal lovers. "Smells Like Teen Spirit" genre-hopped in a way Nirvana's heroes the Pixies had failed to.

★ ★ ★ ★ ★ ★ ★ ★ ★ ★

Nirvana found Tori Amos's version hilarious. In the press, David Grohl hailed it enthusiastically as "an abomination".

★ ★ ★ ★ ★ ★ ★ ★ ★ ★

The Pixies are important – when Kurt Cobain played "Teen Spirit" to the other members of Nirvana, they heard a powerful Pixies influence. It was a very Pixies notion to have quiet verses followed by screaming choruses. The singer of the Pixies, Black Francis, had also perfected the art of putting the most nerve-shredding screams on the most innocuous words in the song. The result, for the listener, was a kind of baffled exhilaration. So it was with "Smells Like Teen Spirit", a scream song *par excellence* but with something extra, something magical: from its title inwards, you instinctively knew you were hearing a rock anthem.

The story behind the song is absurd and endearing. In 1989 Cobain was living in Olympia, a college town in Washington State about 50 miles east of his birthplace Aberdeen. The apartment, he later told Nirvana's biographer Michael Azerrad, was "a filthy pigsty". One night, he and his friend Kathleen Hanna, who played in a local band called Bikini Kill, drunkenly decorated the walls of the apartment with graffiti. At one point, Hanna wrote the words "Kurt smells like Teen Spirit". Teen Spirit happens to be a deodorant in America. Cobain, proud to be a deodorant-free zone, claimed not to know of its existence "until months after the single came out".

Azerrad's book *Come As You Are* reprints a page from Cobain's notebook showing an early lyric for "Smells Like Teen Spirit". Only four lines will eventually make his final cut; the rest are either jarringly strange ("dyslexic idiot savant with bad hearing") or eerily prophetic ("who will be the king and queen of the outcasted teens?" – written at least two months before Cobain met his future wife Courtney Love). Nirvana unleashed the song on tour in America in April 1991, subsequently recording it as the first track on their second album, *Nevermind*, released in September.

Privately, they were sceptical about its chances; when it wasn't sounding like a Pixies song it was sounding naggingly like Boston's 1977 hit "More than a Feeling". However, Nirvana's producer, Butch Vig, who had done a remarkable job of fine-tuning their aggression on *Nevermind*, recognised "Teen Spirit" as a classic, and their record company, Geffen, agreed. "Smells Like Teen Spirit" was released as the first single from *Nevermind*. It came out in September in the States and in November in Britain.

It begins with a staccato guitar rig on four chords, played twice by Cobain. Just as he completes the second one, he is swamped in a primal instant by David Grohl's violent drums, Chris Novoselic's grinding bass and his own overdubbed, distorted guitar. The riff is repeated twice, with thrilling intensity. It then pulls back to make space for a chiming, vaguely ominous two-note guitar signature and, 33 seconds in, Cobain starts to sing. Slightly plaintive, slightly anguished, his voice delivers a childlike, sing-song melody with a coded message that is now deeply poignant: "Load up on guns, bring your friends, it's fun to lose and to pretend". The sense of seditionary intent is blurred at once by a seemingly unrelated couplet about a girl who is "overboard and self-assured", which leads into a sneering, taunting refrain of "hello, hello, hello, hello . . ." It's a very strange song.

Just as suddenly, it jack-knifes back into rage. The chorus is a triumph of screaming and mystique. Those who had bought *Nevermind* could actually locate fragments of the song's chorus in Cobain's incomplete lyric sheet, which tantalisingly provided a mere six or so lines from each song. And here it was: "With the lights out, it's less dangerous/ Here we are now, entertain us/ I feel stupid and contagious/ Here we are now, entertain us/ A mulatto, an albino, a mosquito, my libido . . ."

Just as only a select band of trivia addicts know that the first line of the Rolling Stones' "Brown Sugar" goes "Gold Coast slaveship bound for cottonfields" but everyone can give a decent phonetic rendition thereof, "Teen Spirit" flew into the public domain in a giant blur. Many had reason to thank *Smash Hits* for printing the lyrics in full when the song entered the Top 10.

An article on Nirvana in *NME* in September had shown Cobain still unclear about the message of the song. "It's about – hey, brother, especially sister, throw away the fruit and eat all the rind," he suggested unhelpfully, before adding, more politically, that any teenage revolution would have to start "from the inside . . . with the custodians and the cheerleaders".

Two years later he was denying any political intent, telling Azerrad: "I just felt that my band was in a situation where it was expected to fight in a revolutionary sense toward the major corporate machine. I just thought, 'How dare you put that kind of fucking pressure on me.' It's stupid. And I feel stupid and contagious."

It soon became tempting to view "Teen Spirit" as an anthem of the slacker generation – the lethargic, apathetic young adults of the moment, born in the late sixties and early seventies. It was true that when the song ran out of arguments ("oh well, whatever, never mind") it used the age-old device of screaming randomly. But by then Cobain was thinking of more subtle ways to wax seditionary.

On 4 December Nirvana appeared on *Top of the Pops*, and gave a surreal performance that pushed the song up to its peak of No 7. Cobain, singing live, crooned it in a bizarre Gothic drawl an octave lower than on the record. The opening lines were amended to "load up on drugs and kill your friends". He had glimpsed the immediate future – a wave of designer "grunge" bands; the usurping of his vision by unscrupulous industry bigwigs – and he didn't fancy becoming a totem. From that day on, Nirvana were always prone to mischief and irreverence when they played "Smells Like Teen Spirit".

The first of the inevitable cover versions came from an unexpected direction. Tori Amos, the American singer-songwriter who had created a stir with her album *Little Earthquakes*, put "Smells Like Teen Spirit" on a limited-edition CD of her third single, "Winter" (East West, March 1992). She turned it into a prissy piano ballad. Substituting tremulous longing for blind fury, she sounded woefully gauche on lines like "I feel stoopid and contagious".

Nirvana found Amos's version hilarious. When they played some dates in Ireland in June 1992, they used it as their intro tape, bounding onstage and pirouetting like ballerinas. In the press, David Grohl hailed it enthusiastically as "an abomination".

By then, they had heard, and approved, a clever pastiche of "Teen Spirit" by America's foremost rock'n'roll spoofer, Weird Al Yankovic. Yankovic's reputation in Britain at that time rested on his 1984 hit "Eat It", a parody of Michael Jackson's "Beat It". On his droll "Smells Like Nirvana" (Scotti Bros Records), a minor hit in July 1992, he showed impressive research. His rhythm section's recreation of Grohl and Novoselic's chaos was spot-on, as was his send-up of the chorus: "Here we are now, we're Nirvana/ Sing distinctly, we don't wanna". In the gaps, he replaced Cobain's "yay" with sheep noises.

It wasn't that Nirvana's balloon needed to be pricked. It was simply that "Teen Spirit" was now fair game. The Reading Festival in August witnessed a superb take-off by Australian Abba-clones Bjorn Again, but for the most sacrilegious spoof-mongering you had to look to Nirvana themselves, appearing later on the same day. Striking up the famous riff to tumultuous cheering, Cobain launched straight into "More than a Feeling" by Boston.

In 1993, Nirvana publicly dismissed *Nevermind* as too clean-sounding and released a nightmarish follow-up, *In Utero* (Geffen). On an album loaded with cryptic self-references, they teased the "Teen Spirit" generation one last

139

time. "Rape Me", a song that saw Cobain skirting controversy with mind-boggling recklessness, was clearly inspired by a fraught year in the spotlight during which he admitted an addiction to heroin and almost lost custody of his daughter to the Los Angeles County Department of Children's Services. The first four bars of "Rape Me" are intended to startle; on slightly different chords, it's the introduction to "Teen Spirit".

In May 1993, the four "Teen Spirit" bars were sampled by British rappers Credit To The Nation for the beginning of their single "Call It What You Want". It was a well-known device: Soho had done likewise with the Smiths' "How Soon Is Now?" on their 1990 single "Hippy Chick". It transpired that Credit To The Nation had been granted copyright clearance by Cobain only two days before the single's release.

"Call It What You Want" quickly became a crossover hit in student discos and clubs. It left "Smells Like Teen Spirit" shrouded in delicious irony. For all its notoriety, for all its units sold and feathers ruffled, for all that it arguably defined the early '90s, for all the awful events of April '94, no one can ever be sure, when those four chords start jangling, whether they are about to hear a Nirvana song or a Credit To The Nation song.

140

NOTES ON CONTRIBUTORS

IN ALPHABETICAL ORDER

Marcel Berlins is a leading writer and broadcaster on the law.

Mike Butler writes about the arts for *City Life* in Manchester.

Robert Butler is the *Independent on Sunday*'s theatre feature writer. He is the author of several plays, including *A Drop of Fred*, about Fred Astaire and Liverpool, which has been bought by Granada Television.

David Cavanagh writes about rock music for *Q, Mojo* and the *Independent on Sunday*.

Robert Cushman is a regular presenter of BBC programmes on musicals and popular song. He was theatre critic of the *Observer* 1973-84, and now lives in Canada where he has three times won the Nathan Cohen Award for theatre criticism.

Geoff Dyer is a freelance critic and the author of five books: *Ways of Telling*, a critical study of John Berger; *But Beautiful: a Book about Jazz*, the novels *The Colour of Memory* and *The Search*; and *The Missing of the Somme* (Hamish Hamilton, October 1994).

Mary Harron is a former rock critic on the *Guardian* and New York editor on BBC Television's *The Late Show*. She is now in Los Angeles, making films.

Nick Hornby is the author of *Fever Pitch*, probably the most successful book ever written about football, and editor of *My Favourite Year*, a collection of fans' memoirs. He is a regular contributor to the *Independent on Sunday* and the *Sunday Times*.

Barney Hoskyns writes for several leading magazines, including *Vogue* (UK) and *Mojo*. Among his books are *Say It One Time for the Brokenhearted*, a map of where country meets southern soul, and *Across the Great Divide*, the official biography of The Band.

Allegra Huston is editorial director of the publishers Weidenfeld & Nicolson.

Phil Johnson writes on jazz for the *Independent* and the *Independent on Sunday*.

Rhoda Koenig is the book reviewer for *American Vogue*. She used to be a nightclub singer.

Justine Picardie is assistant editor of the *Independent on Sunday* Review, and co-author with Dorothy Wade of *Atlantic Records and the Godfathers of Rock'n'Roll* (4th Estate, 1993). Ewan MacColl was her father-in-law.

Jasper Rees writes regularly about television for the *Independent*, football for the *Daily Telegraph*, and music for the *Independent on Sunday*.

Tim Rostron is deputy arts editor of the *Daily Telegraph*. He used to be features editor of *Elle* (UK), and, some time before that, a choirboy.

142

Giles Smith is rock editor and a feature writer on the *Independent*, and one of the authors of *My Favourite Year*, the best-selling book of football fans' memoirs.

Robin Stummer is a sub-editor on the *Independent on Sunday* Review. He is a former media researcher, and has written on Eastern Europe for the *Independent*.

Ben Thompson was rock critic of the *Independent on Sunday* from 1991 to 1994. He is now the paper's comedy critic.

Richard Williams is a former editor of the *Independent on Sunday* Review, *Time Out* and *Melody Maker*, and former rock and jazz critic of *The Times*. He is now chief sports writer on the *Independent on Sunday*, and author of books on Bob Dylan (*A Man Called Alias*) and Miles Davis (*The Man in the Green Shirt*).

James Woodall is a publisher turned journalist and the author of a book about flamenco, *In Search of the Firedance* (Sinclair-Stevenson, 1992).

ACKNOWLEDGEMENTS

THERE are a lot of people without whom this book would not have been possible. At the *Independent on Sunday*, Laurence Earle, Isabel Lloyd, Allison Pearson, Jenny Gilbert, Carole Mansur, Jenny Turner and Rosanna de Lisle helped with the editing. The editor of the Sunday Review, Liz Jobey, was always encouraging. The editor of the whole paper, Ian Jack, smoothed the passage of the series from news-stand to bookshop. The designers, Jo Dale, Jacqui Zabarauskas and Janet Folland, made the idea work on the page, not least by commissioning the superb illustrations from Paul Burgess, who also did the cover of the book. Giles Smith and Richard Williams made a vital intangible contribution, quite apart from the ones on the contents pages. Thanks to all of them, and to the *Independent* library, Maggie Chambers in the computer room, Mark Cooper at BBC Television, Elly Smith at Virgin 1215, and Brian Stephens at BBC Radio 2.

Special thanks go to my agent, Araminta Whitley, who negotiated one of the more complex, and probably less lucrative, deals of her career; my assistant, Jane Duncan, who took on a lot of extra work without complaint; the commissioning editor, Trevor Dolby, whose enthusiasm started the book rolling; my editor, Rachel King, who cracked a sympathetic whip as deadlines came and went; and to my wife, Amanda, and our son, Daniel, who tolerated a lot of moonlighting without losing their cool, or their warmth.

On the practical level, we received endless help from everyone at the National Sound Archive, and especially Andy Linehan, the popular-music curator. The Sound Archive is a well-kept secret: a little gem of a library, just up the road from the Science Museum in London, which will let anyone listen to anything, given a day or two's notice. If you're a music buff, the only difference between this and heaven is that heaven doesn't close at five o'clock. At the risk of letting a cat out of a bag, we dedicate the book to the National Sound Archive.

Tim de Lisle
London
May 1994

PICTURE CREDITS

The editor and publisher would like to thank the following for their permission to reproduce the images within the book:

Barney Hoskyns: page 10 (top)

BFI Stills, Posters and Designs: pages 1 (middle), 13 (bottom right), 15 (bottom right)

DG/Susech Bayat, Berlin: page 1 (bottom)

Redferns: pages 7 (top right, photograph by David Redfern), 8 (top, photograph by William Gottlieb), 9 (bottom, photograph by GEMS), 12 (bottom right, photograph by Steve Richards), 13 (top), 16 (bottom, photograph by Brian Shuel)

Rex Features Ltd: pages 1 (top), 2, 3, 4, 5, 6 (bottom, photograph by Robert Taylor), 7 (centre), 8 (bottom), 9 (top), 10-11 (centre, top and bottom right), 12 (top and bottom left), 13 (bottom left), 14, 15 (top), 16 (top).

INDEX

Note: Songs are indexed by title only; albums are not indexed.

144

145

146

147

148